Information Security
Risk Assessment Toolkit

Information Security Risk Assessment Toolkit

Practical Assessments through Data Collection and Data Analysis

Mark Ryan M. Talabis

Jason L. Martin

Evan Wheeler, Technical Editor

AMSTERDAM • BOSTON • HEIDELBERG • LONDON
NEW YORK • OXFORD • PARIS • SAN DIEGO
SAN FRANCISCO • SINGAPORE • SYDNEY • TOKYO

Syngress is an Imprint of Elsevier

Acquiring Editor:	*Chris Katsaropolous*
Development Editor:	*Heather Scherer*
Project Manager:	*Priya Kumaraguruparan*
Designer	*Alan Studholme*

Syngress is an imprint of Elsevier
225 Wyman Street, Waltham, MA 02451, USA

Library of Congress Cataloging-in-Publication Data
Application Submitted

British Library Cataloguing-in-Publication Data
A catalogue record for this book is available from the British Library.

ISBN: 978-1-59749-735-0

Printed in the United States of America
13 14 15   10 9 8 7 6 5 4 3 2 1

Working together to grow
libraries in developing countries

www.elsevier.com | www.bookaid.org | www.sabre.org

ELSEVIER   BOOK AID International   Sabre Foundation

For information on all Syngress publications visit our website at *www.syngress.com*

Jason:

I would like to dedicate this book to my Mom for always supporting me, my Wife for being so understanding when I try to do too many things at once and never holding it against me, and for Carter who was too young to care but would come by and tap on my keyboard while I tried to work on the book.

Ryan:

I would like to dedicate this book to my father, Gilbert; my mom, Hedy; my sister, Iquit; my brother, Herbert.

CONTENTS

Acknowledgments

Jason would like to thank his co-author Mark Ryan Talabis for all his support, patience and hard work. Also, in no particular order: his co-workers at Secure DNA for providing input into the process; Ernest Shiraki Jr. for supporting the idea of putting this book together; Evan Wheeler for his insight and feedback during the editing process; and finally his wife and son, Kaleen and Carter Martin, for being understanding when working on the book took away valuable time that he could have been spending with them.

Ryan would like to thank his co-author Jason Martin for making all of this possible. And to everyone who in one way or another, played a part in this book: Joanne Robles, Heather Scherer, Evan Wheeler, Daisy del Moral, Carlo Monteverde, Joseph Tee, Aldwin Mamiit, Jiffy Armas, John Ruero, Dr. John Paul Vergara, Dr. Joe Santiago, Yvonne Feng, Lorenzo Sy, Benjamin Reodica Jr, Fedeliza Talabis Reodica, Anne Michelle Santos, Rosario Acierto, Howard Van De Vaarst III, Ernie Shiraki, Secure-DNA, Harvard University Extension School, Ateneo de Manila University, University of Santo Tomas, San Beda Alabang and last but not the least, my family: Gilbert, Hedy, Iquit and Herbert Talabis.

About the Technical Editor

Working in the IT and Security industries for over 15 years, **Evan Wheeler** is accustomed to advising clients on all aspects of information assurance. Specializing in risk management, digital forensic investigations, and security architecture development, he offers an expert insight into security principles for both clients and security professionals. Evan currently is a Director of Information Security for Omgeo (A DTCC | Thomson Reuters Company), an instructor at Northeastern University, the author of the Information Security Risk Management course for the SANS Institute, and has published the popular book "Security Risk Management: Building an Information Security Risk Management Program from the Ground Up." Previously he spent several years as a Security Consultant for the U.S. Department of Defense. More details about his work and several free resources are available at: http://www.ossie-group.org.

About the Authors

Mark Ryan M. Talabis is a Manager for the Secure DNA Consulting practice. Prior to joining Secure DNA he was a consultant in the Asian Development Bank (ADB). He has extensive experience in information security risk assessments, information security policy and program development, vulnerability assessments and penetration testing and has specialized expertise in security analytics and data mining as applied to information security. He has a Master's degree in Information Technology; Certified Information Systems Security Professional (CISSP); Certified Information Systems Auditor (CISA); a GIAC Certified Incident Handler Certification (GCIH); a GIAC Security Essentials Certification (GSEC); Certified in Risk and Information Systems Control (CRISC); and a Microsoft Certified Professional (MCP) on SQL Server Administration;. He has presented in various security and academic conferences around the world including Blackhat and Defcon and has a number of published papers to his name in various peer-reviewed journals. He is an alumni member of the Honeynet Project and is currently taking a Master of Liberal Arts (ALM) in Extension Studies in Harvard University.

Jason L. Martin is the President and CEO of Secure DNA, an Information Security Company that provides security solutions to companies throughout the United States and Asia. Prior to joining Secure DNA he was a Manager within KPMG's Information Risk Management group. In his professional services role Mr. Martin has successfully designed, implemented, and operated security programs for multi-billion dollar organizations within Hawaii and the US Mainland as well as provided subject matter expertise as an executive level security advisor to companies throughout the world. He is a Certified Information Security Manager (CISM), a Certified Information Systems Security Professional (CISSP), a Certified Information Systems Auditor (CISA), Certified in the Governance of Enterprise IT (CGEIT), and holds the designation as Certified in Risk and Information Systems Control (CRISC). He has advised Lawmakers on emerging cyber security risks and is working with legislatures to enhance state privacy laws. He is a frequent speaker and instructor at security and audit training events and seminars, is a founder of the Shakacon Security Conference, and is on the board of advisors for the Hackito Ergo Sum security conference in France. He is a former board member for the Hawaii chapter of ISACA and is a current board member for the Hawaii chapter of INFRAGARD.

Introduction

So frequently in our careers we have heard these words "I need an IT Security Risk Assessment done before my regulators get here, and they get here in three weeks!" As security consultants we pride ourselves on helping our customers find solutions to tough problems but hearing those words can make a seasoned security professional quake in the knees. The genesis of this book was born during some of those dark times as we had to put our heads together and formulate a framework that would allow us to quickly, but effectively, pull together the information that was needed and present it in a manner that would be useable and defensible.

Information Security Risk Assessment Toolkit details a methodology that adopts the best parts of some established frameworks and teaches you how to use the information that is available (or not) to pull together an IT Security Risk Assessment that will allow you to identify High Risk areas. Whether your objective is to forecast budget items, identify areas of operational or program improvement, or meet regulatory requirements we believe this publication will provide you with the tools to execute an effective assessment and more importantly, adapt a process that will work for you. Many of the tools that we've developed to make this process easier for us are available as a companion for this publication at http://booksite.syngress.com/9781597497350. We hope that you find our methodology, and accompanying tools, as useful in executing your IT Security Risk Assessments as we have.

Information Security Risk Assessments

INFORMATION IN THIS CHAPTER:

- What is Risk?
- What is an Information Security Risk Assessment?
- Drivers, Laws, and Regulations

INTRODUCTION

The past two decades or so have been routinely called the Information Age. In the Information Age, names like Google, Facebook, and Twitter have become as commonplace in our vernacular as Ford, GE, and Wal-Mart. When you stop and think about it these companies don't sell cars, refrigerators, or diapers. So what makes them relevant in these times? Information! These companies deliver services based on the collection and dissemination of information.

Information is valuable and as with any valuable asset it has to be protected. In order to properly protect an asset one needs to understand the dangers that the asset is exposed to. In the context of information as an asset this is where information security risk assessments come in to play.

In this chapter, we will be providing a primer on information security risk assessments with a focus on providing foundational knowledge regarding risk and its various components. We will then provide a high level overview of the components that make up a information security risk assessment, the major frameworks that provide guidance for conducting an assessment, and the laws and regulations that affect these assessments.

WHAT IS RISK?

All human endeavors carry some level of risk. This explains why throughout history risk has been a common topic of discussion. Strangely enough, even with all the discourse around risk it remains a very ambiguous concept. If you were to ask someone to provide you a definition of risk, they will very likely be able to provide you a reasonable answer; however, if you ask ten people, or even a hundred, you will likely receive a different definition from each person.

The ambiguity associated with defining risk is a fairly common roadblock to truly understanding risk. This is highlighted in the following statement from the Society of Risk Analysis:

> *"Many of you here remember that when our Society for Risk Analysis was brand new, one of the first things it did was to establish a committee to define the word "risk". This committee labored for 4 years and then gave up, saying in its final report, that maybe it's better not to define risk. Let each author define it in his own way, only please each should explain clearly what that way is (Kaplan, 1997)."*

It is safe to say that there have been many discussions about risk but there have been few definitions provided or accepted. Of the definitions that we do have, the only thing that they share in common is the very fact that they share so little in common. This does not mean that people disagree on the meaning of ristk, it just highlights the fact that each person interprets risk, and the definition of risk, in a very different way.

"It is our opinion that when defining Risk, it is important to discuss risk in the proper context". Different fields or disciplines will have different interpretations and perceptions of risk. For example, the definition of risk will vary between Information Security, Economics, Finance, Healthcare, and even within Information Technology itself. Understanding that the definition of risk will vary depending on who you are talking to will help you more effectively communicate your risk assessment within your organization.

Another key point to remember is that the information security risk assessment process you are undertaking is very likely not the only risk assessment being conducted at your organization. Usually there are multiple risk assessments occurring within your organization being driven by different departments. In a well run organization these reviews will be funneled into a centralized risk management function for consolidation and reporting. By providing a solid definition of risk in the context of your field you will be able to avoid misunderstandings when the time comes to report your conclusions to these various centralized risk management functions.

When you start the risk assessment process you will have to interact with other people and many of these people won't be familiar with risk assessments and will only have a layman's understanding of what risk is. If you start talking about the more technical concepts of risk, which we will delve into later in this chapter, you will more than likely confuse them or at the very least make them uncomfortable. Remember that not all people are familiar with risk assessments so it is always good to start off with the most basic definitions of risk when meeting with someone so that the person you are meeting with can easily relate to the topic.

As an example, when interviewing non-technical business unit representatives, one of the best ways to communicate about what you are working on is to tell them that you are assessing the exposure of the department to possible data breach or loss. This may not be entirely accurate as risk assessments are much more thorough than just that but it does provide a simple way to put your interviewee into the proper state of mind for you to ask other more detailed questions.

IMPORTANT DEFINITIONS

So even though it gave the Society for Risk Analysis heartburn, let's start trying to define Risk. It would be impossible to define Risk without first looking at its entomology. As with most English words, risk is likely of Greek origin; however, the earliest and possibly closest origin is from the Latin word "Riscum." "Riscum" in turn could be the origin of various other words such as "Riscare" (Italian), and "Risque" (French), which is supposedly the origin of the English word "Risk."

"The list below shows the possible etymology of risk as well as the first definition:

- Riscum(Latin)—Danger, venture, crisis [1].
- Riscare (Italian—To hazard, to aventure, to jeaopard, to endanger [2].
- Risque(French)—Perill, jeopardie, danger, hazard, chance, aduenture (Costgrave, 1611).
- Risk (English)—Peril, jeopardy, danger, hazard, chance.

One thing that you'll notice immediately is the commonality between the definitions associated with the word, or some derivative of the word, "Danger"—which connotes an exposure to harm. Thus it is fair to say that Risk can be defined as a situation that exposes an object to harm. This is probably one of the most common definitions of risk that you will encounter and frankly, although seemingly simple, not a bad one at all. Using this definition of risk is actually a good way to describe what you are doing to people in your organization who are not familiar with the concept of risk or risk assessments.

Going Deeper with Risk

Using the common definitions of risk would suffice; however, when we start delving into the subject, we need something more substantial. One of the most famous definitions of risk comes from Frank Knight, a renowned economist, in his work "Risk, Uncertainty, and Profit":

> *Uncertainty must be taken in a sense radically distinct from the familiar notion of Risk, from which it has never been properly separated... The essential fact is that "risk" means in some cases a quantity susceptible of measurement, while at other times it is something distinctly not of this character; and there are far-reaching and crucial differences in the bearings of the phenomena depending on which of the two is really present and operating... It will appear that a measurable uncertainty, or "risk" proper, as we shall use the term, is so far different from an unmeasurable one that it is not in effect an uncertainty at all [3].*

Frank Knight's definition focuses on the difference between uncertainty and risk. Uncertainty is a state of having limited knowledge where it is impossible to exactly describe the existing state or future outcome [4]. Simply put, uncertainty is the state of not knowing.

Risk on the other hand can be defined as the quantitation or measurement of uncertainty. When we start measuring uncertainty, it is at this point when it becomes risk. Thus, risk is measureable while uncertainty is not.

Though this definition does have its critics, we believe that this definition presents a simple yet elegant description of risk because of the key concept of "measurement." Risk assessments are primarily an exercise of measurement. An organization without a risk assessment process cannot identify, much less measure, their risks and their level of exposure will remain in an uncertain state. An organization that is in an uncertain state cannot protect against possible dangers to itself until it is able to identify and measure them.

It is important to note that Knight's definition is heavily influenced by probability theory, which during that time was just taking hold. In fact, in most common risk assessment methodologies, probability is an integral component, which now brings us to a discussion of the various components of risk.

Components of Risk

So far, we have provided high-level definitions of risk; however, you have probably heard the concept that "An entity is a sum of its parts." Risk can be described in a very similar manner (see Figure 1.1). In order to break risk down to its individual components, let us use the definitions that we have used so far as illustrated in Figure 1.2.

Our first definition of risk has already provided us with the majority of the components that are needed to continue with this discussion. As we mentioned in the previous sections, without a form of measurement, than we are really just dealing with the definition of uncertainty. We need components from our second definition to complete our overall description of risk.

Risk is a **situation** that exposes an **object** to **harm**

Event   **Asset**   **Outcome**

Figure 1.1 Individual Components of Risk

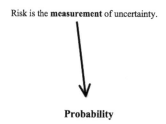

Risk is the **measurement** of uncertainty.

Probability

Figure 1.2 Probability as Component of Risk

The addition of the components from our second definition helps to appropriately define risk for purposes of our discussion. Based on our definitions, risk is the sum of the following components:

- Event.
- Asset.
- Outcome.
- Probability.

Let's go over these components one by one.

Event

An event is a chance or situation that is possible but is not certain. An event in the context of a risk assessment is always a future event. An event could also be an action or inaction. This action or inaction will have a direct or indirect influence on the outcome.

Also, though there are different ways to view the polarity of an event. In the context of this book, we will always treat an event as a negative occurrence, which represents something undesirable or unwanted.

Identifying events is one of the key activities of a risk assessment. In information security risk assessments, these events will be our threat actions, which will be discussed in greater detail in later chapters. Hackers gaining unauthorized access to an application or an unencrypted backup tape data being lost and then read are examples of events in the context of information security.

Asset

An asset is the direct or indirect target of an event. The outcome always has a direct consequence and is applied to the asset.

More often than not, an asset is something valued in your organization. In information security, these assets are typically applications, databases, software, hardware, or even people. In our event example above, the application and the backup tape are the assets that are the object of the event.

Outcome

An outcome is the impact of the event. In the context of this book, an outcome will always be an adverse or unwelcome circumstance such as a loss or potential for loss. This loss in turn always has a direct effect on the whole or part of the asset.

Using the same examples provided in the event definition; a lost backup tape being read or unauthorized access by hackers to an application could have a similar outcome; that being the potential disclosure of sensitive information.

Probability

As previously mentioned, measurement is the cornerstone of any risk assessment. Ultimately, the goal of a risk assessment is to measure the probability or likelihood of a future event occurring.

Looking back at the examples that we have used so far regarding hackers accessing an application and the unencrypted backup tapes, the probability component will attempt to answer the following questions:

- What is the probability that hackers may be able to gain unauthorized access to the application?
- What is the probability that data on unencrypted backup tapes may be disclosed?

Probability typically revolves around the determination of the exposure and frequency of an event and can be very subjective in nature. The basis for determining probability will be discussed in more detail in the proceeding chapters.

Putting it All Together

Figure 1.3 illustrates the components of risk and their interaction with each other. Now that we have all the pieces in place, let's put them together:

- The first component of risk is a future event, which can either be an action or inaction.
- The second component of risk is the probability or likelihood of that future event happening.
- The third component of risk is the asset, which is directly or indirectly affected by the event.
- The fourth component of risk is the outcome, which is the impact of the event on the asset.

Information Security Risk

Now that we have a high level definition of risk as well as an understanding of the primary components of risk, it's time to put this all into the context of information security risk. As we mentioned at the beginning of this chapter each field or discipline has its own definition of risk because each field has their own perception of what risk is.

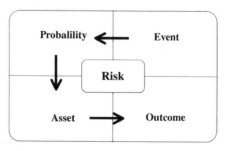

Figure 1.3 Components of Risk and their Interactions

In information security, risk revolves around three important concepts: threats, vulnerabilities and impact (see Figure 1.4).

1. *Threat* is an event, either an action or an inaction that leads to a negative or unwanted situation.
2. *Vulnerabilities* are weaknesses or environmental factors that increase the probability or likelihood of the threat being successful.
3. *Impact* is the outcome such as loss or potential for a loss due to the threat leveraging the vulnerability.

Sounds familiar? Of course it does. We have talked about all of this before. Figure 1.5 shows how to apply them to our risk components illustration.

We see that threat, vulnerability, and impact are just different interpretations of event, probability and outcome. This is important to note, as this will assist you in explaining your risk definition to other people reviewing your assessment. As we talked about earlier in this section, other people who are involved in risk management functions within your organization may not be familiar with the concepts of threats and vulnerabilities and may be more familiar with the generic risk concepts of event and probability.

As seen in Figure 1.5, we can overlay our hacker and backup tape examples to see how the components work together to illustrate a real risk statement.

In this example, the full risk statement is:

- Unauthorized access by hackers through exploitation of weak access controls within the application could lead to the disclosure of sensitive data.

Our second example is illustrated in Figure 1.6.
For the example in Figure 1.6, the full risk statement is:

- Accidental loss or theft of unencrypted backup tapes could lead to the disclosure of sensitive data.

Now that we have covered defining Risk and it's components, we will now delve deeper into the background, purpose, and objectives of an information security risk assessment.

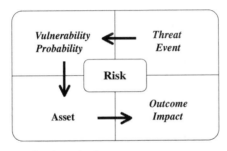

Figure 1.4 Risk and Information Security Concepts

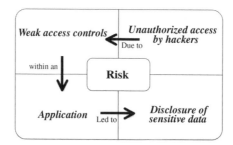

Figure 1.5 Illustration of an Information Security Risk Statement (Unauthorized Access)

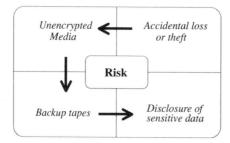

Figure 1.6 Illustration of an Information Security Risk Statement (Unencrypted Media)

THE REAL WORLD

Jane has extensive experience in IT, particularly in application development and operations; however, she is relatively new to the information security field. She received a battlefield promotion to the role of information security officer at the financial organization she worked for (ACME Financials) after a data breach occurred. Focusing on information security she obtained her CISSP designation and built up the security program at her company by aligning with well-known information security frameworks.

Jane excelled in her position, and came to the attention of a large healthcare organization after one of the auditors of ACME Financials mentioned her to the CIO at the healthcare organization. After some aggressive recruiting the CIO convinced Jane to join the hospital system as their information security officer. Although she had limited exposure to the Healthcare Insurance Portability and Accountability Act (HIPAA) she is comfortable with working in a regulated environment as her previous organization was subject to Gram-Leach-Bliley Act (GLBA) requirements. The position is new to the hospital system and was created in response to an audit comment noted in a HIPAA audit performed by an external party.

One of the primary tasks that the CIO has for Jane is to build up the information security program. Jane is actually a little hesitant since the organization is significantly larger than her prior company; however, she is up to the challenge. Throughout this book we will keep coming back to Jane's situation and see how risk assessments play a role in her journey to keep her new company, and frankly her new job, safe!

Let's talk about Jane's first day on the job. She wasn't expecting much. Just show up at HR, get her keys, badges, and attend the new employee orientation. Basically, just ease into her new job and allow hereself to adjust and get a feel for the organization. As you well know, that seldom happens in the real world. Instead of sitting in new employee orientation the CIO of the hospital decided at the spur of the moment to ask her to speak to the IT managers, some members of the hospitals risk committee, audit department, and other select department heads of the hospitals about what she believes the organizations primary information security risks are!

Whoa! Definitely not the first day Jane was expecting. But she wasn't going to let this rattle her. Well, she was rattled a little but she was not completely unprepared. In her prior company she had implemented her program using a risk-based approach so she was familiar with the concept of risk. She also knew that with this diverse group of people, they would probably come to the meeting with their own preset ideas on the definition of risk in the context of their specific department or field. Since it was her first day, she really didnt want to ruffle any feathers by minimizing or highlighting specific risks since she didn't feel like she knew enough about the organizations operating environment to make that call.

With all of that in mind, instead of going up and enumerating risks from out of the air, Jane decided to start with a conciliatory note:

"Each one of us here would most likely have their own ideas of what the "primary" risks are. For example, for audit, you would probably be concerned about the possibility of a lack of compliance to HIPAA. For the department heads here, this could be the possibility that we'll be unable to deliver service to our patients. For others, it could be a possible inability to protect our patient's personal information. All of these are valid risks and all could produce a negative impact to our organization. But in order to answer the question of which ones are the "primary" risks to the organization, we need to start measuring risk through a documented and repeatable process. This is one of the main things that I plan to start with, a formal risk assessment process for information security. Though ultimately risk is always based on perception, a formal process will allow us to look at all the risks in a more objective manner. What I would really like to do now is go around the table and ask each of you to tell me what risks are of primary concern to your department."

As Jane waits for a response from the group she is met with blank stares! Not one to give up, she decided to just start with the person immediately on her left and then work her way around the room, helping each of the participants to convey their risk in a structured way by utilizing her knowledge of the definitions and components of risk. For example when she was talking to the applications manager:

Jane:	"What security event are you worried about?"
Application Manager:	"Hmmm. Not much really. But I guess hackers might be able to get into our hospital website?"
Jane:	"That's is worth looking into. What things to do you have in place to protect from hackers?"
Applications Manager:	"Hmmm. Nothing on our side. But we do have a firewall. Besides the website is just html and I don't think they'll be able to use anything there."
Jane:	"But they can deface the website right?"
Applications Manager:	"Right. That's true, they can deface the website by changing the files."

CIO: "Hmmm. I think we'll want to look more into that. That would be really embarrassing to the hospital. If people think we can't protect our website, then how would they be comfortable that we can protect their sensitive information?"

By going around the table, Jane is beginning to see trends in the risks that the people in the room are most concerned with and equally as important is able to start identifying preconceptions that may be wrong. You've also probably noticed that she is doing it in a very structured way; ask for the threat, then the vulnerability, and finally the asset. It's good to know the basics since if push comes to shove you can fall back onto basics to guide a productive conversation about risk.

By going around the room and letting other people talk, with some gentle guiding, she was able to quickly learn quite a bit about the perception of risk within her new organization. She did run into some snags, one of the attendees was adamant that the risk assessment could be done in a day and was under the impression that the meeting they were having was the risk assessment, not understanding why the process would actually take some time and require meetings with multiple groups. Now the meeting was probably not what Jane's CIO was expecting but hey, it's her first day and she knows she is going to educate her new boss as much, or probably even more, than anyone else in the organization. Although done indirectly, Jane was able to convey that one person cannot identify all risks alone since different perspectives are needed and that this would ultimately be an organizational effort. She also demonstrated her knowledge of the concept of risk and used that knowledge to create a structured information gathering approach for questioning the meeting participants.

All in all, not a bad first day for our information security officer!

WHAT IS AN INFORMATION SECURITY RISK ASSESSMENT?

In the past few decades, modern society has become increasingly dependent on information systems. We have also seen massive efforts to collect personal information by the private and public sector. This might be best evidenced by the rise of social networks and the use of "the cloud" as a repository for personal information. In many ways, people have started to out-source parts of their lives to service providers.

These changes in our information landscape have led to newer non-traditional risks to organizations and individuals. These risks have also moved into the warfare arena where nations are struggling with moving from a kinetic landscape to the amorphous cyber landscape.

All these changes are placing an increasing importance on security and privacy. Understandably, there has been a commensurate increase in the need for requirements to identify risks in information systems. This is reflected in the number of laws and regulations that have been implemented that require some level of security and privacy controls be implemented over sensitive data. This process of identifying risk, as we already know, is called an information security risk assessment.

An information security risk assessment, also known as an information security risk analysis, involves identifying and assessing risks to the confidentiality, integrity, and availability of information systems and resources. This process should be a fundamental requirement for any security program in any organization.

Why Assess Information Security Risk?

In the previous section, we talked about how risk assessments are all about measurement. In order to protect something, we need to identify first what we should be protecting and what we should be protecting it from. As the old saying goes "Being forewarned is being forearmed."

Performing an information security assessment allows an organization to "know themselves" with respect to their risk exposures. As Sun Tzu stated in "The Art of War":

> *So it is said that if you know your enemies and know yourself, you can win a hundred battles without a single loss.*
>
> *If you only know yourself, but not your opponent, you may win or may lose.*
>
> *If you know neither yourself nor your enemy, you will always endanger yourself.*

Knowing what dangers the organization is exposed to is an essential step that must be completed prior to trying to prioritize or implement safeguards or controls to protect the organization.

This knowledge ensures that controls, and ultimately the expenditures needed to implement and support these controls are commensurate to the risk the organizations assets are exposed to. Thus if the assessment shows that there is greater risk to one asset, then greater protection and resources should be applied to that asset versus an asset shown as being at lower risk. This not only allows the organization to provide an appropriate level of security it also helps determine the acceptable level of risk that the organization is willing to accept based on the effort or expenditure involved in the application of the control or safeguard.

As an information security professional, it is essential to understand why it is critical to perform an information security risk assessment. Obviously it makes good sense to perform an assessment but ultimately it is one of the most effective tools for justifying necessary activities to management and other people in the organization who might question the need for security requirements or expenditures.

Depending on the framework used and the approach taken, the manpower and resources involved in performing an information security risk assessment may be substantial. Thus at one time or another, you will need to explain why you need to perform this activity and ultimately budget for it. Depending on who is asking you why the work needs to be performed, your best bet will be one of the following responses:

- This will enable us to identify our high-risk information assets.
- This will enable us to identify what assets we need to protect.
- This will enable us to determine what safeguards we need for high-risk assets.
- This will enable us to determine how much protection we need to apply to an asset.
- This will enable us to determine what security initiatives we need to implement.
- This will enable us to determine whether we are at risk of non-compliance for [put law and regulation here].

- This will assist us to determine how much manpower and what skillset we need to protect our assets.
- This will assist us to determine an accurate budget for the security program.
- This will assist us to determine what security technologies that we need to procure for the organization.

Of course this cheat sheet of responses is not all encompassing but is intended to help you answer questions regarding the usefulness of an information security risk assessment. In our experience, the most useful answers are probably the ones related to determining the risk of non-compliance with laws and regulations since the organization is required to be compliant as well as the ones relating to determining a security budget because anything that would streamline spending is awlays an easy thing to justify.

Risk Assessments and the Security Program

As we mentioned earlier in this section, we believe that information security risk assessments should be a fundamental requirement for any security program. An information security function should be able to utilize this process as a guide to achieve three primary objectives:

1. First and foremost, an information security risk assessment is the first step to determine safeguards needed to secure information systems that store and process information. By undergoing this process, it assists the security function in the discovery, correction, and prevention of security problems. This will also allow for the creation of security requirements from the resulting conclusions and documentation stemming from the process. Ultimately, through regular assessments, this will allow the organization to consistently devise, implement, and monitor security measures to address the level of identified risk.

2. An information security risk assessment will allow an organization to comply with internal and external requirements. Internal requirements are typically organizational policies that are the result of an audit requirement or guidance from standard security frameworks such as ISO 27001 or NIST SP800-53 both of which require a risk assessment as part of the overall framework. External requirements are typically federal laws and regulations that require an organization to conduct an information security risk assessment. Examples include the Gramm-Leach-Bliley Act (GLBA), Health Insurance Portability and Accountability Act (HIPAA), and Federal Information Security Management Act (FISMA). There has also been a trend towards state specific security and privacy laws requirements that demand the same.

3. From a management perspective, an information security risk assessment can enable the information security function to make well-informed decisions. The results and conclusions of the assessment can be used as leverage to justify expenditures, manpower, time, budgeting, technology purchases, and service procurements.

Additionally, an information security risk assessment has great value to an organizations information security practitioners. A risk assessment can be particularly helpful if the security program is just starting. Ideally, if you are in charge of setting up or redesigning an organizations security program, an information security risk assessment is a good way to kick off your program. For one, it is easily justifiable since most security frameworks recommend a risk assessment and it also shows management and other key stakeholders your commitment to a standardized approach and a dedication to the responsible allocation of resources. The results of the assessment can be used to have information driven discussions with executive management when discussing appropriate levels of controls and security program requirements for the organization.

Information Risk Assessments Activities in a Nutshell

Just as there are multiple definitions of risk, there are many different risk assessment frameworks. Over the course of this book, we will introduce you to a number of frameworks such as ISO 27005, NIST SP800-30, FAIR, OCTAVE, ENISA, CRAMM, EBIOS, and RiskIT. With the number of different frameworks it can get confusing at times, particularly when a group or individual insists that their way is the right way. What we will illustrate in some of the chapters to come is that some frameworks, in certain situations, are just not feasible to use.

Just like the definition of risk, information security risk assessments themselves have common generic components and activities that are shared across all of the frameworks. Knowing these basic components will allow you to distill the fundamental principles from all of the assessment frameworks, which in turn will allow you to conduct a defensible risk assessment no matter what approach, methodology, or technique you may use.

Most, if not all risk assessment frameworks revolve around the six activities shown in Figure 1.7. You might find these terms familiar since in one way or another these are related to our definition of risk.

Let us walk through a high level overview of each activity in order to allow you to put into context the different frameworks and methodologies that we will be discussing in the coming chapter. Each individual activity will also be discussed in greater detail within future chapters.

Identify Threats

This activity is focused on identifying possible information security threats. These threats are events, sources, actions, or inactions that could potentially lead to harm of your organizations information security assets. Many of the frameworks represent threats as a combination of threat actions and threat sources as illustrated in Figure 1.8.

In this example, a hacker is a threat source, while unauthorized access is the threat action. Therefore, the threat in this scenario is unauthorized access by a hacker.

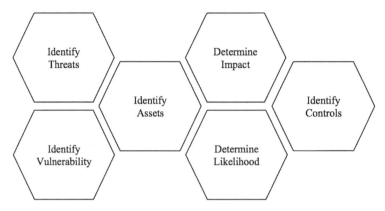

Figure 1.7 Primary Activities in a Risk Assessment

A threat source can typically have more than one threat action. For example, a hacker could also conduct a denial of service attack, manipulate or delete data, or use the resource for other purposes aside from just simply unauthorized access.

The objective of this activity is to identify all possible threats to an asset. The result of this activity is typically a list or "catalog". Threat determination can be very subjective so it helps to use a standard threat catalog. As with the definition of risk, and risk assessment frameworks, there are also a variety of threat catalogs to choose from. No one catalog is the authoritative source for threats; however, some catalogs provide decent listings including catalogs provided by ISO27005, NIST SP800-30, OWASP, and BITS. Further discussion about these catalogs will be provided in upcoming chapters.

Identify Vulnerabilities

This activity is focused on identifying vulnerabilities that could be exploited by the threats that you have identified. The existence of a vulnerability is a major contributing

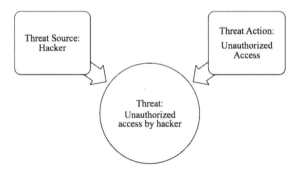

Figure 1.8 Threat Actions and Threat Sources

factor for calculating the probability of risk. If an asset has a vulnerability that can be exploited by a threat, then the risk to that asset is much higher when compared to an asset that does not have the same vulnerability.

As in the example in Figure 1.9, if a system has weak passwords, a hacker who is able to find and leverage a "weak password" in an information system has a greater chance of achieving unauthorized access. Therefore, we can see here that a vulnerability increases the probability of a threat source achieving its threat action.

The objective of this activity is to determine all potential vulnerabilities to the asset that could be leveraged by a threat source. The outcome of this activity is typically captured in the form of a vulnerability listing. There are actually two possible approaches to take here. Either you make a comprehensive vulnerability listing of all possible vulnerabilities that you can think of or you can focus only on the vulnerabilities that have already been identified within the organization. These approaches will be discussed in more detail in Chapters 3 to 6 but ultimately the final goal here is to prepare a list of vulnerabilities. If the second approach is used, that of listing down identified vulnerabilities, you will be largely dependent on the availability of documentation in your organization. Sources of good vulnerability data for your organization can include penetration testing reports, previous risk assessments, vulnerability assessments, security incident data, security metrics, and other third party or internal audit reports.

Identify Assets

Before any assessment can be conducted, there needs to be an asset or assets to be assessed. Typically, a risk assessment encompasses all critical assets of the organization that have a direct impact to the confidentiality, integrity, and availability of the organizations information resources. But identifying critical assets is definitely easier said than done.

One of the first questions that you will encounter when you begin trying to identify an asset is "What does the organization consider a critical asset?" This is very subjective and you will receive a variety of different answers in response to this question depending on who you ask. As with risk, defining what a critical asset is, will often be based on perception. For example, in a hospital a person who works on a radiation therapy system would consider that the most important system in the hospital while another who works on the financial systems would consider that as the most important. The critical part here is to be able to obtain all possible perspectives in order to make the most informed decision possible.

Figure 1.9 Threat Source Leveraging a Vulnerability

The objective of this activity is to identify to the best of your knowledge, all the critical assets of the organization. The result of this activity is typically a list of applications, databases, hardware, software, processes, and people. Though there will be differing views as to what is considered a critical asset, most of the time you will end up with a list consisting of the main enterprise applications and databases. These assets are typically those that are tied to core processes within the organization. Regardless of the type of industry you are in you can almost always expect to see your HR and Financial systems on the list along with those systems that support customer management, e-commerce, or corporate reporting.

The most important part of this activity is primarily data collection. Important documents that you will want to procure and review include business impact analysis documents, asset inventory reports, previous risk assessments, and third party audits. Aside from these documents, it is very helpful to set up asset scoping workshops to obtain feedback from various people in order to obtain their views on what the critical systems of the organization are.

Determine Impact

In all risk assessment frameworks that you will encounter, there will be in some form or another, a measurement of impact. As previously mentioned, impact is the outcome, typically harmful, of a threat applied to an asset. This is also one of the primary components for computing a risk rating.

The objective of this activity is to produce a measurement for impact. This will be part of an impact and likelihood matrix, which will ultimately produce your risk ratings. There are many different ways to determine impact and contrary to what you may read in some literature there is no single correct method for determining impact.

Quantitative risk assessments, deal with estimating loss based on a financial perspective by using calculations like Single Loss Expectancy (SLE), Annualized Rate of Occurrence (ARO), and Annualized Loss Expectancy (ALE). As an example, a HIPAA violation not due to willful neglect carries a penalty of $100 for each violation, with the total amount not to exceed $250,000; therefore, we know that if a database with several thousand patient records was compromised, the impact to your organization will be $25,000. But if this was due to willful neglect, the impact could be as much as $1.5 million. This may be the most objective way to determine impact, but in reality, this is highly dependent on information that may not always be readily available.

Qualitative determination of impact differs from quantitative in that qualitative risk assessments do not try to put a financial value to the asset and the subsequent monetary losses stemming from the threat. In this approach one measures relative values. For example, if we have a health information system that handles all enterprise wide information processing, a business owner might say that losing the system will affect virtually all operations of the hospital. In this scenario, one might not be able to assign an accurate monetary value without going through hospital financials and working closely with the accounting department, which for all intents and purposes, though helpful, is not the primary objective of an information security risk assessment. In qualitative analysis you would typically assign a relative value. This would be a statement such as "Loss of system availability for the target system will have a HIGH impact in terms of availability of information processing across the organization and could cause significant financial losses."

Determine Likelihood

Likelihood is the probability that a threat would exploit a vulnerability to affect an asset. Together with impact and control maturity, this is a primary component in determining a risk rating for an asset.

The objective of this activity is to measure the possibility of the threat happening by assigning a likelihood value. This value will be part of an impact and likelihood matrix, which will ultimately produce your risk ratings.

As with most aspects of a risk assessment, there is a subjective component that comes into play; however, as security professionals, this subjectivity is tempered by the assessors' expertise, experience, and judgment.

For instance in Figure 1.10, an experienced information security professional would know that the likelihood of unauthorized access from an external hacker is higher for an Internet facing system when compared to a system that is accessible only through the local Intranet. This scenario utilizes exposure as a basis for likelihood and is directed at the asset. Another example would be that the threat of loss of availability due to a physical data center accident is higher when compared to say a volcanic or other geological event. This scenario utilizes frequency as a basis for likelihood determination and is directed towards the threat source.

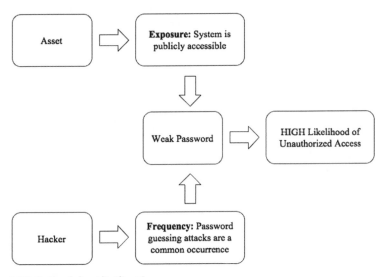

Figure 1.10 Determining Likelihood

Identify Controls

Controls are mechanisms that detect or prevent threats sources from leveraging vulnerabilities and thus are closely tied to likelihood as it affects the probability of a risk.

The objective of this activity is to identify what controls are currently in place for the asset that would have an effect on the threat that is being assessed. For example, if you are assessing a threat of a hacker leveraging weak passwords in a system, one needs to identify if there are existing controls that would affect the probability of that risk actually happening. Let's say the system being assessed supports and enforces password complexity, as this control directly affects the potential vulnerability of weak passwords, this would affect the probability of the threat successfully exploiting the vulnerability and thus have a proportionate effect on the risk rating.

Typically, in the various risk assessment frameworks, you will be providing a control score, of some type, for each of the threats assessed. As a rule, the stronger the control, the less likely the risk is to occur. This concept will be discussed in greater detail within the coming chapters.

THE REAL WORLD

Jane has now been working at the hospital system for two weeks. After multitudes of orientations, introductions, and meetings she has her first weekly working meeting with the CIO.

CIO: "So let's get this going. Internal audit has been riding me about our security program and initiatives. Can you draft up something so I can give it to them?"

Jane: "Sure, I've been doing some research about that and I think we should go with a standard framework. Maybe ISO 27001 or this health care specific security standard called HITRUST. We can't go wrong with following a standard. Those are the documents I emailed to you last week."

CIO: "Ah, yep. I saw those. Is that what those were? Seems like a lot of work and honestly, I don't think we have the budget or manpower to do all of those. And besides, we're a hospital not a bank. We need to prioritize."

Jane: "I totally agree. Actually, in HIPAA, we are required to do an information security risk assessment or analysis. That's how we'll be able to identify our high-risk areas and focus on them. That way, we know what we need to protect and can focus our money on protecting the resources that are worth protecting."

CIO: "Hmmm. That makes sense. Tell me more about this information security risk assessment. I'm going to a budget meeting very soon and I'll need to bring up why we need it."

Jane: "Well for one, aside from being required by HIPAA, I think it just makes sense. For the purposes of our overall goal of developing a sound security program and corresponding initiatives, conducting a risk assessment will really allow us to memorialize our decision-making process and demonstrate that we took a risk-based approach. I know you mentioned to me that one of the things you wanted to bring up with the budget committee was the need for backup tape encryption. A risk assessment will use a structured approach to show that this is an area of

> high risk for the organization which will likely make it much easier for us to get the initiative approved."
>
> CIO: "Interesting. So how will it show we need backup encryption? I'd really like to discuss that with the committee."
>
> Jane: "It would be good if you gave an example based on the risk assessment process. It starts with threat and vulnerabilities. For example identify the threat first: our backups being stolen or lost. Then the vulnerability: our backups being unencrypted."
>
> CIO: "Ok, sounds good so far"
>
> Jane: "After that discuss the impact and likelihood. Our backups are being shipped to an offsite location on a daily basis so there's a chance that they could be lost or even stolen while in transit. Then you can tell them of the impact if our unencrypted backups, which include ePHI, got lost. Based on some rough calculations I did after our last discussion I think the HIPAA penalties alone could be around $1.5 million."
>
> CIO: "Really? Hmmm. That will certainly raise a few eyebrows in the budget meeting, especially when I'm only asking for $125,000."
>
> Jane: "Yea, and we will do this for all the significant risks in the organization and base the prioritization of our security initiatives on the results of the analysis. I think that would be a good start for our security program."
>
> CIO: "Good. It seems that you've thought this out. I knew there was a reason why I hired you. Can you give this risk assessment of yours to me next week?"
>
> Jane: "Say what!?"
>
> So in this single meeting with the CIO, using her basic knowledge of the objectives and components of an information security risk assessment, Jane was able to convey why we need to do a risk assessment and even gave a quick walkthrough of the process involved. Of course, our CIO still has the wrong idea of the actual resources and time needed to conduct a information security risk assessment from scratch but otherwise Jane appears to have been able to convince the CIO of the value of doing the assessment.

Now that we have covered information security risk assessments, we will have a quick discussion about some of the key US laws and regulations that require us to conduct information security risk assessments.

DRIVERS, LAWS, AND REGULATIONS

In this section, we will be discussing the most common US laws, regulations, policies and frameworks related to information security risk assessments. As previously mentioned, risk assessments are often executed as part of an organizations obligation to meet a regulatory requirement. Thus, being knowledgeable about some of the major regulatory requirements that mandate risk assessments is of benefit to the information security practitioner, especially if they operate in one of the affected industries.

The diagram in Figure 1.11 represents the major risk assessment "drivers" in the United States.

Federal Information Security Management Act of 2002 (FISMA)

For federal agencies, one of the primary regulations around information security compliance is the Federal Information Security Management Act of 2002 or FISMA.

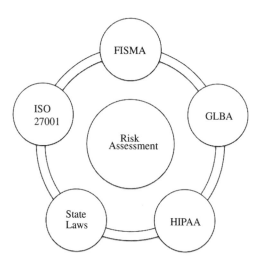

Figure 1.11 Primary Information Security Risk Assessment "Drivers"

This act requires all federal agencies to develop, document, and implement an information security program to protect information and information systems that support the assets and operations of the agency. This is meant to protect agency operations, which includes its mission, functions, image, and reputation.

FISMA is a requirement for all federal agencies and the Office of Management and Budget (OMB) is tasked to provide oversight for FISMA. As part of their responsibility, OMB has provided Memorandum 99-20, which provides guidelines on the security of federal automated information resources.

This memorandum or circular reinforces the tenet that federal agencies should have a continual assessment of risk in computer systems and maintain adequate security commensurate with the risk. Risk is mentioned multiple times within the circular from OMB. The OMB states that federal agencies should consider the risk when deciding what security controls to implement and recommends implementing a risk-based approach to security. This means that security should be commensurate with the risk and magnitude of harm such as loss, misuse, unauthorized access, and modification. Based on the circular, when determining the adequacy of security, federal agencies should be considering the major risk factors, which are the value of the system, threats, vulnerabilities, and the effectiveness of controls and safeguards.

Now hopefully none of this should surprise you. Since we already had a primer regarding the concept of risk and the components of the risk assessment, the considerations such as the value of the asset, the threat, the vulnerabilities and effectiveness of the controls should sound familiar when we talk about risk.

Overall, the basic concepts of FISMA and the OMB circulars are very sound. They highlight the need for a risk-based policy through which an agency could have a "foundational" level of security. As you can imagine, an essential part of setting this "foundation" is to gain an understanding of what risks the organization is exposed to and thus a risk assessment must be performed. Accordingly, OMB points to the National Institute of Standards and Technology (NIST) for specific standards regarding risk assessments. The standards released by NIST will be discussed in Chapter 2 of this book.

Gramm-Leach-Bliley Act (GLBA)

The Gramm-Leach-Bliley Act, or GLBA, primarily affects financial institutions. GLBA defines financial institutions, as companies that offer financial products or services to individuals, like loans, financial or investment advice, or insurance.

Specific sections of GLBA, particularly the Information Security Guidelines of section 501(b), require institutions to establish standards and safeguards around administrative, technical, and physical security. These safeguards are meant to protect against anticipated threats and hazards and ensure the security and integrity of company and customer information and information systems.

As such, security practitioners in institutions that need to maintain GLBA compliance are required to assess the risks of reasonably foreseeable threats, and in particular those that could result in unauthorized disclosure, misuse, alteration, and destruction of information and information systems. In fact, the institution is required to report to its board at least annually on its information security program with a focus on risk assessments and risk management.

GLBA also states that following the assessment of risk, the organization should design a program to assess the identified risk and develop and maintain appropriate measures to address these risks.

Within GLBA most of the discussions about risk assessments, and what is required for a compliant risk assessment, are high level and rather broad; as is the term "financial institution". This leaves room for specific regulators or bodies to provide their own interpretation regarding various security related topics. Some such regulatory bodies include:

- Federal Deposit Insurance Corporation (FDIC).
- Office of the Comptroller of the Currency (OCC).
- National Credit Union Administration (NCUA).
- Consumer Financial Protection Bureau (CFPB).
- MAIC Mergers & Acquisitions International Clearing.

As a result of there being multiple regulatory bodies evaluating various organizations for GLBA compliance, the Federal Financial Institutions Examination Council (FFIEC) was empowered to create standards in order to promote uniformity in the supervision of financial institutions.

In our experience, the various sets of guidance, with specific focus on the IT Examination Handbook published by the FFIEC, are quite useful. This document actually includes a specific section on information security risk assessments.

The guidance provided by this document will be discussed in more detail in the information security risk assessment framework section of this book.

Health Insurance Portability and Accountability Act (HIPAA)

The Health Insurance Portability and Accountability Act (HIPAA) focuses on health-care providers, insurers, and employers. Specific sections of HIPAA, particularly the Security Rule, focus on the need to adequately and effectively protect Electronic Protected Health Information or ePHI by adhering to good business practices for systems handling ePHI.

Specifically, in the Security Rule, HIPAA requires all covered entities (healthcare providers, insurers, etc.) and their Business Associates (vendors, contractors, etc.) to conduct an accurate and thorough Risk Analysis (or a Risk Assessment). This Risk Analysis should assess the potential risks and vulnerabilities that could affect the confidentiality, integrity, and availability of ePHI.

The Department of Health and Human Services (HHS) is tasked to provide oversight over HIPAA. HHS has provided a significant number of guidance documents and memorandums regarding the security rule. One in particular focuses specifically on Risk Analysis (HIPAA Security Standards: Guidance on Risk Analysis).

This guidance document states that Risk Analysis is foundational and is the first step in identifying safeguards or controls as well as ultimately implementing these safeguards. It also states that risk analysis allows the organization to determine the appropriateness of these safeguards or at the very least, document the rationale as to why these safeguards are in place.

There are also some specific guidelines that HHS includes in the requirements associated with risk analysis, particularly whether the organization has identified the locations of ePHI, external sources that handle ePHI, as well as identifying human, natural, and environmental threats.

Though HIPAA or HHS does not prescribe a specific methodology, its guidance is based primarily on the recommendations of NIST, which we discussed during our overview of FISMA. According to HHS, following NIST guidance provides a framework, which can be considered an industry standard, for assisting in securing an organizations ePHI.

While HHS bases its guidance primarily on NIST, there are also several other referenced methodologies that are provided by HHS to assist in performing Risk Analysis including:

- Guidance from the Office of National Coordinator for Health Information Technology (ONC).
- Healthcare Information and Management Systems Society (HIMSS).
- Health Information Trust Alliance (HITRUST).

In our experience, NIST's methodology appears to work well in dealing with HIPAA related risk assessments. The use of this standard, and others, will be discussed in more details in the Framework and Methodologies section of this book.

State Governments

Though regulations that require risk assessments are mostly federal in nature and focused on a specific industry, we have seen the beginning of state level laws and regulations that require risk assessments in one form or another. From what we have seen, most of the current state level laws or regulations are usually based on existing federal ones such as FISMA or HIPAA.

As an example, we will use the Massachusetts Commonwealth Enterprise Information Security Policy, which is one of the most mature state based information security regulations in the United States. This particular policy statement provides specific guidance for state agencies to perform risk assessments. According to the policy statement, their risk assessments must include the identification of risk factors and the identification of threats. Additionally, agencies are required to identify risk, quantitate risk, and prioritize risk based on operational and control objectives so as to provide reasonable assurance that risk is managed at an acceptable level.

The policy specifically recommends the CMS (Centers for Medicare & Medicaid Services) Information Security Risk Assessment Procedure, which is based on NIST SP800-30, which will be discussed extensively in the coming chapters.

ISO 27001

ISO 27001 is not a law or regulation but is one of the most widely adopted security frameworks in the world. It is a framework for establishing an effective information security management system (ISMS). This framework is considered a top down and risk-based approach, which is technology neutral.

Not surprisingly, one of the first requirements for ISO 27001 compliance is to define the risk assessment approach of the organization. According to the framework, the risk assessment methodology should be based on business, information security, legal and regulatory requirements and should have a criterion for accepting and identifying acceptable risk levels. Another important aspect that the framework states is the risk assessment approach should be able to produce comparable and reproducible results.

ISO 27001 also mentions that the organization should be able to identify risks by identifying the assets and asset owners, identifying threats, and identifying vulnerabilities which impacts confidentiality, integrity, and availability. As we've talked about in this chapter, these are common paradigms that are seen over and over again throughout the major risk assessment frameworks.

Aside from just identifying risk, ISO 27001 requires the organization to analyze and evaluate risks. This evaluation is based on the business impact of the security failure, the realistic likelihood (considering current controls), estimation of the risk, and a determination for accepting the risk. Basically, these are just different way of saying that an organization needs to evaluate the impact and likelihood of the risk, components of risk management that we discussed previously.

ISO 27001 primarily refers practitioners to ISO 27005, which is the techniques document that focuses on Information Security Risk Management. This document will be discussed in further detain within the methodologies section of the book.

As previously stated, ISO 27001 is not a law; however, in this period of internationalization, it has become a way for one business to attest to another business that they are sufficiently exercising an acceptable level of security controls.

Now that we have covered the different laws and regulations that your organization might need to be complaint with let us proceed with the next chapter and talk about the various risk assessment frameworks that we can use.

THE REAL WORLD

Wow. It was a hectic first two weeks for our new information security officer but fortunately she came prepared. She knew that knowing about risk and risk assessments was going to be an important part of her job as well as the fulcrum for forcing changes onto the organization and as a frame for discussions with the organizations senior leadership team. Not only that, she knew how to convey risk in a manner that different people from different departments were able to relate to. This highlights why knowing the basics is always a good idea.

Finally, with the week winding down, she decided to go to a meeting of the local ISACA chapter. The topic was risk management. At her table, she met a couple of information security professionals there that worked in other industries including one from the public sector and one from her old familiar world of finance.

Jane:	"Hi guys, glad to see there are other security officers here. And what a coincidence we ended up at just one table!"
Federal Agency ISO:	"Yea, that's great! I used to attend more regularly but I've been so busy lately doing our annual risk assessment."
Bank ISO:	"Boy I can relate! That's a pain but we have to do it. No choice in the matter."
Jane:	"No choice on the matter? Your bosses are forcing you?"
Federal Agency ISO:	"Nope, since I work for a federal agency, a risk assessment is required because of FISMA."
Bank ISO:	"Same here. But in our case it's complying with GLBA."
Jane:	"That's interesting. I knew that financial institutions had to comply with GLBA; however, I had no idea that Federal agencies had to conduct a risk assessment."
Federal Agency ISO:	"Yup, risk assessments are pretty much standard nowadays. Honestly, even if you're not required, it's just good practice."
Bank ISO:	"Yea, aside from that, we adopted ISO 27001 as our framework and we are trying to get certified. Risk Assessments are required as part of the ISO 27001 framework so even without GLBA, we would have done it anyway."
Jane:	"Wow! I'm glad I attended. It feels like I'm with other people in the same situation! Just like therapy!"

So our information security officer left the ISACA meeting feeling much better. She didn't care much about the speaker since the talk ended up being pretty bad; however, she did enjoy meeting two like-minded information security officers who she feels will be a great resource for her in the coming months.

SUMMARY

What is Risk?

In this section we primarily learned about the meaning of risk. More specifically, we learned these key points:

- Risk is perceived differently in different fields and disciplines.
- Risk can be defined as a situation that exposes an object to harm.
- Risk can be defined as the measurement of uncertainty.
- The generic components of risk are:
  - Event.
  - Probability.
  - Asset.
  - Outcome.

- The components of information security risk are:

  - Threat.
  - Vulnerabilities.
  - Asset.

What is an Information Security Risk Assessment?

In this section we had a quick review of Information Risk Assessments. More specifically, we learned about these key points:

- Information security risk assessment or analysis is a fundamental requirement for any security program.
- The main objectives of an information security risk assessment is:
  - To determine safeguards needed to secure information systems that store and process information.
  - To assist an organization to comply with internal and external requirements.
  - To enable the information security function to make well-informed decisions.

- Components of an information security risk assessment:
  - Identify Threats.
  - Identify Vulnerabilities.
  - Identify Assets.
  - Determine Impact.
  - Determine Likelihood.
  - Identify Controls.

- Knowing why you are doing an information security risk assessment and knowing its components can help you make sense of the different methodologies and frameworks out there.

Drivers, Laws, and Regulations

In this section we primarily learned about the major US laws and regulations that directly or indirectly require organizations to conduct risk assessments. More specifically, we learned about the:

- Federal Information Security Management Act of 2002 or FISMA for federal agencies.
- Gramm-Leach-Bliley Act or GLBA for financial institutions.
- Health Insurance Portability and Accountability Act or HIPAA which is focused on healthcare providers, insurers' and employers.
- ISO 27001 which is not a law but an internationally recognized and widely adopted security standard.
- Various state government security policies.

REFERENCES

[1] Andrews. A Latin dictionary. Founded on Andrews' edition of Freund's Latin dictionary. Revised, enlarged, and in great part rewritten by Charlton T. Lewis, Ph.D. and Charles Short, LL.D. Clarendon Press: Oxford; 1879.

[2] Florio J. A vvorlde of wordes, or Most copious, and exact dictionarie in Italian and English, collected by Iohn Florio. Printed at London by Arnold Hatfield for Edw. Blount; 1598.

[3] Knight FH. Risk, uncertainty, and profit. Boston, MA: Hart, Schaffner & Marx; Houghton Mifflin Company; 1921.

[4] Hubbard Douglas. How to measure anything: finding the value of intangibles in business. John Wiley & Sons; 2007.

Information Security Risk Assessment: A Practical Approach

2

INFORMATION IN THIS CHAPTER:

- A Primer on Information Security Risk Assessment Frameworks
- Hybrid Risk Assessment Approach

INTRODUCTION

There has been quite a bit written about information security risk assessments. In fact, there are numerous published information security risk assessment frameworks and numerous books about the subject that are currently in circulation. But with so many frameworks to choose from why do organizations continue to struggle with the concept?

It can easily be stated that theory is not the problem with risk assessments. For the most part, risk assessment frameworks are based on the foundational concept of risk as was discussed in Chapter 1. The real difficulty lies in the implementation of these frameworks. Except for a few of the frameworks, most focus on concepts and principles represented in many cases as various risk formulas. What is almost universally missing is a practical approach on how to bring these frameworks into the workplace. For example, it is easy to say to someone that they need to identify assets and threats, but how do you actually go about doing this in an organization?

This chapter will attempt to address the gap between conceptual risk frameworks and actual workplace implementation. Coverage over major information security risk assessment frameworks such as OCTAVE, FAIR, NIST SP800-30, and ISO 27005 will be provided as well as a brief introduction to some lesser-known frameworks. This chapter will also introduce the reader to a hybrid approach to conducting risk assessments, which should not be seen as a competing framework but as a collection of practical ideas and techniques to implement the best parts of the aforementioned frameworks based on their underlying principles and individual strengths.

A PRIMER ON INFORMATION SECURITY RISK ASSESSMENT FRAMEWORKS

First and foremost, we need to understand what a framework is. A framework is some form of logical structure to organize information or activities. Thus, an information security risk assessment framework provides the logical structure or model to guide a user through the process of executing an information security risk assessment. Typically, these frameworks won't go into implementation details but will focus on foundational concepts associated with risk elements, high-level activities, formulas, and decision matrices, all of which are components essential to successfully conducting an information security risk assessment within an organization.

In this section, we will be focusing on the major information security risk assessment frameworks commonly used within the United States such as OCTAVE, FAIR, NIST, and ISO27005; however, we will also provide information on some additional frameworks and provide you with guidance on where you can obtain more information and resources regarding them.

This section is meant to be a primer so it will be a high-level overview instead of a detailed discussion regarding the different frameworks. This is only meant to be a guide and not a replacement for actually reading and going through the actual framework documents.

Do I Use an Existing Framework or Should I Use My Own?

One of the common challenges that we have encountered in our various engagements are the variety of different approaches that companies, professional service firms, or regulators will use to conduct or evaluate a risk assessment. We often run across organizations that use custom or modified frameworks that they have developed themselves. There is nothing wrong with this approach; however, in Table 2.1 we discuss some of the important pros and cons associated with use of a custom versus standard framework for conducting a risk assessment.

Obviously, the choice is yours but we recommend using a framework that gives you as much flexibility as you need, so that you can tailor it to your organization, while still maintaining a defensible position against the naysayers and people who always think they have a better way of doing things. The key is finding a balance between flexibility and soundness of concept. If you choose to customize your approach it is important to map it back to one of the major frameworks to show that you are following key tenants of a broadly accepted framework; however, it is equally as important to clearly document your rationale for the areas that you are not going to follow since those will be the most likely areas of challenge.

What follows is a primer on the different risk assessment frameworks to help provide you a sound background for assessing what framework, or combination of frameworks, will be best for you organization. One thing that you might find helpful is to have the actual framework document available while you read through the primer.

OCTAVE

OCTAVE is a collection of tools, techniques, and methods for risk based information security assessments. This framework was developed by the Software

Table 2.1 Standard and Custom Frameworks

	Pros	Cons
Standard Frameworks	There is less initial work since all you have to do is read and understand the framework A standard framework makes your work easier to defend. It is like using ISO 17799:2005 or COBIT. When you are asked why you are doing something you have a defensible position since you are using what is considered to be an industry standard	Frameworks were not created specific to your organization. The more detailed a framework is, the greater the chance that some aspect of it will not be applicable or will be difficult to implement in the context of your organization
Custom	More initial work since you will have to build all the formulas, activities and decision matrices for yourself	Depending on how knowledgeable the people building the custom framework are, they might miss some important key concepts regarding risk. Remember though that all "standard" frameworks were once custom as well
	If the people creating the custom framework are well versed with the theory behind risk assessments they can make a framework that is tailored to your organization and thus easier to implement	If you are using a custom non-standard framework, meaning it is not widely used, it may be more difficult to defend to stakeholders and auditors. For example, when asked the question, "Why are we using the Jane Smith Framework and not ISO 27005?." would you be able to answer that? Since a custom framework is often subjective in nature it is open to interpretation and opinion and may provoke challenges from parties that disagree with the results or are just trying to discredit you

Engineering Institute (SEI) of Carnegie Mellon through its CERT program. This is a highly regarded framework. Depending on the version of OCTAVE used, it is also very detailed, which tends to make it closely resemble a methodology instead of a framework. Many risk assessment practitioners agree that the detail level and complexity of the OCTAVE assessment approach has made it hard to adopt on a wide scale. Each revision to OCTAVE has been an attempt to streamline the approach; however, this has been met with mixed success. OCTAVE seems to work best when there already is a process, like an SDLC or large project, that requires assessing. OCTAVE can be very difficult to implement in the shorter everyday risk assessments.

Details

Currently OCTAVE has 3 different versions:

1. OCTAVE;
2. OCTAVE-S; and
3. OCTAVE-Allegro.

OCTAVE or (Operationally Critical Threat, Asset, and Vulnerability Evaluation) is the original framework and is the basis for all OCTAVE types of frameworks. It is recommended for large organizations (according to SEI this typically means an organization with more than 300 employees) that have the ability and resources to conduct internal security evaluations and workshops across the organization. Among the three, this version is the most prescriptive and very closely resembles a methodology. It is very comprehensive and contains various templates such as surveys, meeting minutes, and guidelines on how to conduct workshops. This framework recommends the involvement of a wide variety of people, many of whom are not directly involved in the risk management function.

OCTAVE-S was developed for smaller organizations. According to SEI, OCTAVE-S was made for organization with less than 100 employees and would require a team of 3–5 people who are knowledgeable about the company in order to complete the evaluation. This framework assumes that the people doing the assessment know about the company's assets, security requirements, threats and security practices and thus do not require the company-wide workshops and meetings that are prescribed in the original OCTAVE framework. The assumption that a company of only 100 employees could dedicate 3–5 people for the execution of a risk assessment is indicative of one of the major shortcomings of OCTAVE in general; an overall underestimation of the level of effort it takes to execute an assessment and the reasonable amount of resources that would have to be applied to be successful.

Finally, OCTAVE-Allegro is the most recent version of the framework. OCTAVE-Allegro was specifically streamlined for information security risk assessments. Similar to OCTAVE-S, this framework does not require extensive organizational involvement. We will be focusing on the Allegro iteration of OCTAVE and all future references of OCTAVE in this book will be regarding OCTAVE-Allegro.

The OCTAVE-Allegro framework describes eight steps and provides various worksheets and questionnaires as a guide and model on how to assess risk for the organization or more specifically the assets of the organization. What follows is a brief introduction to the eight steps of OCTAVE-Allegro.

Establish Risk Measurement Criteria

The initial step of OCTAVE-Allegro is to establish a way to measure risk. The idea here is that every organization would have a different view of risk and would place more importance on some aspects than on others. This simply means that at the very start you identify the main areas of possible impact that a threat could affect. You will also have to create the different impact criteria for each of the impact areas.

Some of the areas that octave recommends evaluating are (the first 5 are prescribed by OCTAVE-Allegro, the Sixth is intended to be customized by your organization):

1. Reputation/Customer Confidence.
2. Financial.
3. Productivity.
4. Safety and Health.
5. Fines and Legal Penalties.
6. User-defined Impact Criteria.

An interesting thing that you will see in the OCTAVE-Allegro risk computation which is a little bit different than the other frameworks, is that, not only will you provide scores for each of the impact areas, you will also provide a ranking which will be then be incorporated into the impact score. We will dive into this concept in more detail later on.

Develop an Information Asset Profile

The second step of OCTAVE-Allegro deals with collecting a list of information assets based on their importance to the organization. This list is created by focusing on the concept of identifying a "critical few" assets by executing a brainstorming session to rank assets based on a specific criteria. Several important activities included in this step are:

1. Documenting the owners.
2. Providing a description of the critical assets.
3. Identifying Confidentiality, Integrity, and Availability (CIA) requirements.
4. Identifying which of the CIA requirements is most important.
5. Rationale as to why the asset is important.

Identify Information Asset Containers

The third step of OCTAVE-Allegro is identifying the "information asset containers." This might be confusing at first but asset containers are simply assets that contain information. The information being collected here can be categorized into:

1. Technical—Hardware, Processes, Type of Information, Vendor, Partner Information, etc.
2. Physical—Location of the hardware/data, Data Centers, etc.
3. People—Asset Owners, Technical Contacts, etc.

Identify Areas of Concern

According to the OCTAVE-Allegro documentation, "Areas of Concern" are a descriptive statement that details a real-world condition or situation that could affect an information asset in your organization. OCTAVE has a tendency to use different terminologies but all this means is that you start identifying possible weaknesses or vulnerabilities for the system that is being reviewed. For example, this could be: On the web server, weak application security practices (vulnerability) from our developers. Or sensitive HR records left on the desks in the HR department.

Identify Threat Scenarios

One of the first things you may notice when reading through the OCTAVE-Allegro document is the difference between the previous step (*Identify Areas of Concern*) and this one. In *Identify Areas of Concern*, you are more focused on a condition derived from a potential weakness or vulnerability. In this step, you focus more on the threat leveraging that vulnerability thereby creating a threat scenario. For example, weak application security practices (vulnerability) from our developers could lead to potential unauthorized access by hackers (threat).

This threat scenario consists of a statement that combines the following factors:

1. Asset.
2. Access/Means.
3. Actor.
4. Motive.
5. Outcome.

This overall step description is not very detailed in the OCTAVE-Allegro documentation but one way to think of it is as if you were building a list of threats that could affect the asset. Other frameworks would call this process "building a threat catalog." A very helpful resource provided in this framework are the Threat Scenario Questionnaires provided toward the end of the Allegro document. These questionnaires provide a guide for preparing the threat scenarios through the use of a standardized list of questions.

Identify Risks

This step identifies the risk for the asset by simply creating a table listing down the threat and the impact. This is represented in the following formula:

Risk = Threat (condition) + Impact (consequence)

A sample table would look something like Table 2.2.

Table 2.2 Identify Risks	
Threat and Weaknesses	**Impact**
On the web server, weak application security practices from our developers could lead to unauthorized access from external hackers	Our website does not contain any confidential data but a public defacement could cause damage to the hospitals reputation as patients or potential patients may question the overall security of the organization
Sensitive patient records left in the open at nursing stations could be stolen or viewed by unauthorized personnel	Loss and disclosure of patient records could lead to fines up to $200,000 based on HIPAA regulations

Analyze Risks

The analysis computation of OCTAVE-Allegro is a little bit different from other frameworks as it focuses primarily on impact. Other frameworks typically use the "Impact × Likelihood" formula. It is not too say that Allegro does not consider likelihood but the likelihood value is in fact incorporated in a step associated with the selection of mitigating factors. Table 2.3 illustrates a threat to impact analysis table that could be completed. Going through this analysis helps establish a rationale to support the assignment of scores using Octave's impact scoring worksheets. An example of what the scoring for this threat would be is shown in Table 2.4.

The computations given in Table 2.4 are based on standard OCTAVE worksheets.

One thing that Allegro states, and which we tend to find holds true with most of the frameworks, is the scoring provided is only for the purposes of prioritization and is not to be used as an absolute indication of the level of risk. For example a score of 28 versus 10 only means that the 28 is relatively more important than the risk with 10 but it does not mean that the difference in 18 points means anything else.

Select Mitigation Approach

As mentioned in the previous step, the likelihood or probability is considered in the mitigation approach. This approach can be seen in this relative risk matrix in Step 8 Activity 1 of the Octave Allegro document.

Table 2.3 Analysis of Risk

Threat	Impact
On the web server, weak application security practices from our developers could lead to unauthorized access from external hackers	Our website does not contain any confidential data but a public defacement could cause damage to the hospitals reputation as it would cause customer concern with the overall security of the organization. Recovering from a public defacement and performing incident response activities would incur costs associated with IT services, lost productivity, as well as potential acquisition of outside services to assist with the incident investigation

Table 2.4 Sample Octave Scoring Worksheet

	Ranking	Impact Value	Score
Reputation	5	High (3)	15
Financial	3	Low (1)	3
Productivity	4	Moderate (2)	8
Safety and Health	1	Low (1)	1
Legal	2	Low (1)	2
		Overall Score	28

This relative risk matrix provides a means to categorize risk. The categorized risk will then fall into certain mitigation approaches, which brings us to the concept of "pools." These pools are determined by the intersection of the Risk Score computed in the previous step and the Probability of the threat happening.

In OCTAVE, there are four pools:

1. Pool 1—Mitigate.
2. Pool 2—Mitigate or Defer.
3. Pool 3—Defer or Accept.
4. Pool 4—Accept.

Once the pools are determined, the pools become the source of the mitigation strategy. For example, if the risk score falls under "Pool 2," the organization has the option to mitigate the risk or defer it to another time. This is a concept that provides a great deal of flexibility to an organization in its approach to mitigating risk since it provides options within the mitigation approach category that the risk falls into. For a more detailed discussion regarding the OCTAVE "pools," please refer to the OCTAVE documentation.

Strengths and Weaknesses of OCTAVE (see Table 2.5)

Table 2.5 Strengths and Weakness

Strengths	Weaknesses
Worksheets, decision/criteria matrices, and questionnaires are provided with the framework. This means that less preparation time for creating supplementary materials is needed	Even if Allegro is the streamlined version of OCTAVE, it is still relatively long and complex if followed to the letter when compared to other frameworks
Prescriptive though not as prescriptive as the original OCTAVE framework	No threat catalog is provided. It uses threat questionnaires which are very subjective. For inexperienced assessors, they may miss specific threats, which is less likely to happen if they are using a pre-made listing of threats. For threat catalogs, you might want to look at ISO27005, NIST SP800-30, or the BITS threat listing
Provides good impact criteria tables. It might be useful as a supplement even if you choose to use a different framework	Preparation of threat scenarios assumes that the assessor has good knowledge of the organization and the system (though this is an underlying assumption of Allegro), which in some cases may not possible
The document provided is fairly easy to follow	Adjustment based on controls is not explicitly computed. Sometimes, stakeholders and auditors have questions regarding how controls are incorporated and would like to see the impact of controls explicitly called out in the computation of risk

Table 2.5 Strengths and Weakness *Continued*

Strengths	Weaknesses
The concept of pools and how to categorize risk based on them is a good method of choosing mitigation approaches. May be useful even if you are using another framework	Likelihood is not explicitly computed in the risk analysis step but is part of the probability computation in the selection of mitigation approach. This does not make the framework incorrect but it's just a different way to approach it. People with a more traditional risk assessment background may find this a little unusual and may need some additional explanation

---

HELPFUL LINKS

OCTAVE-Allegro Homepage and Download link: http://www.cert.org/octave/allegro.html
    Additional OCTAVE-Allegro introduction and documentation: http://www.cert.org/archive/pdf/07tr012.pdf
    Original OCTAVE: http://www.cert.org/octave/octavemethod.html
    OCTAVE-S: http://www.cert.org/octave/octaves.html

Fair

The FAIR framework was developed by Risk Management Insight and has a strong following with several groups including the Open Group and ISACA. This framework has a heavy focus on objectivity. In fact, according to the developers of the FAIR framework, the shortcomings of current risk assessment practices are primarily the result of information security being practiced as an "art" rather than a science.

One thing that you will immediately notice with FAIR is that it has many complex sounding terms and formulas. For the uninitiated reader it may seem intimidating but it is actually pretty straightforward and the FAIR documentation provides the criteria, charts, and explanations to get through them.

Details

The FAIR framework uses the term "stages" to break down its activities. There are four primary FAIR stages outlined below.

Stage 1: Identify Scenario Components

The first FAIR stage consists of two primary activities:

1. *Identify asset at risk:* According to FAIR, an asset would be anything that would have a value or liability. This includes anything, including credentials, applications, systems and the information within the asset.
2. *Identify the threat community:* The threat community is the source of the threat. A threat community is FAIR's interpretation of what other frameworks refer to as threat sources, threat agents, or threat actors. For example, these threat communities could be actual groups of people (e.g. visitors, cleaning crews, hackers).

HELPFUL LINKS

FAIR Documentations link:
http://www.cxoware.com/resources/

FAIR is more of a high-level framework and is more conceptual when compared with the OCTAVE-Allegro framework, which really tends to be more of a methodology.

Stage 2: Evaluate Loss Event Frequency

This stage of the FAIR framework is a bit longer than the others. It essentially has five steps. An easy way to look at it is that for each step, you will end up with a value. This value will then be used in either some intermediary computation for the stage or in the final risk computation.

What follows is a brief description of each of the activities. For more details around the specific steps refer to the FAIR documentation.

1. *Threat Event Frequency (TEF):* FAIR defines this as the probable frequency, within a given timeframe, that a threat agent will act against an asset. Basically this tries to answer the question: How frequent can the attack occur? FAIR uses a 5 point scale with corresponding frequency ranges from Very High (>100) to Very Low (<.1 times) (see Table 2.6).

   For example using this table, what would be the Threat Event Frequency for an automated mechanism (e.g. a worm) attacking an externally facing system such as a company website? Using Table 2.6, this would be given a "Very High" rating as this event could possibly occur more than 100 times a year (due to the number of worms that are in the wild).

2. *Threat Capability (Tcap):* FAIR defines this as probable level of force that a threat agent is capable of applying against an asset. Additionally, it is a measure of the threat agents' resources and skill and how it can be effectively applied to the asset. All this means is you need to answer this question: What is the capability of the attacker to conduct the attack? (see Table 2.7).

Table 2.6 TEF Ratings and Description

Rating	Description
Very High (VH)	>100 times per year
High (H)	Between 10 and 100 times per year
Moderate (M)	Between 1 and 10 times per year
Low (L)	Between .1 and 1 times per year
Very Low (VL)	<.1 times per year (less than once every 10 years)

Table 2.7 Threat Capability Table

Rating	Description
Very High (VH)	Top 2% when compared against the overall threat population
High (H)	Top 16% when compared against the overall threat population
Moderate (M)	Average skill and resources (between bottom 16% and top 16%)
Low (L)	Bottom 16% when compared against the overall threat population
Very Low (VL)	Bottom 2% when compared against the overall threat population

While this may seem confusing, all this is trying to do is address the level of skill an attacker would need to have to successfully conduct a given attack. So let's say we have three threat sources: A secretary, a systems administrator, and a hacker. Who would have the greatest Threat Capability to perform unauthorized activities on a server? It is reasonable to conclude that a systems administrator would probably be within the top 2% that could actually do this attack, followed by a hacker, and then a secretary.

3. *Estimate Control Strength (CS):* FAIR defines this as the expected effectiveness of controls, over a given timeframe, as measured against a baseline level of force or the assets ability to resist compromise. In other words, how strong are the controls and protective mechanisms in place to prevent the attack? (see Table 2.8).

This is another rather confusing table but simply put, what we are trying to measure, is the strength of the control. If we used the example of the compromise of sensitive data on lost or stolen storage media, an encrypted hard drive would certainly have a much higher control strength (probably at the top

Table 2.8 Control Strength Table

Rating	Description
Very High (VH)	Protects against all but the top 2% of an avg. threat population
High (H)	Protects against all but the top 16% of an avg. threat population
Moderate (M)	Protects against the average threat agent
Low (L)	Only protects against bottom 16% of an avg. threat population
Very Low (VL)	Only protects against bottom 2% of an avg. threat population

2%) compared to a hard drive that has not been encrypted. Unfortunately the difficulty with an evaluation like this is the subjectivity in identifying which controls fall into which categories.

4. *Derive Vulnerability (Vuln):* FAIR defines this as the probability that an asset will be unable to resist the actions of a threat agent. To obtain this value, you consider two previous values which are the Threat Capability (Tcap) and the Control Strength (CS). Deriving the Vuln value is as simple as plotting the Tcap and Control Strength and finding the point where the two intersects. This is a fairly logical derivation as the capability of the attacker is inversely proportional to the control strength. For example, a system will be more vulnerable to unauthorized access if the threat source was a hacker and there was a weak control (e.g., lack of password complexity enforcement) that was unable to prevent a hacker from gaining access to the system.

5. *Derive Loss Event Frequency (LEF):* FAIR defines this as the probable frequency, within a given timeframe, that a threat agent will inflict harm upon an asset. To obtain this value, you consider two previously computed values: Threat Event Frequency (TEF) and Vulnerability (Vuln).

Obtaining the LEF is done by simply plotting the TEF and the Vuln and identifying where the two intersect. The concept here is focused on determining how likely a threat source would be able to successfully leverage the vulnerability in a system. For example, if you consider a threat scenario of a worm infecting an unpatched system on the Internet you would have a very high LEF. This is because worms have a high TEF, as there are so many constantly probing the Internet, and the Vuln rating would be high since the control strength would be considered weak due to the lack of patching.

It is important to note that many of the tables in the FAIR documents are suggestions about how to quantitate these risk elements, and FAIR allows room for customizations.

Stage 3: Evaluate Probable Loss Magnitude (PLM)

This step is concerned with evaluating the impact if the threat event does happen. The goal of this stage is to determine the severity of the loss if the event does happen. There are two main activities in this stage:

1. *Estimate Worse Case Scenarios:* FAIR defines this step as determining the threat action that would likely result in a worst-case outcome. The magnitude is determined using a loss form table provided in the FAIR documentation.

   As an example, let's say we are evaluating the threat of patient records being stolen from a nursing station (see Tables 2.9 and 2.10).

   For this sample threat scenario, we have chosen disclosure as the worst-case scenario. Then based on the magnitude table provided, you simply assign it

Table 2.9 Worst-Case Scenario Table

Threat Actions	Productivity	Response	Replacement	Fines	Competitive Advantage	Reputation
Access						
Misuse						
Disclosure	L	H	L	SV	L	SV
Modification						
Deny Access						

Table 2.10 Worst-Case Scenario Criteria

Magnitude	Range Low End	Range High End
Severe (SV)	$10,000,000	–
High (H)	$1,000,000	$9,999,999
Significant (Sg)	$100,000	$999,999
Moderate (M)	$10,000	$99,999
Low (L)	$1000	$9999
Very Low (VL)	$0	$999

to the proper magnitude category. So let's say that if you believe that the fines due to the disclosure of the medical records could go up to $10,000 then you would put it in the "SV" category. When you go through the FAIR introduction document, it will tell you to "Sum" the loss magnitudes. This simply means that you add up the magnitudes. Also note that the low and high end ranges presented in Table 2.11 are just samples.

Adding up the values in the table; we calculate $21,002,000 which falls under the Sever (SV) rating.

Thus overall, the worst-case scenario would fall under a "Severe" magnitude. The values given above are just guesses to illustrate the point and are not in any way indicative of a real life disclosure threat scenario.

2. *Estimate Probable Loss Magnitude (PLM):* FAIR defines the PLM as the most likely threat community action or actions. The only difference between this step and the previous step is that this is the "most likely," meaning the event that could have the highest probability to occur as compared to the "worst-case," which is the event that could cause the most significant loss. For example, in the stolen medical records scenario, for all intents and purposes, the most likely threat could just be "Misuse" which would have a much lower overall loss magnitude than the worst-case scenario (see Table 2.12).

Table 2.11 Worst-Case Scenario Table

Threat Actions	Productivity	Response	Replacement	Fines	Competitive Advantage	Reputation
Access						
Misuse						
Disclosure	L=$1000	H=$1,000,000	L=$1000	SV=$10,000,000	L=$1000	SV= $10,000,000
Modification						
Deny Access						

Table 2.12 Probable Loss Magnitude

Threat Actions	Productivity	Response	Replacement	Fines	Competitive Advantage	Reputation
Access						
Misuse	M=$15,000	M=$10,000	M=$20,000	L=$5000	L=$1000	L=$1000
Disclosure						
Modification						
Deny Access						

Table 2.13 Deriving Risk

PLM	Risk				
Severe	H	H	C	C	C
High	M	H	H	C	C
Significant	M	M	H	H*	C
Moderate	L	M	M	H	H
Low	L	L	M	M	M
Very Low	L	L	M	M	M
LEF	VL	L	M	H	VH

Similar to the process of the worst-case scenario, you simply add up the magnitudes to get the overall magnitude. In our example, the overall PLM will be Moderate (M) since our calculation is $521,000, which falls within the moderate category.

Derive and Articulate Risk

This is the final step and probably the simplest as this only entails plotting the Loss Event Frequency (LEF) and the Probable Loss Magnitude (PLM). The intersection will be your final Risk score (see Table 2.13).

Above we have mapped a threat that has a PLM of Significant (Sg) and an LEF of High (H) which yields a risk of "High." This is fairly logical as it simply means that a threat that has a high likelihood to occur (from LEF analysis) and could lead to a significant loss (from PLM analysis) should be considered a High risk.

Strengths and Weaknesses (see Table 2.14)

NIST SP800-30

The "Risk Management Guide for Information Technology Systems" or NIST SP800-30 was developed by the National Institute for Standards and Technology

---

IMPORTANT VALUES IN THE EVALUATE LOSS EVENT FREQUENCY STEP

Let's go through a brief rundown of the values you have right now:

1. Threat Event Frequency (TEF)—Estimate how often the threat can happen.
2. Threat Capability (Tcap)—Estimate how capable the threat is.
3. Control Strength (CS)—Estimate how effective the controls are
4. Vulnerability (Vuln)—Plot Intersection of Tcap and CS.
5. Loss Event Frequency (LEF)—Plot Intersection of Vuln and TEF.
6. Probably Loss Magnitude (PLM)—Estimate the most likely threat and magnitude.
7. Risk—Plot intersection LEF and PLM.

Table 2.14 Strengths and Weaknesses of FAIR

Strengths	Weaknesses
Very objective. This makes it very defensible and very repeatable.	Can initially appear to be overwhelming because of the terminologies and matrices involved
Very good for organizations that have strong metrics	Some of the criteria are difficult to interpret in a real scenario. For example, how would you decide which controls are in the "top 2% of the average population" in control strength?
	Might be difficult for organizations with immature programs due to lack of objective data particularly regarding loss magnitudes
	Might be difficult for inexperienced assessors due to lack of knowledge in specific areas such as threat frequencies
	Might be difficult to articulate in a cross-disciplinary group

REFERENCES

Website:
    http://fairwiki.riskmanagementinsight.com/
    A Draft FAIR Introduction:
    http://www.isaca-cincinnati.org/Resources/Presentations/FAIR_introduction.pdf
    Basic Risk Assessment Guide:
    http://www.riskmanagementinsight.com/media/docs/FAIR_brag.pdf

(NIST). NIST is a standards organization that is sponsored by the US Federal Government. It regularly publishes many guidelines and standards related to all kinds of information security topics from cryptography to incident response processes. You will find that many government standards in the US are based on the guidelines developed by NIST. This particular risk assessment framework is heavily adopted not only by federal agencies but also local governments. Organizations that are under federal regulations, particularly FISMA or HIPAA, typically refer to this framework to conduct risk assessments and operate risk management programs. If you are not familiar with the resources available for NIST, you are strongly encouraged to look through their website (http://crsc.nist.gov/).

SP800-30 is a high-level approach to risk management and is not as prescriptive as OCTAVE or FAIR. Overall, SP800-30 appears to have been made with a lot of flexibility and "wiggle-room" to take into consideration the wide range of organizations that would adopt this as a standard. Also note that while 800-30 is a risk management lifecycle document for purposes of this publication only the risk assessment portion will be discussed.

Details

The SP800-30 framework uses the term "steps" to break down its activities. There are nine steps in SP800-30 which are described below.

System Characterization

The first step of SP800-30 focuses on creating descriptions of systems or assets that are in scope for the risk assessment. This step assumes that you already have a list of systems on hand. Based on the framework, the following details should be collected for each asset:

1. Hardware.
2. Software.
3. Interfaces.
4. Data & Information.
5. Person Support.
6. System Mission.
7. System and data criticality.
8. System and data sensitivity.

The objective of this step is to create a good picture of what the system is and the environment that the system resides in and depends on. This process of detailing out the characteristics of an asset is a typical initial step for many of the risk assessment frameworks and is a very important one at that. How can you properly assess risk to your organization if you don't fist know what you are trying to protect?

One very useful aspect of SP800-30 is that it provides some recommendations on how to go about collecting the information needed above. Based on the standard, some information gathering techniques that could be used include:

1. Questionnaires.
2. On-site interviews.
3. Document Review.
4. Automated scanning tools.

Ultimately, at the end of this step, you should have a list of systems in scope for the assessment and a characterization of each of the systems in scope. A more detailed discussion of these information gathering techniques and approaches will be provided in the next chapter dealing with Data Collection.

Threat Identification

The objective of this step is to create a threat statement. A threat statement is a list of threat sources that is applicable to the system. A threat source in turn is something that may leverage a weakness in the system. For example a "hacker" is a threat source as this threat source may leverage a system or application weakness or vulnerability.

SP800-30 provides a table listing several threat sources that an assessor may be able to leverage. This list of threat sources is categorized as natural threats, human threats, and environmental threats. SP800-30 also points to several informational resources that could be used as references such as various Intelligence agencies, the Federal Computer Incident Response Center, and security websites like SANS and Security Focus. Though the list and the references provided by NIST are good, many of them are somewhat dated, and there are actually several better resources for threat sources such as ISO27005 Annex C and BITS that a user might want to consider using in this step. At the end of this step, you should have a threat statement for each asset in scope which contains all applicable threat sources that could leverage weaknesses in the application or applications being assessed.

Vulnerability Identification

In the previous step, SP800-30 required a list of threat sources. Once this list has been compiled, the next step deals with identifying vulnerabilities that can be leveraged by these threat sources.

Basically, a threat source plus the vulnerability that leverages it produces what we call a threat and vulnerability pair. This is a very important concept in SP800-30 and with all risk assessment frameworks. Here is an example of a threat and vulnerability pair:

- *Threat Source:* Hacker.
- *Vulnerability:* Lack of System Patching.

Then for each of the threat and vulnerability pairs that have been identified, a threat action is then created. The threat action of the threat and vulnerability pair outlined above would be:

- *Threat action:* A hacker using an exploit against a system vulnerability and gaining access to the system.

Probably one of the most useful aspects of the SP800-30 is that it provides possible inputs or sources of information for each of the steps. For vulnerability identification, SP800-30 identifies the following sources to assist in identifying vulnerabilities:

1. Previous risk assessments.
2. IT system audit reports.
3. Vulnerability Listings.
4. Security advisories.
5. Vendor advisories.
6. CERT.
7. System security testing.
8. Security requirements checklist.

In SP800-30, one very important source of information in the vulnerability identification step as well as in other steps is the Security Requirements Checklist. This is a checklist of the security controls that are "standard" for an asset to comply with in order to have a baseline level of security. A resource that can be utilized is

SP800-53 or the "Recommended Security Controls for Federal Information Systems and Organizations." Any "non-compliance" or control gaps that were found through this checklist could be identified as a vulnerability in the system being assessed. At the end of this step, you should have a list of vulnerabilities for each of the threat sources identified for the system.

Control Analysis

The main objective of this step is to take into account the current and planned controls in assessing the likelihood of the vulnerability being leveraged by a threat source. Obviously, the stronger the control, the less likely that a vulnerability can be leveraged and vice versa.

SP800-30 discusses different control methods, control categories, and analysis techniques but we have found that an effective way to conduct the analysis is to use the security requirements checklist, the one used to identify vulnerabilities in the previous step, as a reference to determine control deficiencies.

SP800-30 does not expound too much on this step and is very open-ended regarding determining the effectiveness of controls. At the end of this step, the main output is to create a list of current or planned controls for the system.

Likelihood Determination

The main objective of this step is to determine the probability that a vulnerability may be exploited based on the threat source and environment. As an example, how likely is it that a hacker would be able to leverage application weaknesses on a web server that was exposed to the Internet considering that the organization does not perform any application security reviews? There's a high likelihood that hackers might be able to exploit some undetected weakness in the application right? This is basically the process you'll have to go through in determining the likelihood for each of the threat and vulnerability pairs.

SP800-30 provides a three level likelihood scale for this determination (see Table 2.15).

Based on the rating scale provided one can see that it considers:

1. Motivation and capability of the threat source.
2. Strength of the control.

Let's walk through the example of trying to determine the likelihood of a hacker leveraging an application vulnerability against an e-commerce site. Based on your security checklist review, you determined that the organization did not have any security application review process, does not have a web application firewall, and the developers who work on the site have never had any application security or secure coding training. Based on the scale provided, this scenario would end up with a high rating as hackers are highly motivated and sufficiently capable and the controls that the organization has to prevent hackers from leveraging application flaws are non-existent.

Table 2.15 SP800-30 Likelihood Scale

Rating	Description
High	The threat source is highly motivated and sufficiently capable, and controls to prevent the vulnerability from being exercised are ineffective
Medium	The threat source is motivated and capable, but controls are in place that may impede successful exercise of the vulnerability
Low	The threat source lacks motivation or capability, or controls are in place to prevent, or at least significantly impede, the vulnerability from being exercised

Table 2.16 SP800-30 Impact Scale Based on the Rating Scale Provided Above, One Can See That it Specifically Considers: (1) Cost, (2) Effect to the Organization Mission and Reputation, and (3) Human Injury

Rating	Description
High	Exercise of the vulnerability (1) may result in the highly costly loss of major tangible assets or resources; (2) may significantly violate, harm, or impede an organization's mission, reputation, or interest; or (3) may result in human death or serious injury
Medium	Exercise of the vulnerability (1) may result in the costly loss of tangible assets or resources; (2) may violate, harm, or impede an organization's mission, reputation, or interest; or (3) may result in human injury
Low	Exercise of the vulnerability (1) may result in the loss of some tangible assets or resources or (2) may noticeably affect an organization's mission, reputation, or interest

Like most of SP800-30, the criteria here is flexible and open-ended and has a high level of subjectivity. At the end of this step, you will be providing a likelihood rating for each threat vulnerability pair identified in the assessment.

Impact Analysis

The main objective of this step is to determine the adverse impact to the asset if a vulnerability is successfully leveraged by a threat source. For impact, SP800-30 primarily focuses on the CIA security triad of Confidentiality, Integrity and Availability. In addition, SP800-30 also focuses on impacts such as loss of public confidence, loss of credibility, and damage to an organization's interests as other possible impact types to consider.

SP800-30 provides a three level impact scale for this determination (see Table 2.16).

In the context of discussing impact let's say a hacker is able to deface the main website of Amazon? Obviously even though it was only a defacement of the site this

Table 2.17 Determination of Risk

Likelihood	Impact		
	Low (10)	Medium (50)	High (100)
High (1.0)	Low $10 \times 1.0 = 10$	Medium $50 \times 1.0 = 50$	High $100 \times 1.0 = 100$
Medium (0.5)	Medium $10 \times 0.5 = 5$	Medium $50 \times 0.5 = 25$	Medium $100 \times 0.5 = 50$
Low (0.1)	Low $10 \times 0.1 = 1$	Low $50 \times 0.1 = 5$	Low $100 \times 0.1 = 10$

would have to be considered high impact because there is a significant effect to the reputation of the organization and the event could undermine consumer confidence in the perceived security of the company.

At the end of this step, you will be providing an impact rating for each of the threat and vulnerability pairs identified in the assessment.

Risk Determination

Risk computation for SP800-30 is traditional and straightforward. It is simply:

- $Risk = Impact \times Likelihood$

SP800-30 has provided a risk matrix table to assist in the determination of risk (see Table 2.17).

The determination of the final risk rating is based on the intersection of the Impact and Likelihood for each of the threat and vulnerability pairs that were identified. For purposes of illustrating this process let's say that you have determined that a successful hacker defacement of your e-commerce website will have a high impact. You have also determined that the likelihood of a successful attack leveraging application flaws in your website is medium due to the fact that your organization has just procured an inline 24/7 monitored web application firewall that's on block mode. Using the risk matrix above, this will fall under Medium risk, as it is the intersection between High impact and Medium likelihood.

At the end of this step, a risk rating will be provided for the threat and vulnerability pairs for each of the systems or assets that are scope.

Control Recommendations

In some risk assessment frameworks, the assessment is completed once a risk rating is provided; however, since NIST SP800-30 is a risk management framework, it takes into account the remediation and mitigation aspect in its overall process and it's worth remembering that control recommendations are part of the risk assessment report.

Once the risk rating is derived from the previous step, control recommendations are provided to mitigate the risks which are identified. NIST also recommends performing a cost benefit analysis to make sure that the cost of control implementation does not exceed the estimated loss associated with a given event but it does not provide specific guidance on this process.

Results Documentation

This step just entails putting together an official report or briefing based on the risk assessment. According to SP800-30, this report helps senior management and the mission owners make decisions on policy, procedures, budget, as well as system operational and management changes. The standard characteristically leaves this step open-ended but it does recommend that the report should contain:

1. Threat Sources.
2. Vulnerabilities.
3. Risks Assessed.
4. Recommended Controls Provided.

Finally, one interesting thing that SP800-30 does mention and is an important concept to remember during the course of a risk assessment project is:

Strenghts and Weaknesses of NIST (see Table 2.18)

Table 2.18 Strengths and Weaknesses	
Strengths	**Weaknesses**
The framework is open-ended and provides a lot of flexibility to the assessor. Useful for highly diverse environments.	Not as objective and data driven as other frameworks.
Provides good sample interview questions and a sample report outline (although it is a per asset reporting style).	There is a lack of criteria and decision guides. Some of the matrices provided in the standard are high level and highly subjective. Results will be heavily dependent on the experience and opinions of the individual executing the assessment leaving it open to interpretation and challenge.
Many organizations in the United States, particularly in the federal space, align to the standard.	Narrative is short and broad and does not provide a lot of details. Implementation examples are also sparse.
Good discussion regarding the concept of threat and vulnerability pairs.	Threat sources are primarily geared for government and military scenarios.
The risk mitigation section, though not technically part of a risk assessment, is very thorough and may be useful for risk management implementations.	
Inputs and outputs for each of the steps are clearly identified.	

Unlike an audit or investigation report, which looks for wrongdoing, a risk assessment report should not be presented in an accusatory manner but as a systematic and analytical approach to assessing risk so that senior management will understand the risks and allocate resources to reduce and correct potential losses.

ISO 27005

ISO 27005 is the "Information Technology—Security Techniques—Information Security Risk Management" standard released by the international standards body ISO to provide guidance over information security risk management processes that are needed for the implementation of an effective information security management system (ISMS). Though this standard is considered a risk management standard, a significant portion of the standard deals with risk assessments, which are of course a key part of a risk management program.

ISO 27005 is heavily aligned with NIST SP 800-30 and is written from a high-level perspective when compared to the other frameworks that we have discussed so far. The ISO 27005 standard has 6 major topic areas:

- Context Establishment.
- Information Security Risk Assessment.
- Information Security Risk Treatment.
- Information Security Risk Acceptance.
- Information Security Risk Communication.
- Information Security Risk Monitoring and Review.

In the context of this book, we will be focusing on the "Information Security Risk Assessment" section of the ISO 27005 standard.

Details

ISO 27005 has 3 steps for the section dealing with risk assessment: Risk Identification, Risk Estimation, and Risk Evaluation.

Risk Identification
Risk identification consists of 5 main activities, as follows:

1. *Identification of Assets*—The objective for this activity is to identify the assets that are in scope for the risk assessment. This includes identifying the asset owner for the asset that was identified. In ISO 27005, assets are categorized as either primary or secondary. Primary assets are core process/activities and information. Secondary assets are hardware, software, network, personnel, site, and structure. The list of asset types in ISO 27005 is fairly comprehensive and can be seen in Annex B of the standards document.
2. *Identification of Threats*—The objective of this step is to prepare a list of potential threats for the asset. According to ISO 27005, people such as asset owners, users, human resources staff, and facilities management could assist in identifying the threats to an asset. ISO 27005 also states that internal experience, particularly based on incidents that have occurred or previous assessments that

have been performed, should be considered. One of the most useful contributions of ISO 27005 is the inclusion of standardized threat catalogs. A sample threat catalog is provided in Annex C of the standard. This is a great reference for risk assessment practitioners, regardless of which risk assessment framework they are choosing and will be discussed in more detail in the Data Analysis chapter.

3. *Identification of existing controls*—The objective of this activity is to identify existing controls. The guidance provided within ISO 27005 for this activity is fairly open-ended and does not specifically address criteria or scale for the control review. It does provide references to information sources that may be able to assist in this activity. Some examples identified as good sources for conducting this part of the review are:
   * Documents that have information about controls.
   * People responsible for information security.
   * On-site reviews.
   * Review of internal audit results.

4. *Identification of vulnerabilities*—As the name implies, the goal of the activity is to identify the vulnerabilities for the asset. Though the narrative does not provide much information, Annex D of the standard does provide examples of vulnerabilities, which can be used as a helpful guide. ISO 27005 also provides specific information sources that can be used to identify vulnerabilities in assets. Some samples are:
   * Vulnerability Scanning and Penetration Testing.
   * Code Reviews.
   * Interviews.
   * Questionnaires.
   * Physical Inspection.
   * Document Analysis.

5. *Identification of consequences*—The objective of this activity is to determine the possible damage or consequences caused by an "incident scenario" or what other frameworks call a threat scenario. ISO 27005 provides a list of impact factors that can be used to identify and measure consequences. Interestingly, when compared to most of the other frameworks, ISO 27005 leans towards identifying quantitative aspects of impact such as financial replacement value, and cost of suspended operations. Samples of these quantitative aspects of impact are provided in Annex C of the standard.

Risk Estimation

The risk estimation phase consists of three primary activities. These are:

1. *Assessment of consequences*—The main objective of this activity is to assess the impact cause by an incident scenario. Some of the consequences that the standard recommends you evaluate are:
   * Investigation and repair time.

- Work time lost.
- Opportunity lost.
- Health and safety.
- Financial cost of specific skills to repair the damage.
- Image reputation and goodwill.

Annex B of the standard breaks the consequences into direct and indirect operational impact and provides more details and examples of consequences that may need to be assessed. Annex B also discusses an important concept in impact evaluation.

As you may have noticed ISO 27005 focuses on objectives, guidance, and concepts. The standard is not prescriptive; it does not really provide criteria, scoring, or decision matrices unlike some of the other frameworks.

2. *Assessment of incident likelihood*—The main objective of this activity is to assess the likelihood of an incident scenario using qualitative or quantitative estimation techniques. As with most of ISO 27005, it is not prescriptive but it does recommend that while performing this activity, one should consider the following factors:
   - Frequency of occurrence of the threat (statistics).
   - Motivation and capability of the source.
   - Geographical factors and the environment.
   - Vulnerabilities.
   - Existing Controls.

3. *Level of risk estimation*—The main objective of this step is to provide values ot the likelihood and consequences, which will ultimately result in a risk value. The narrative for this activity is relatively short but ISO 27005 provides a fairly comprehensive list of approaches to risk estimation in Annex E of the standards document. Annex E also provides various examples of tables and computation matrices to allow for the computation of risk based on likelihood and consequence.

Risk Evaluation
Once risk estimates have been determined, the final step in the Risk Assessment stage of ISO 27005 is to prioritize the risks that are identified based on the risk evaluation criteria and the risk acceptance criteria. Determining the priority for these risks would allow the following risk management actions to be determined:

- Whether an activity should be undertaken.
- Priorities of risk treatment considering estimated levels of risk.

A Comparison of the Major Activities for the Four Frameworks
See Table 2.20.

Strength and Weaknesses (see Table 2.19)

Table 2.19 Strengths and Weaknesses

Strengths	Weaknesses
The Annexes provided in ISO 27005 provide very useful information and examples. ISO 27005 provides good examples of a threat catalog, vulnerabilities, and various computation and plotting techniques for rating risk	Very open to interpretation. Since it is not prescriptive, there is a higher risk that different organizations and different assessors would conduct an activity differently. Similarly, stakeholders and auditors might also have different interpretations of the standards
ISO is an international standard and stakeholders and auditors would be hard pressed to contradict your approach	
It is very flexible. As with most ISO standards, ISO 27005 is fairly high level and focuses on objectives, which leaves organizations a lot of "wiggle-room" in terms of how the standard is implemented	

A Comparison of the Major Activities for the Four Frameworks Based on Activities

Looking at Table 2.21, one can see that in general, the major risk assessment frameworks have some measure of alignment based on several overarching activities or steps. Of course, one should note that although there are common concepts across frameworks, each framework may have a different ay of accomplishing the assessment; however, the overall objective is still the same. The hybrid approach covered in this book is based on those common activities or steps.

Our Risk Assessment Approach

The goal of this book is to be able to successfully complete a quick and defensible risk assessment project. When we talk about implementing a risk assessment project, these are organizational and project activities that would encapsulate the frameworks and methodologies discussed to use both an efficient and structured approach to collect, analyze and evaluate data. We have written this approach with five main considerations:

1. *The approach will be practical*—The main goal for the approach provided in this book is to provide something that will bridge the frameworks and methodologies into something that can be easily understood, executed, and

---

The risk assessment frameworks presented above are the major ones that you will most likely encounter as a practitioner. There are also quite a few other frameworks out there that may be of use. A good comparison of these various frameworks can be found at the ENISA website:

http://rm-inv.enisa.europa.eu/rm_ra_methods.html

Table 2.20 Comparison of Frameworks

OCTAVE	FAIR	NIST SP800-30	ISO 27005

1. Establish Risk Measurement Criteria	1. Identify scenario components
	  • Identify asset at risk
	  • Identify the threat community
		1. System Characterization	1. Risk Identification
			  • Identification of Assets
			  • Identification of Threats

2. Develop an Information Asset Profile		2. Threat Identification	• Identification of existing controls
3. Identify Information Asset Containers	2. Evaluate Loss Event Frequency	3. Vulnerability Identification	• Identification of vulnerabilities
4. Identify Areas of Concern	• Calculate Threat Event Frequency (TEF)	4. Control Analysis	• Identification of Consequences
5. Identify Threat Scenarios	• Calculate Threat Capability (Tcap)	5. Likelihood Determination	2. Risk Estimation
6. Identify Risks	• Estimate Control Strength (CS)	6. Impact Analysis	• Assessment of consequences
7. Analyze Risks	• Derive Vulnerability (Vuln)	7. Risk Determination	• Assessment of incident likelihood
8. Select Mitigation Approach	• Derive Loss Event Frequency (LEF)	8. Control Recommendations	• Level of risk estimation
	3. Evaluate Probable Loss Magnitude (PLM)	9. Results documentation	3. Risk Evaluation
	• Estimate Worse Case Scenarios		
	• Estimate Probable Lost Magnitude (PLM).		
	4. Derive and articulate Risk		

Table 2.21 Comparison of Framework Activities

	OCTAVE Step	FAIR Step	NIST Step	ISO 27005 Step
Identifying the asset and asset components	Develop an Information Asset Profile	Identify asset at risk	System Characterization	Identification of Assets
Identifying Threats	Identify Threat Scenarios	Identify the threat community	Threat Identification	Identification of Threats
		Calculate Threat Event Frequency		
		Calculate Threat Capability		
Identifying Vulnerabilities	Identify Areas of Concern	Derive Vulnerability	Vulnerability Identification	Identification of Vulnerabilities
Identifying and Analyzing Controls	Identify Risk Analyze Risk	Estimate Control Score	Control Analysis	Identification of Existing Controls
Analyzing Likelihood	Select Mitigation Approach	Evaluate Loss Event Frequency	Likelihood Determination	Assessment of Incident Likelihood
Analyzing Impact	Identify Risk Analyze Risk	Evaluate Probable Loss Magnitude (PLM)	Impact Analysis	Assessment of Consequences
Determining Risk	Establish Risk Measurement Criteria Analyze Risk	Derive and Articulate Risk	Risk Determination	Level of Risk Estimation

defended. Risk assessment frameworks are structured based on risk concepts. In our approach, we will be encapsulating these concepts into specific activities. For example, where FAIR recommends the activity of "Identify Scenario Components," our methodology will break it down into much more specific organizational activities such as "Conduct scoping meetings," "Conduct executive surveys," "Prepare an asset spreadsheet," as well as others.

2. *The approach will be based on common denominators*—In the risk assessment primer provided in this chapter, you have seen that there are quite a few risk assessment frameworks out there. This chapter has provided a brief description of the major risk assessment methodologies used within the United States. At first glance, they seem to be structured rather differently but each one of them will have similarities. Risk is Risk and the components of risk do not really

change. One of the goals of our approach is to stick with the concepts that are common in all of the methodologies. For example, all methodologies have the concept of "Threat Identification." Though terminologies between frameworks may be different, we believe it all amounts to the same thing since at the end of the day they are all trying to help the practitioner derive conclusive data to assist in decision making related to risk mitigation. Our approach will identify these commonalities and will provide activities that will assist in implementing them no matter what framework you are using.

3. *The approach will be data driven*—One of the main objectives of our approach is to have sufficient data to back up and defend the results of your risk assessment. Granted that in many cases this will be qualitative data; however, it will still be data that you will be able to show your executive sponsors and auditors and prove that the methodology was not based solely on guess work and that your conclusions are based data that was collected throughout the organization and with the assistance of key stakeholders.

4. *The approach will use automation as much as possible*—One of main things that you will see throughout the course of this book is the authors use spreadsheets. The main point behind the use of the spreadsheets is that you can leverage commonly available tools to assist in conducting the assessment and managing diverse datasets.

5. *The approach will be consistent and repeatable*—One of the most important aspects of our approach is that it aims to make the risk assessment repeatable and provides for the ability to leverage the work put forth in your first execution of the assessment to make future iterations richer and easier. In large organizations, you will typically have a core team responsible for conducting a risk assessment. Our goal is to ensure that each member of the team will be able to have a consistent result regardless of their background or experience. Contrary to what some risk assessment frameworks may say, consistency is a very hard thing to achieve. This is widely due to the fact that we are not measuring absolute risk. Risk assessments encompass the whole organization and no matter how data driven we want to be or what we do, people will be involved and when people are involved, you will end up recording and dealing with perceived risk, which will vary from person to person.

Main Phases in Our Methodology

What follows are the main phases in implementing an information security risk assessment project using the approach in this book. We will be providing a quick description of these phases before we do a deep dive into each one.

Data Collection

Before performing an analysis of your organization's risk, it is important to obtain data to support your analysis. One common mistake we see is that security officer's end up performing an "isolated island" analysis whereby they conduct the assessment by themselves. Though this is not necessarily wrong and may even be perfectly acceptable if the organization is small, making it likely that the security officer is typically knows most of what is going on, it definitely does not scale for medium to large sized organizations. As much as possible you should always try to include various business units in the risk assessment process. Proper data collection is by far the most rigorous and encompassing activity in the overall methodology. Some of the activities in this phase include:

- Identifying a project sponsor.
- Executive interviews and discussion regarding strategic objectives and risks.
- Collection of asset inventories, asset owners and technical contacts.
- Management scoping workshops.
- Interviews with asset owners.
- Interviews with technical owners.
- Interviews with system and security control resources.
- Preparation of collection mechanism and storage matrix.
- Preparation and collection of an asset owner system profile and characterization survey.
- Preparation and collection of a technical contact control scoring survey.
- Asset owner and technical contact interviews and communications.

This phase does not actually take a lot of manpower in terms of the security office but it does take a long time because the activity mainly relies on collecting data from different parts of the organization. Needless to say, the successful completion of this phase requires strong support from executive management and sponsors as you may need to push other departments to complete the data collection activities. Depending on how many assets are being analyzed and the turnover time for collection from other departments, this phase could last from a few weeks to several months. The main output for this phase is a matrix containing all the systems, asset owners, technical contacts, description of the system, system profiles, and the results of control maturity self assessments.

Data Analysis

Once all the necessary information has been collected from the different data sources the next step is to start risk analysis activities. Some of the activities in this phase may be performed while working on the data collection phase, allowing the overall process to be more efficient. For example, while waiting for the various resources to complete the surveys in the data collection phase, which may take a while, the assessor could start reviewing previous third party assessments. The data analysis phase is the part of our process where the assessor will start applying the risk concepts discussed in the frameworks that were previously discussed in this chapter. The activities in this phase are:

- Review of organizational risks and controls.
- Review of previous or third party assessments.

- Review of organizational security metrics.
- Preparation of threat and vulnerability catalogs.
- Normalizing system profile and control maturity score results.
- Designing and performing the Impact Analysis scheme.
- Designing and performing the Likelihood Analysis scheme.
- Designing and performing the Control Analysis scheme.
- Preparing the Risk Scores.

If prepared correctly this phase is actually rather fast. Once the analysis schemes and computations have been automated, using some simple macros and a spreadsheet, it usually becomes a simple matter of recreating the computations across all assets using their various scores. As part of the chapter on Data Analysis, we will be providing sample excel macros to help with the different scoring and analysis schemes. Depending on the complexity of the schemes used, and the number of threats to assess, this may take a minimum of one week to a month. The main output for this phase is a "risk assessment toolkit." This could be a spreadsheet, database, or application that contains a list of threats and vulnerabilities with corresponding impact, likelihood, control, and risk scores for each of the assets being reviewed.

Risk Analysis, Prioritization, and Treatment

Once the data has been analyzed, this is the time to stand back and look at the results of the data. Compared to the past two phases, the activities in this phase require a lot more thinking and discussion, as this is where you will ultimately derive the findings of your assessment. In some risk analysis frameworks, treatment is not included in the assessment activities as it is sometimes considered as a separate activity within the overall risk management process. The "Risk Analysis, Prioritization, and Treatment" activities are:

- Preparing and designing a "Risk Threshold."
- Prioritizing the risks for individual systems and preparing treatment recommendations.
- Preparing organizational level risk statistics and findings.
- Conducting team discussions, obtaining feedback, validating, and adjusting results.

Remember that no matter how closely a framework is followed; sometimes there will be things that need to be adjusted to more accurately reflect the real-world situation so feedback on and verification of the results is critical.

Though there are fewer activities in this phase, the assessor should spend quality time on this phase since the results of this part of the assessment will be the basis of the findings that ultimately end up in the risk assessment report and executive management.

Reporting

Reporting is a critical activity and could make or break your risk assessment. Weeks or even months worth of risk assessment work will need to be summarized into what will likely be just a few pages that will be provided to executive management. This does not mean that a detailed report is not required since you will need to have a full report to substantiate your results, it just means that ultimately the decision makers within the organization neither have the time nor inclination to want to read more than is necessary. The reporting activities are:

- Preparing a risk assessment memo for executive management.
- Preparing a risk assessment slide deck.
- Preparing a detailed risk assessment report.
- Preparing the supplementary materials.
- Conducting the debrief.

Note that multiple report formats are necessary as each format is directed at different audiences. For example, a memo is geared to be the most concise and is targeted at executives that have little time and want to obtain only the important points to support their decision making while the detailed risk assessment is geared for technical people, internal or external auditors, or other individuals who may want to go through the data collected and evaluate the overall methodology used.

Maintenance

Once the initial assessment is complete, the hardest part is over and you can celebrate for a short period. However, for those of us who have done enough risk assessment projects, you will know that inevitably you encounter some roadblocks and there is always room for improvement in either the execution or methodology that you used. The final phase of our methodology consists of activities that will help make the transition and the overall experience of the risk assessment better. The activities in maintenance are:

- Conducting a "lessons learned" discussion.
- Preparing and engaging the risk management process.
- Keeping aware of changes and adding new assets and threats.
- Defending your risk assessment.

The maintenance phase is more of a "pseudo" phase since, except for "lessons learned" discussion, there are really no preset activities that you will be conducting since most of the activities are reactive, based on the outcome of your assessment and changes in the organization. For example, one of the most common scenarios is that you will need to defend your risk assessment. This is not an uncommon occurrence since as with most organizations, people in your organization will have different views, and will have different opinions on the findings of your risk assessment and some people may outright disagree with your conclusions.

THE REAL WORLD

Jane, our information security officer is back! After the rigors of the first month and getting settled in while adjusting to her new boss, she is ready to tackle the risk assessment!

She has been given the go ahead from her CIO to begin preparing the risk assessment. Unfortunately, her previous job does not give her the opportunity to conduct a risk assessment from scratch so she has never done an end-to-end assessment. She knows it will be an uphill climb but she's enthusiastic and ready for the challenge.

One of the first things she did was Google "information security risk assessment." Not surprisingly, she got hits on most of the major ones: NIST, OCTAVE, ISO 27005 and FAIR. She downloaded all the PDFs and materials then spent a couple of long days, nights, and weekends trying to understand all the different approaches. Unfortunately, although she understands the theory and concepts, her lack of experience in actually conducting an assessment makes it difficult to put the risk assessment into a "real-life" context. Fortunately, she is not alone and she did make some new friends in the local ISACA chapter meeting that she attended. Many of them have been conducting risk assessments for years at their respective organizations. Knowing that one of the best ways to learn is to discuss her questions with others she decides to give them a call and pick their brains regarding information risk assessments.

The first person she decides to call is the information security officer who works for a Federal Agency.

Jane:	"I'm trying to put together a risk assessment from scratch for the hospital I work in. Do you have any recommendations for me on how to get this going?"
Federal Agency ISO:	"Hmmm... I would say decide on a framework first. For me, I really didn't have much choice about it since federal agencies typically go with what NIST provides which is SP800-30."
Jane:	"Oh, yea, I read about that one. How is it?"
Federal Agency ISO:	"It's ok. Initially, when I saw it I thought, well... this isn't helpful. It's too high level!"
Jane:	"Really? That was my first thought too!"
Federal Agency ISO:	"Yea, I guess NIST comes from the perspective that frameworks and standards are not meant to be prescriptive and need to allow flexibility so they can be applied to the readers situation. This is especially important to federal agencies, since we have very diverse environments. But the funny thing is, there are always exceptions. In fact, although NIST is flexible, sometimes Federal agencies take out all the flexibility by prescribing a lot of stuff themselves!"
Jane:	"Hmmm... yea that does make sense. So how did you start going about implementing it?"
Federal Agency ISO:	"That's the interesting thing. Managing and implementing a risk assessment project is an entirely different beast compared to just assessing risk."
Jane:	"What do you mean by implementing a risk assessment project and assessing risk? Aren't they one and same?"
Federal Agency ISO:	"They are related but what the NIST standard will give you are principles you can use to assess risk like what elements to look for, computations to use and other things. But you'll need to encapsulate those activities in a project right?"
Jane:	"Hmmm. Ah... I'm not getting it."

Federal Agency ISO:	"For example, in SP800-30. There's a step called control analysis. Conceptually, it makes sense. You need to adjust the risk based on the controls. But how do you go about doing this control analysis? Who are the people in your organization that you need to talk to? What controls will you be analyzing? How will you do your "analysis," will you be assigning control scores? What will be the basis of those scores? How do you get those scores? Will you be assigning those yourself or will you be conducting interviews or surveys? I can go on and on with this…"
Jane:	"Oh. I understand now. You are right. I've read through several risk assessment frameworks and I can't answer even half of what you asked. I know the theory and concepts but risk assessments are projects and I need to know how to implement the project."
Federal Agency ISO:	"Yea, that's exactly right. It looks simple but there are so many things that could go wrong or become a bottleneck. When I first started our risk assessment, I actually tried to do everything. When I gave my first draft to the committee I was reporting to, I was peppered with questions. Ultimately, what I learned is you really can't rely on just your knowledge. You have to collect information from all over the organization because some people will know more about the risk of a system than you."
Jane:	"Makes sense. I think I see what you are talking about. Anyway, I won't keep you. I'll ponder what you said and I'll start doing some project planning."

That was a good conversation. Next up, she decided to pick the brains of the bank information security officer that she met at the local ISSA chapter meeting.

Jane:	"I'm trying to get started on a risk assessment for our hospital. Any suggestions on what framework to use?"
Bank ISO:	"That's an interesting question. I really didn't use any framework per se. What I did do was read up on the FFIEC requirements and decided to just wing it."
Jane:	"Wing it? What do you mean?"
Bank ISO:	"This was maybe 5 years ago. Back then, I thought I had a pretty good idea of what risk is so I decided to put together a spreadsheet and based on my knowledge of risk, make my own computations to compute for the risk of our assets."
Jane:	"Wow. That must have been tough!"
Bank ISO:	"Yea, and unfortunately I went pretty far down that path before I realized just how tough it was going to be. I created all sorts of stuff. I used data mining techniques like clustering, tree maps, and bell curves. It was really fancy. I'm sure that our auditors were impressed but I doubt they understood any of it!"
Jane:	"Haha! That's funny. Then it's not so bad after all?"
Bank ISO:	"Yea, but the upkeep is so difficult. There are just so many moving parts that I can barely complete it every year. Also, although no one has said anything yet, the more I learned about risk during the 5 years since I started this process, the more I'm beginning to see inconsistencies in my approach. Unfortunately, since we've been using this through the years, I can't change anything anymore since it would make the results inconsistent with prior years and raise too many questions with executive management."

Jane:	"Hmm. Thanks. These are good insights. I read up on several frameworks and I've began playing around with the idea of just making up something of my own too since some appear too high level."
Bank ISO:	"I think it's not too bad to deviate a little as long as you stay within the concept. My suggestion is: Make it simple! You'll understand the importance of that statement after going through one risk assessment project."
Jane:	"Thanks. Also, someone told me that managing a risk assessment project is a bit different than just assessing the risk."
Bank ISO:	"I think I know what you mean by that. We actually have a project management office here that asked me to prepare a project plan when I said I was going to do our risk assessment. Initially, what I wrote up in the plan was something like asset identification, likelihood determination... impact assessment and risk scoring. They told me that this is well and good but what they needed from me were actual activities that would occur, the departments that would be involved, and when those activities were going to take place. For instance, they wanted to know what specific activities would occur in the "asset identification" step and what resources in the organization would be required? They wanted to know who the people where that I needed to make this happen? How much time did I need from them and when? Would I be conducting workshops? Would we need surveys? If so, do I need any resources or software to conduct those surveys? How much time will this all take?"
Jane:	"Ah that makes sense. We don't have a project management office but I can see where they are coming from. This was very helpful! Thank you very much for sharing with me!"

After Jane got off the phone calls she was a bit overwhelmed. Those conversations were really an eye opener. What dawned upon Jane was that risk assessments are more than just reading the framework. In order to successfully implement an assessment one has to think about project planning and management as well. She also needs to make it as simple as possible and collecting information in the organization was important.

Armed with more information, she decides to do some additional research on frameworks since she doesn't think she can make one of her own. She makes a short list of the major frameworks that seem to be used a lot in the United States. These were Octave-Allegro, NIST SP800-30, ISO 27005 and FAIR, which was pretty much what Google gave her in her initial research.

She has heard of Octave before and knew it was very in-depth. She wasn't too familiar with OCTAVE-Allegro but based on her research it appears to be a more streamlined version of the original OCTAVE. She looked through FAIR and its objectivity was very appealing but looking through he document, she's worried that it may not have enough information to help her through the decision matrices. On her first review of ISO 27005 it appeared to be too high level for her.

Then, while reading up on HIPAA, she stumbled across a memo from the HHS that discusses the "Risk Analysis" clause in HIPAA. Lo and behold it looks almost exactly like NIST SP800-30. With further reading she realized that HIPAA's Risk Analysis requirements were based on NIST SP800-30 and the memo was recommending that hoslpitals use the framework.

| Jane thinks: | "Ok, first step is "System Characterization." Hmmm. What system is NIST talking about? Was I supposed to know what they are?" |

Suddenly she realizes that this may be harder than she thought.

SUMMARY

What have we learned?

There are numerous information security risk assessment frameworks out there. Some of the more popular ones in the United States are

- NIST SP800-30.
- ISO 27005.
- Octave.
- FAIR.

While we have provided a primer for these frameworks there are many more frameworks out there. A good reference for this can be found in:http://rm-inv. enisa.europa.eu/rm_ra_methods.html.

The methodology presented in this book consists of

- Data Collection.
- Data Analysis.
- Risk Analysis.
- Reporting.
- Maintenance.

This chapter provided a primer on risk assessment frameworks and a quick preview of the methodology that we will be going through in the book. In the next chapters we will be delving into each of the activities in more detail.

Information Security Risk Assessment: Data Collection

3

INFORMATION IN THIS CHAPTER:

- The Sponsor
- The Project Team
- Data Collection Mechanisms
- Document Requests
- IT Asset Inventories
- Asset Scoping
- The Asset Profile Survey
- The Control Survey
- Survey Support Activities and Wrap-Up
- Consolidation

INTRODUCTION

The cornerstone of n effective information security risk assessment is data. Without data to support an assessment there is very little value to the risk assessment and the assessment you perform can be construed as mere guesswork.

Data collection is by far the most rigorous and most encompassing activity in an information security risk assessment project. There are many factors that affect the success of the data collection phase; however, the single most important factor is planning. Since all of the subsequent phases of the assessment will rely on the information gathered in this phase, not properly planning the data collection phase will have significant repercussions. This phase is also one where you will have to coordinate with people throughout your organization, so effective and appropriate communications are an essential element. We emphasize the word appropriateness in your communications since providing too much or too little information may impair your ability to effectively interact with the individuals or groups that you will rely on for data collection.

Throughout this chapter, we will also be highlighting several critical success factors that you should be trying to ensure are in place within your organization. This includes identifying a strong executive sponsor or sponsors, regular follow-ups with all involved groups, building strong relationships with system owners and contacts, proper asset scoping, leveraging automated data collection mechanisms, identifying key people with strong organizational knowledge, and use of a standard control framework. The existence of these and other factors will be good predicators of how successful your data collection phase will be.

The main output for this phase is a data container with relevant information about the organization, environment, systems, people, and controls that will be used in the various analyses throughout the project. Depending on the size of the organization, the number of assets, and support from the organization, this phase may take a few weeks or several months.

A sample Gantt chart enumerating the data collection activities is provided in the companion website of this book.

THE SPONSOR

An information security risk assessment is usually seen as a project or an initiative that is part of the overall enterprise information security program or enterprise risk management process. Like any good project, a strong project sponsor is needed and it is no different for an information security risk assessment. In many cases this sponsor may very well be the executive or group of executives (e.g. Enterprise Risk Committee) that oversees the information security function within the organization.

The project sponsor, whomever it ends up being, will be your torchbearer. This individual, or group, will be who you ultimately report to and will "have your back" throughout the whole project. Typically, the decision of who the project sponsor should be is not a difficult one. As mentioned previously, it should be the person, or group, who has the highest level of accountability for security or risk within the organization. Typically this could be the:

- VP of Information Technology.
- Chief Information Officer.
- Chief Technical Officer.
- Chief Information Security Officer.
- An executive board or committee (e.g. Risk Committee).

The project sponsor is typically a senior official in your organization whose area of responsibility also encompasses governance over the information security function. Sometimes, IT directors and managers can take on this responsibility; however, they may not have enough clout to spearhead activities that require cross-functional participation throughout different areas of the organizations. One thing to remember is that different sectors (e.g. military) may call these positions by different names. The important thing to consider is they should be high enough in the hierarchy to be able to make decisions related to your assessment without the need to pass it on to another level of approval.

Typically, you won't have any choice regarding the personality and the skill set of your project sponsor as your CIO will be your CIO no matter what you may wish. It is good to try and determine from the very start whether your project sponsor will have the characteristics that you will need to rely on when the project hits some rough patches. Another thing to always keep at the front of your mind while doing these assessment is corporate politics. For example, the CIO and CTO's agenda may conflict with the findings of your assessment, meaning it might make their programs look bad, and you need to be aware of this potential conflict of interest when looking for support.

Some of the characteristics of a good project sponsor include:

1. Has a high level of independent decision making capability (e.g. can make decisions without continually consulting someone else in the hierarchy).
2. Positioned at an executive level, preferably within the C and VP level hierarchy.
3. Has direct access to the highest level (e.g. the CEO or President) of leadership within the organization.
4. Has strong relationships with other decision makers in the organization.
5. Thinks that Information Security is an important aspect of supporting the organizations mission.
6. Has some base knowledge around the concepts of confidentiality, integrity, and availability.
7. Has enough clout and authority that people from different departments will cooperate and respond to requests from them.
8. Has experience dealing with internal audit and is not rattled when auditors challenge the process.
9. Is patient and has a basic level of understanding around the complexity of the process.
10. Strong communications skills and is approachable.
11. Supports and has "bought off" on your approach.
12. Someone who is not too hands on in the actual process as you will need some room to do your work.

Once a project sponsor has been identified, the next step is to set up a meeting with your project sponsor. This can be an informal meeting; however, the primary objectives should be to lay out your expectations for the project sponsor and outline what their responsibilities are within the process.

Finding an appropriate sponsor is often much easier said than done. In most cases the person who is an ideal fit will be someone who is a bit above your pay-grade. Don't let that dishearten you. Shoot for the top and you might be able to obtain the sponsorship you are looking for. If you have to work your way through several levels of hierarchy ensure that at each subsequent level you explain the benefit of having an involved sponsor as high up within the organization as possible. If you are able to gain access to an appropriate sponsor make sure you manage expectations early in the project since this will ultimately lead to a better and more fluid working relationship between you and your project sponsor.

So what is the role of a project sponsor? These will vary depending on the situation; however, here are some of the important roles played by a project sponsor:

1. Provides the primary backing for the initiative and project, this includes but is not limited to allocating budget, time, and personnel to the project.
2. Review and approve the approach that will be used to conduct the information security risk assessment.
3. Send out high-level communications (e.g. to senior leaders of other divisions) and assist in removing roadblocks to assessment activities that the project teams may be experiencing.
4. Review the findings and activities and provide input and insights.
5. Communicate the findings that are derived from the risk assessment to the executive team.
6. Provide a point of escalation for any issues or roadblocks encountered in the assessment.
7. Be in high-level meetings (e.g. meeting with Internal Audit) if necessary.

There may be cases where the project sponsor and the individual implementing the information security risk assessment are one and the same. This is fairly uncommon but can occur in smaller organizations.

THE PROJECT TEAM

The project team is the group of individuals that will be conducting the information security risk assessment. The size of the project team for an information security risk assessment can vary greatly depending on the size of the organization and scope of the assessment. In some cases the team could end up being a team of one or multiple teams.

So, how do you decide on the size of the project team? There are many factors that determine this. Some factors include:

The Size and Breadth of the Risk Assessment

The size of the assessment often directly correlates to the size of the organization. Obviously, a Fortune 500 company will have a much larger risk assessment team when compared to a small company.

One indicator that is helpful in judging the potential size of your risk assessment is the number of assets that could be in-scope. Though there are exceptions, typically, the larger the size of the organization, the more assets could be in-scope for the assessment, and with more assets, the bigger the team will need to be.

The size of the team also depends on the complexity of the assessment and the data collected. The simpler the assessment, the less effort and thus less manpower needed. For example, the more systems considered in-scope, the more survey items need to be completed, the more people need to be interviewed, and the more documents need to be reviewed. These factors, along with the time constraints you be under to complete the assessment, all contribute to the decision regarding the size of the team. Another contributing factor could be the risk assessment framework or control catalog that you choose for evaluating the in-scope assets.

Scheduling and Deadlines

As briefly mentioned above the deadline to complete the assessment can also directly impact the required size of the team. The more compressed the duration, the more people you may need to complete the assessment. As is often the case, you will not necessarily have the liberty of deciding when you need to complete the risk assessment. For example, if your estimate is it will take two months to complete the risk assessment by yourself but there is an audit scheduled one month from now that requires that you have completed your assessment prior to the start of the audit, you will obviously need more people to complete it. It is important to remember though that just throwing people at the project won't necessarily make it move any faster as there are quite a few external constraints (e.g. availability of interviewees or documentation) that could still stall the assessment.

Assessor and Organization Experience

Another important factor is the assessor's experience in conducting risk assessments. If this is the first time that you will be conducting an information security risk assessment, you will definitely need more help. This also holds true if this is the first risk assessment that the organization has been through. Typically, there are some growing pains whenever a new process is instituted within an organization. The challenges associated with instituting the risk assessment process include but are not limited to:

- Friction from various departments and individuals.
- Availability and tracing down resources such as documents and reports.
- Creating collection and analysis tools from scratch.
- Preparing a report for the first time.
- Individuals who will challenge your methodology and findings.

You may require a larger team if you run into these issues and if this is the first risk assessment within the organization you should plan on running into most of these issues.

Workload

As an information security practitioner within your organization it is probably safe to say that you have much more to do other than just the performance of the information security risk assessment. Your day is likely filled with meeting and various operational day-to-day activities. At the very least you will need someone who you can offload tasks to like sending out and compiling the results of surveys.

In order to effectively estimate the size of the team, one needs to determine the appropriate composition of the team. A good team should include:

1. The Information Security Officer (ISO).
2. A Senior Security Analyst.
3. A Junior Security Analyst.

There are often instances where an organization may not have sufficient full-time staff in place to support the performance of the risk assessment. In this case, it is very common to see the Senior and Junior Security Analyst roles being filled by contractors or consultants with experience performing such assessments. In many cases this may be a more cost-effective method for dealing with the short-term resource spike that results from the need to complete the assessment in a short period of time.

The ISO is the bridge between the project sponsor and the team. Since the ISO typically has other day-to-day responsibilities, they will typically provide the strategy and the direction for the review but will seldom do the hands on work associated with the risk assessment. Strategy and direction includes but is not limited to, designing or approving the methodology, deciding which aspects of the environment to assess as well as those that should be out of scope, going to various meetings and interviews, and presenting the results and findings of the assessment.

ISOs usually have a solid view of the organization and will be best positioned to review the results and determine during different points of the assessment whether the assessment is going smoothly and if the initial observations and findings appear to be valid. Most of the time, the ISO assumes the role of project manager, and this approach is what is reflected in this book.

It is not uncommon to see the ISO conducting the information security risk assessments themselves; however, in large organizations this may not be feasible as the ISO has other initiatives and projects to worry about. This is the reason why a Senior Security Analyst is typically brought in to assist in the day-to-day aspects of the risk assessment. The Senior Security Analysts responsibilities often include designing surveys, conducting interviews, collecting information, reviewing documents, preparing the analysis tools, and writing the draft reports. Important characteristics of a security analyst that you should look for are their familiarity with the framework that is being used as well as the process and approach that the ISO has outlined. It is very important that the Senior Analyst is in sync with the ISO's vision and project plan for the assessment. In large organizations this position is often a full-time staff member; however, as previously mentioned, in small- to medium-sized organizations, this role may be filled by a consultant or contractor.

In particularly large assessments, Junior Security Analysts may be incorporated into the core team. The role of a Junior Security Analysts is mostly technical support. Responsibilities often include creation of the data collection mechanisms, spreadsheets, databases, or if your vision is to create an application to support current and future assessments, they may be involved in programming. In the case where there are a significant number of assets to be reviewed, work might even be distributed in terms of collecting the surveys, performing follow-up activities, and assisting in interviews. Ideally though the interviews should be performed by either the Senior Analyst or the ISO to ensure someone with enough knowledge and seniority is involved. This is due to the fact that the data gathered from the interviews is the cornerstone for the entire assessment and many of the results derived from the assessment will be directly correlated to the results of the various interviews. It is important to include the Junior Analyst as much as possible in the interviews and process though since this is a valuable training opportunity for the junior member.

DATA COLLECTION MECHANISMS

The age-old adage "Measure twice and cut once" is not only helpful when building something but applies 100% to performance of the risk assessment. As mentioned previously, the success of many of the other phases of the risk assessment relies heavily on the success of the data collection phase. It is of critical importance that the team prepare properly to ensure that data is collected in a structured manner.

The importance of having a structured and streamlined collection process will not only make sure there is efficiency in the collection process but also provides you with a means to defend your findings and conclusions. Structuring everything and making sure that everything ties together to support a finding will allow you to easily substantiate your finding when discussing the results of the assessment with executive management, auditors, or regulators.

One part of proper preparation is to decide what data collection mechanisms are going to be used. Data collection mechanisms can be divided into two categories:

- Collectors.
- Containers.

Collectors

Collectors are simply the means to obtain data from a source. There are a number of important data sources that we will be discussing in more detail in the proceeding sections. Some of the data to be collected includes but is not limited to:

- System Profiles.
- Control Profiles.
- Audit Reports.
- Vulnerability Assessments.
- Various Information Security Events and Metrics.

For these data sources, typical collectors are:

- Document Request Lists.
- Surveys.

- Interviews.
- Workshops.

Very often, requesting existing documentation is the easiest part of the collection process. This is typically just an email to the asset owner or steward requesting a document such as any audit reports or/and previous vulnerability assessments. An asset owner is the person who is responsible for the process and the data that is being handled by the application (e.g. a VP or director of a department). The steward is the person who the asset owner delegates the responsibility for the process, the data and ultimately the application (e.g. a manager of the department).

When requesting documents, it is important that the requestor is very clear on what they are looking for otherwise the team will likely receive and have to sort through unnecessary information.

In terms of ease and general efficiency, conducting surveys is the next process after document requests. Designing and implementing surveys, as a data collection mechanism is often much easier said than done and a poorly designed survey will ultimately give you nothing of value or worse, could affect the integrity of your findings. Surveys by their very nature are also impersonal and if the purpose of the exercise is not properly conveyed, recipients of the survey may be hesitant to answer the items, may be guarded in their responses, the questions may be misunderstood/ misinterpreted, and even in some cases people may outright lie. Techniques associated with composing proper surveys will be discussed in more detail when the system and control profiles are discussed in the upcoming sections.

Interviews are very effective mechanisms and actually a preferred way to gather information when compared to surveys. This is because you are able to explain, verify, and confirm answers to questions at the time you are collecting them. These interviews also give the assessor the chance to explain the process to the interviewee and make them more comfortable in sharing information in the future if required. It is not unusual for interviewees to think that they are being audited and the face-to-face interaction allows the assessor to explain the rationale and deliverables associated with the process. The value of the answers derived from interviews significantly outweigh the value of answers derived from surveys; however, interviewing individuals can take significantly longer, so a balanced approach of using both surveys and interviews is necessary.

One way to tackle the problem of having to interview so many people is to conduct workshops. Workshops are great ways to obtain views from multiple people on one particular subject or gain consensus about a certain topic. For example, workshops are very helpful when trying to determine the organizational impact of a specific event on an enterprise system (e.g. breach of data or outage) as it would affect multiple departments. In fact, some frameworks advocate workshops as the primary source of information gathering. Effective as it may seem, in reality workshops are something that can only be used sparsely as the logistics involved in setting one up, especially a cross-departmental workshop, can be very difficult. We advocate the use of workshops only during important critical points of the assessment where findings or information needs to be verified by people involved.

Containers

Containers are resources where the collected data is stored. Containers could be in the form of a database, a spreadsheet, flat files, or even paper documents. There are many pros and cons regarding the choice of the container and each should be evaluated on a case-by-case basis. For example, databases are probably the most flexible in terms of mining and extracting information especially for very large assessments; however, they are the most complex and difficult to implement. Spreadsheets on the other hand have a lower learning curve; however, you may run into issues when it comes to efficiently extracting and correlating data. Ultimately, there will be many options available for storing the collected data and the decision primarily should be centered around what type of container the project is most comfortable using.

While the choice of the container is certainly important, especially since you will be utilizing this container throughout the assessment, it is not as important when compared to how the project team will structure the data. Structuring the data means identifying the high-level data elements and encapsulating them into the container. This allows the project team to organize the data in a structured way which will then allow them to extract findings efficiently and properly correlate the data with the findings from the assessment. As discussed earlier, each finding within the risk assessment will need to be backed up by data that was collected. Structuring your data with that end result in mind will make substantiation of your findings much easier.

One structure that we have found useful is setting up four containers, one for each of the following high-level data elements:

- Findings.
- Assets.
- Risk.
- Reference data.

The Finding container is for the issues and observations that have been collected throughout the assessment. One possible structure for this container could be:

- Finding:
  - Finding Statement.
  - Description.
  - Asset.
  - Source.
  - Risk Rating.
  - Status.
  - System.

For purposes of illustration here is a hypothetical finding taken from a review of the security incidents in the organization:

Finding State-ment	Description	Asset	Source	Risk Rating	Status	System
Phishing incidents	A review of security incident data collected over the past year shows that a large number of the incidents documented were related to some form of phishing or social engineering attack. Either a user provided their user name and creden-tials or clicked on a malicious link or attachment	Users	Security Incident Metrics collected by ISO	High—was considered an incident	No action taken	None but attempts were through the email system

The Asset container contains the data elements pertaining to the asset reviewed. An asset could be construed as one system (system risk analysis) or the organization (strategic risk analysis) itself. This Asset container is very important since the information contained here is typically used in substantiating findings. At a high level, the data elements for the Asset container would be composed of:

- Asset:
  - Asset Name.
  - Asset Classification.
  - Asset Profile (multiple sub-elements).
  - Control Information (multiple sub-elements).

Asset information, environment, and control information can still be broken down into multiple sub-elements. We will be discussing this approach in more detail in the proceeding sections dealing with the asset and control profiles.

Many of the elements that are listed below will be discussed in much more detail in the data and risk analysis phases. In the meantime, here is a sample of what the Risk container could look like:

- Risk:
  - Asset/Application.
  - Threat.
  - Vulnerability.
  - Impact.
  - Likelihood.
  - Control.
  - Risk.

This container could be structured similar to the table below. The process to derive this container will be discussed in more detail when we start the data and risk analysis portion of the assessment.

Application: Hospital Information System				
Threat (Agent and Action)	**Vulnerability**	**Impact Score**	**Likelihood Score**	**Risk Score**
Users	Eavesdropping and Interception of data	Lack of transmission encryption leading to interception of unencrypted data	5	2	10

Finally, the Reference container is composed of various reference materials that would support the findings and the asset containers. This is the least structured of all the containers and is extremely variable as it depends on how much and what types of supporting data are collected. An example of a reference container could be:

- Reference Data:
  - Threat Catalog.
  - Vulnerability Catalog.
  - Document Request Lists.
  - Data Sources.
  - Asset Inventory.
  - Interview Notes.

So what are all these containers and how do we use them? If you haven't noticed already, what was presented above is very similar to a database schema. In fact, if you decide to use a database to collect the data, then each of these containers can be structured as tables (after adding the necessary keys). If you decide to use spreadsheets, each one of these containers could actually be a workbook or a worksheet. For flat files, these containers can actually be a tree of folders and files.

Ultimately, it is up to the project team to decide on the container to use but the data elements that compose that container should be fairly consistent with the data elements shown above. For this book, we will be utilizing spreadsheets as our containers and we will be providing samples of how these data elements are used.

EXECUTIVE INTERVIEWS

There is a reason that the people say that the environment within a company is driven by "The Tone at the Top." The direction of a company is dictated from the Board and Executive Management, or the "top." All business decisions and strategies affecting the company will always funnel down from the top of the hierarchy within the company. This holds true for information security as well. This is the reason why one of the most important things to consider in conducting an information security risk assessment is the opinions and perspectives of the people who lead the organization.

In most risk assessments and frameworks, there is a heavy focus on identifying risks to specific systems. What is often overlooked is a strategic alignment of the risks based on the mission and goals of the organization. For example, in a hospital environment, we do know that regulatory pressures are very visible aspects of information security; however, this means that there is often a myopic focus on just meeting regulatory requirements diverting attention away from areas of information security that expose the organization to all types of non-regulatory-related risks. What are the other issues that keep executive management up at night and how many of these may be impacted if an information security risk was realized? These are the questions that are better suited for the organization's top executives to answer and this is the reason that any risk assessment, large or small, needs to gather the views of the decision makers within the organizations.

This information gathering exercise is best conducted early in the data collection process. By engaging with Executive Management to find out what they worry about you will also increase the visibility of the information risk assessment process and make sure they understand why it is being performed. If properly conducted, this exercise will help you in the upcoming activities since if you're able to explain the process clearly and have them understand the importance of what you are doing, you will gain executive support and thus have less resistance from the people within their department who you will be mostly dealing with.

So, who are these "executives" that you'll need to interview? These executives would obviously be all C-Level executives and the EVPs, SVPs, or VPs of various departments. Depending on your organizations structure and hierarchy, you should request to meet the following people:

- Chief Executive Officer.
- Chief Information Officer.
- Chief Technology Officer.
- Chief Operations Officer.
- Chief Financial Officer.
- Chief Information Security Officer.
- Chief Privacy Officer.
- Chief Risk and Compliance Officer or Risk Management Director.
- Internal Audit Director or VP.
- Vice Presidents and/or Directors of various departments.

In reality, especially for large organizations, it will not be feasible to meet with all of these people. The goal should be to aim high and set up meetings with as many as possible. If you were able to obtain the correct project sponsor, they can be an invaluable asset for setting these meetings up for you. These meetings could be a short 15-min interview or an extended 1-h deep dive. Regardless of the duration of the meeting you should make sure you are properly prepared so that you use their valuable time appropriately. Being ill prepared for a meeting with a senior executive could jeopardize your ability to set any future meetings with the individual, it could also impact the success of your risk assessment as it could lead to a loss of executive buy-in and support.

To prepare for the interview, there are several things that you must research. At a minimum you should ensure that you know the following information before you go to the interview:

1. The mission and vision of the organization.
2. What is the background of the executive you are meeting?
3. What department or process is the executive in charge of?

Knowing the mission and vision of the organization will help you not just in performing the interviews but throughout the risk assessment process. Remember, everything that an organization does should tie back to its mission, and understanding how proper information security risk management fits into and supports that mission is a powerful tool. It provides you with focus and the ability to discuss information security risk in a way that they can relate too. Some important things that you may want to consider while reviewing the mission are:

• What are the goals of the organization?
• How does security help achieve these goals?
• Is security seen as a strategic enabler or competitive advantage in delivery of the organizations mission?

This mission can often be found in the charter of the organization or even the employee handbook or the company website.

The background of the executive and the department and processes under their supervision may be bit more difficult to obtain information on. It is usually a good idea to talk to your project sponsor to gather as much information as possible since he or she would most likely have dealt with the executive on other matters. This personal insight can help you structure the interview to your audience and hopefully lead to a more productive meeting.

The next, and obvious step, is to actually prepare what you need to ask the executive. The questions should be high level and non-technical. They should focus on strategic aspects of security. Don't assume that the executive will be familiar with confidentiality, integrity and availability principles, or almost any core concepts of information security for that matter. You should be ready to explain and "dumb it down" and give a brief overview and examples of what information security is.

What follows are some questions that could be used in the interview:

1. Ask the interviewee to rate the importance of each of the mission objectives of the organization. There may be a possibility that they are not familiar with the objectives so make sure you have them with you. This ranking process can be done in two ways, you can ask them to rank each of the objectives in order of importance or have them score each one using a 3- or 5-point scale.

For example, let's say the following are very simplified version of the mission objectives for a hospital:

a. Provide highest level of service to patrons.

b. Ensure full compliance with laws and regulations.

c. Ensure the continued financial viability of the hospital.

You should ask the executive to rate or rank each one based on what he or she thinks is the most important. Typically the rankings will be dependent on the area of the organization that they oversee. A Chief Financial Officer would probably have the financial viability of the hospital as the highest, while a Chief Risk Officer would probably view compliance with laws and regulations as the highest. Whichever the case is, these answers can be leveraged to ultimately answer the question that is important in the process: "What should we be protecting?"

2. Ask the interviewee what assets or resources are the most important to protect in their department or in the organization as a whole. The information that you collect from this question will help you with asset scoping activities. It is important to remember that as high-level executives, they may not be able to give you specifics. They might not even know the name of the application or the database that they want to protect. More than likely they will be able to provide you broad and general terms like "our financial systems that support our billing" or "our databases that holds patient information." This is fine as it is your role to translate the information provided as executive concerns down to the processes and the physical assets that support them.

3. Ask the interviewee in what way security is important in their respective departments and to the processes that they oversee. For example, a Chief Financial Officer will probably say that it is essential that financial systems should be secure so that the integrity of the data is maintained to support the accuracy of financial reporting. A Chief Privacy Officer would probably say that patient records should be secured to ensure that patient privacy and regulatory compliance is maintained.

4. Ask the interviewee to rate the level of security awareness in their department and the organization as a whole. You can use a 3- or 5-point scale but either way it is important to recognize that this is a very subjective question. A useful follow-up to this question is to ask why they rated their department or the organization with that score. For example, if they say that they think security is weak in their department, ask them why they feel that way. This will provide you valuable insights into potential missing controls that will be helpful when you perform your risk analysis.

5. Ask the interviewee what they feel the impact to their department or the organization as a whole would be if a security breach were to happen. It is likely that the impact will be associated with something that affects their area of responsibility. After receiving their response, you should then lead them through a more structured question and answer session where you cover the different types of impacts as it pertains to the organization's mission. For example, in our fictitious hospital setting:

a. Will a breach have an impact on the privacy of the organization's patrons?

b. Will a breach have a legal or regulatory impact?

c. Will a breach have an impact on the reputation of the hospital?

d. Will a breach have an impact on the hospital's ability to deliver its services?

e. Will a breach have an impact on the organization's competitive advantage?

6. Finally, a good question to close out the interview with would be: "When it comes to our IT systems and data, what keeps you up at night?" It is a simple question but it allows you to frame risk in a simple way. Answers to this question will often be very general; however, since they are coming from a top-level executive, the answer should be evaluated as it will carry a lot of weight and will likely align with the mission objectives of the organization.

During the interview make sure that you provide a brief explanation of the objectives of the risk assessment and a brief overview of the methodology. Risk assessments in some organizations are often erroneously perceived as audits which can be detrimental to the process. It is always a good idea to mention that the process is not an audit but in fact an operational activity to continuously improve the security of the organization.

Finally, as we mentioned previously, though you may want to, it is very unlikely that you will be able to interview all the executives in the organization. In fact, in some cases, you may only be able to interview a very small number of executives and likely only those that will have a direct stake in the information security risk assessment process such as the executives in charge of IT, Security, Compliance Risk, and/or Privacy. When you only have a limited pool of executive interviewees, it is also worth considering sending out surveys to the other executives that you're not able to interview. Sending out surveys is rather impersonal and it's easy for the recipient to misunderstand the questions, so surveys should only be used if you are unable to setup face-to-face interviews.

DOCUMENT REQUESTS

One of the items that an assessor should prepare early in the data collection phase is the document request list. A document request list is simply a list of documents that are necessary for the successful completion of the information security risk assessment. The creation and dissemination of a document request list is a fairly common practice in audits, so most of the people you would be sending the request list to should be fairly familiar with the process.

The main question that you will be faced with at this point is "What are the documents that I will need?" In most cases, if the assessor works for the Information Security Office, they should have ready access to most of the documents needed; however, in some cases, the document owner may be in another department. In these cases, aside from identifying the document, it is also necessary to identify the particular source and location of the document. What follows is a sample list of documents that the assessor should be requesting:

1. Previous Information Security Risk Assessments—Request for the last few information security risk assessments or at the very least the most recent risk assessment. This request is usually made to the Information Security Office of the organization.

2. Previous IT Risk Assessments—Request for the most recent IT Risk Assessment. IT Risk Assessments are broader in-scope, typically using COBIT or ITIL as a framework. This request is usually made to the IT director or CIO; however, the request could also be submitted to the Internal Audit department who should be performing periodic IT Risk Assessments as part of their Enterprise Risk Management scoping process.

3. Previous Audit Reports—Request for previous audit reports and/or findings related to IT. Audit reports can be over multiple areas with IT (e.g. change control, access control, security) so you will need to be specific with your request. This request is usually made to Internal Audit.

4. Any previous Regulatory or Framework Driven Assessments—Request for any other assessments that have a regulatory aspect. For example, there could be assessments conducted specific to HIPAA, SOX 404, or ISO27001. This request is usually made to Internal Audit or Information Security.

5. Previous Penetration Testing Reports—Request for previous penetration testing reports. This should include external network, internal network, application, social engineering, and physical assessments if available. This request is usually made to Information Security.

6. Previous Vulnerability Assessments—Request for previous vulnerability assessment results. Vulnerability assessment data can include thousands of entries so a synopsis of the results should be sufficient.

7. Current Security Policies, Standards, and Procedures—Request for the current security policies. Go through all policy areas and request the standard and procedures for each of the policy areas. This request is usually made to Information Security and IT.

8. Disaster Recovery and Business Contingency Plans—Request for the current DRP and BCP plans. Depending on the size of the organization this request may be made to Information Security but ti depends on who has the responsibility for Disaster Recovery and Contingency Planning.

9. Request a copy of the BIA. Similar to the DRP and BCP, this request may be made to Information Security or another group depending on who has the responsibility for the BIA process. In some cases this function may fall under the Enterprise Risk Management group.

10. Asset Inventories—Request for IT asset inventories. This is much easier said than done and we provide more detailed discussions around this process in the next sections.

11. IT and Information Security Metrics—Request for various metrics collected by IT and Information Security over the past year, or longer if available. This is usually requested from Information Security and the Director of IT or the CIO.

12. Facilities Security Plan—Request for the Facilities Security Plan. If there is not a specific security plan then request for the general facilities plan. This is usually requested from the Physical Security or Facilities group.

13. Organizational Chart and Contact List—Request the organizational chart and a contact list for the organization. This is usually requested from the Director of IT or the CIO.

14. Any Previous Security Presentations and Debriefs—Request for various security-related presentations and debriefs that have been made within the organization. These are typically security presentations to the various organizational management committees by the Information Security Officer and IT Director or CIO. These may be a little bit harder to track down; however, the best place to start is the Information Security Office.

15. Security Program, Plans, and Roadmaps—Request for documents pertaining to the overall security program. These could be roadmaps or project plans in support of the overall program. This is usually requested from Information Security.

16. SAS70s/SSAE16—Request for any SAS70s/SSAE16s related to the operations of the organization. This is usually requested from Information Security, Internal Audit, IT Director, or the CIO.

17. Vendor Security Accreditations—Request for all vendor security accreditation documents particularly for in-scope vendor maintained systems. At this point, it is unlikely that the assessor knows what the in-scope systems are. Taking that into account you can ask for a list of vendors that have gone through vendor accreditation. The request for the actual accreditation can be sent after the Asset Scoping phase. At this point, it is unlikely that the assessor knows what the in-scope systems are.

18. Hardening Guidelines and Checklists—Request for the various guidelines and checklists used as baseline security control checklists for applications, operating systems, databases, and processes. This is usually requested from Information Security; however, may be available from IT.

Aside from the documents mentioned here, there could be other security-related documents in your organization that should be requested if available. There will be instances where the document you are requesting will not be available simply because it does not exist. The general idea here is to collect as many documents as you can. By doing so, you will have more references and resources when you perform the data and risk analysis portion of your review. Often, just the act of requesting documents and determining what type of items are not documented can assist you in evaluating the risk within the organization.

The document request list should be sent to the specific individual and groups that are most likely to have the information. The list should include at least the name of the document (e.g. Information Security Audit Report) you are requesting as well as the date or date range of the document (e.g. SAS70 for January 2011–June 2011) and if possible the source of the document (e.g. Change Management Audit Report by KPMG) for clarity.

A sample document request list is provided in the companion website of this book.

IT ASSET INVENTORIES

One of the activities that should be started early during the data collection phase is the compilation of IT asset inventories and IT asset owners. This activity can be initiated at the early stages of the project and be run in parallel with the executive interviews. In fact, having a good knowledge of the IT assets would help you in the executive interviews especially when talking about systems that support the processes being discussed during the interview.

An IT asset inventory, as the name implies, is a list of IT assets that belong to the organization and support a business process or processes. The goal of this activity is to identify as many systems as possible and then, in the scoping phase, narrow the list down to the most important systems. An IT asset inventory basically gives you the building blocks to start your risk assessments for the individual systems.

This process sounds simple enough; however, time after time we have seen this activity be a source of confusion, especially during early implementations of the risk assessment and management process. This is particularly true in organizations that have never done a risk assessment and have a relatively immature control environment especially in the area of asset management.

The first step in this process is to identify sources where you can obtain or collect information for the IT asset inventory. There is rarely a "good" place to obtain this information and it may vary from organization to organization. In fact, depending on the type of organization you are working in there may be no listing or inventory at all. We have compiled a listing of groups that are typically involved with maintaining a rationalized listing of applications. Approaching these groups may give you the best chances of obtaining a good listing:

- Asset Management Group.
- Enterprise Architecture.
- IT Application Support Group.
- IT Operations Group.
- Network Group.
- Head of Individual Departments.
- Finance—Procurement/Purchasing.

If you are lucky enough to be in an organization that has its own asset management group, there is a good chance that you will be able to get a decent listing; however, before you get your hopes up, some asset management groups focus primarily on tracking hardware rather than software and so they may not be able to provide much assistance. The organization's application support group, as well as the enterprise architecture group are also typically great sources of information when trying to compile an IT asset listing.

Ok, so now you know the groups you should approach; however, how do you narrow down the individuals that you should be approaching? The best people to approach would be the operational or line managers for each group, as they are the most involved with actual operations. Going to executives to obtain this information may be of little value since the knowledge of day-to-day operational details tends to decrease the higher you move up the organizational hierarchy. Operational and line managers are more likely to know the key applications and supporting databases that are supporting their operations.

Ultimately, you need to keep in mind that your goal is to gather as much information as possible to allow you to build the closest approximation of all the systems supporting the organization. The information to be collected includes but is not limited to:

- Listings of Enterprise Applications.
- Listings of Databases.
- Software Inventory.
- Hardware Inventory.
- System Diagrams.
- Technical Design Documents.

The goal here is to combine all of the information collected into the form of a single list (e.g. a spreadsheet). Though you shouldn't be picky when obtaining information from various sources in the organization there are certain important data elements that you should try to capture. These are:

- Asset Name.
- System Name.
- Description of the System.
- Hostnames or IP Address.
- Vendor if any.
- System Owner.
- Technical Support Contact.
- Department that uses the Asset.
- Description of Data.
- Classification of Data.
- No of Records.
- If an application:
  - Operating System.

- Database.
- If a database:
  - Operating System.
  - Applications Supported.

There are a variety of different sources for the above information, so it is important to rationalize and normalize the list. One common problem occurs when various groups use different modules of a single enterprise application and refer to the system by the module they use instead of the applications name. As trivial as this may sound, when it happens this can lead to having 10–15 entries on your listing, all of which are for the same system. Another question you will face is whether you should consider a database that supports an application as a separate asset. This is actually a tough question to answer. Let's say that you have identified a database that supports multiple applications. Should you consider the database as a separate asset or would you only identify the application assets and leave the database server off the list? Ultimately, this depends on the application and database architecture. For a database that supports multiple applications such as a database cluster, there is an argument that it should be considered as an asset for purposes of creating your listing. In an instance where the database supports one application and is self-contained, you may just consider the application stack as one asset.

In many cases, the collection and correlation of the data needed to build your listing does not go as well as planned. There are usually large gaps between what information you would like to obtain and what you actually have. The goal here is to gather as much information as you can. At the very least, you should aim to obtain the system name and system owner as this information will allow you to follow-up and gather more detailed information through interviews.

A sample asset inventory is provided in the companion website of this book.

ASSET SCOPING

Asset scoping is an often-overlooked activity in the data collection phase. In most information security risk assessment frameworks, there is an activity focused on characterizing an asset but very few tackle the fundamental question of "Which assets should you characterize in the first place?"

Previously, we discussed using existing asset inventories or trying to build an asset inventory. The problem with this approach, when looking at relatively large organization, is that the list of information processing assets (e.g. applications used by departments to perform their business processes) may be in the thousands. So let's say you complete your initial inventory and you have a list of 300 applications? Does this mean that you'll have to review all 300? If you have unlimited budget and time you might be able to do this; however, being realistic, performing a detailed assessment over 300 applications will be cost and time prohibitive.

Scoping, in the context of this discussion, is basically narrowing down the asset list so that the most important assets are assessed first. The most important assets are those that, if they were affected by an information security event, would have the greatest adverse impact on the organization. Scoping should be viewed as a prioritization activity, more so than an exclusion activity. The idea here is to rank the assets of the organization based on its importance to the organization and by doing so, those assets that are deemed the most important will be given priority in the review.

So how do we choose which assets are in-scope? There are a number of techniques that can be utilized for this purpose:

- Interviews.
- Asset Scoping Workshops.
- Business Impact Analysis.
- Critical Success Factor Analysis.

Interviews

Interviews are the simplest and the least formal method to perform scoping. This simply entails talking to key people in the organization to identify the assets in your inventory that support the processes critical to the enterprise. Typically, the best people to talk to are those that are most familiar with the applications that are used within the enterprise. Usually this is the CIO or the enterprise architect; however, key contributors to this process could also be Vice Presidents, Senior Managers, or Directors that are in charge of key operating areas of the organization. It is important to note that it is very likely that you may miss mid- or lower-tier applications in this process since executive or senior level personnel may not be as familiar with the smaller systems used within each department.

Asset Scoping Workshops

Asset scoping workshops are a bit more formal than simple interviews. An asset scoping workshop is an activity where you try to obtain consensus from the people invited to the workshop in order to identify the assets that will be in-scope for the risk assessment. Ideally, senior executives should be included in these workshops but this is not always possible due to constraints on their time. Assuming that you have completed some level of executive interviews, you should have an idea by now what the important processes within the organization are. It is through these asset scoping workshops that you map these important processes to the actual systems that support those processes. The participants in the asset scoping workshop should be knowledgeable about the systems in use within the organization and particularly what processes these systems support. Valuable participants in these workshops are typically the CIO, enterprise architect, various IT managers, department managers, system owners (when able to be identified), IT administrators, and key third party vendor representatives (if applicable). Ultimately it is up to the assessor to run the meeting in a way that best meets their needs; however, there are some key tips and techniques that might be useful. For example some, if not all, of the following activities could take place in the workshop:

1. Provide participants with the results of the executive interviews. This should include a quick summary of the mission of the organization as well as the critical processes supporting the mission as identified by the executives.
2. Provide them with the asset inventory that you have been able to compile to this point.
3. Ask them to write down the systems that they believe support the critical processes that the executives are most concerned with. A good way to put this into a question would be: "What system is of such importance that if the confidentiality, integrity, or availability of the system was impaired it would have an adverse impact on our ability to execute a key business process?" Prepare a sheet with the critical processes in one column and ask them to write down the systems that meet this criterion in another column. For identifying the systems, at this point, what is needed is just a general description of the system. For example, that could be as simple as identifying the "PeopleSoft" system as supporting the Payroll processes.
4. Gather all the results and consolidate them into one main form.
5. Show the results to the group and ask for comments and feedbacks. Ask the group to force rank the systems in order of mission priority. The force ranking will require the team to make decisions on the priority of the systems and will help keep the list to a manageable level. Sometimes you may want to set a target in advance by stating that: "We need to leave this meeting with agreement on what the top 10 systems to the organization are." You could choose to do the top 15 or top 20; however, the number of systems you choose should be directly proportional to the resources (time and personnel) that you have available to complete your assessment. The more systems you allow into your "top" list the longer your assessment will take. As mentioned earlier, this is not really an exclusion process; you are simply prioritizing your efforts. You will likely find yourself defending this process and will need to make sure you clearly communicate that for this particular assessment the focus was to identify risks with respect to the top 10, 15, or 20 applications with an understanding that risks related to those assets are likely pervasive throughout the organization and extrapolation of the results to support your enterprise IT security assessment would be valid.
6. Ask for agreement and sign-off from the group. Once this is done, the final list of systems, agreed upon by this group, will typically be the list that will be considered in-scope for the assessment.

A sample Asset Workshop Sheet is provided in the companion website of this book.

Business Impact Analysis and Other Assessments

Sometimes, a relatively easy way to identify and then scope out the applications for your assessment is to review the organization's Business Impact Analysis (BIA), typically as part of the overall Disaster Preparedness and Recovery Plan. A BIA is an assessment performed by an organization to identify critical and non-critical organizational functions and activities. A BIA will often map out critical processes within the organization and if done properly will also identify specific systems supporting those processes. Review of the BIA should reveal which systems are critical from a significant business process stand point. Thus, the most critical systems identified in a BIA could very well be the same systems that will be prioritized in the information security risk assessment. Based on our experience there are a number of pitfalls that you should be aware of when using this approach:

1. Not all organizations will have a BIA or the BIA will be hopelessly out of date or incomplete. You would be surprised at the number of fairly large organizations that lack a BIA or have an out of date BIA.
2. A BIA mostly focuses on the availability aspect of security and the operational aspect of criticality. For example, in a hospital scenario, what if there's a large data mining system that is only used for university research and not directly related to any critical operational process such as patient care? And what if this data mining system has millions of ePHI records? A breach would cost the hospital millions even though it is not part of a critical process. There are definite dangers associated with missing key systems from a security perspective if you only rely on a BIA.

Other assessments that may be useful for identifying systems are internal and external audit reports. Depending on the type of audit, auditors will also conduct scoping based on the materiality of the asset. These reports, or related scoping documents, can be a useful resource when identifying in-scope assets. While BIAs and resources such as audit reports can be useful in asset scoping, we definitely recommend that you do not solely rely on such reports when performing your scoping activities as your information security risk assessment needs to take into account multiple factors of risk while the BIA or audit reports may have been focused on only a specific risk area and may not identify all the assets that you need to review.

Critical Success Factor Analysis

Most of the scoping activities described above rely on the judgment of the assessment team and the various people that have been included throughout the interviews and scoping workshops. The results of this type of activity will typically be a more subjective decision based on perceived value. It is human nature for people to generally perceive the functions that they supervise or perform for an organization as being the most important. For example, a system owner or an IT administrator will generally believe the systems that they are in charge of are the most important. Operating from a "big picture" few that is obviously not accurate so you can consider using the Critical Success Factor Method. Think of critical success factors as elements that are essential in meeting the organization's mission goals and objectives. This method utilizes an affinity analysis to map information assets against the organization's critical success factors and provides a more consistent and repeatable method of identifying critical assets.

A discussion of the concepts surrounding Critical Success Factors as well as their use could fill an entirely separate book and we will not spend much time discussing them here. If you are interested in the concept and would like to incorporate it into your process, a Software Engineering Institute (SEI) report called "The Critical Success Factor Method: Establishing a Foundation for Enterprise Security Management" is available to guide you through this method and how you can utilize this as an asset scoping method.

The choice of the technique utilized is ultimately up to the assessor but always try to remember that whatever technique is used, your final asset listing should contain at least the following:

- Name and description of the asset.
- Rationale and factors used to identify the asset as in-scope.

Use of the various asset scoping techniques is not mutually exclusive. They often overlap and should if possible be used in conjunction with each other. For example, you could perform the asset scoping workshop utilizing affinity techniques (critical success factors) as well as supplement your assessment with a review of the BIA and audit reports.

A question often asked in this activity, and touched upon earlier, is how do we identify the right population of assets to put in-scope? This is a very difficult question to answer. Ideally, any asset that is identified in the various scoping activities should be included in the scope but what do you do when your scoping activities identify a hundred or even hundreds of applications? Ultimately, this will all come down to an executive decision that needs to take into consideration time and cost trade-offs. As was emphasized earlier, and it is important so we'll emphasize it again, asset scoping is a prioritization and not an exclusion activity. Any assets that are left out of your initial review can still be reviewed in subsequent risk assessments. While it can be tempting to buy into the rationale that all assets need to be reviewed it is often a good idea, when performing an assessment for the first time, to keep the scope small. The benefits of this approach are twofold, firstly it minimizes the overall impact on organizational resources and secondly it allows you to uncover potential flaws in the assessment process.

A sample scoped Asset Listing is provided in the companion website of this book. This is not representative of the listing that would be derived for a large organization, and for the sake of simplicity, this list only includes a few assets.

THE ASSET PROFILE SURVEY

Once you have all the in-scope assets identified, it is time to build a profile for assessment of the assets. Some frameworks refer to this step as asset characterization and for many of the major frameworks this is the official start of the risk assessment process. The data collected in this activity will ultimately form the basis for the results and findings of the assessment.

Though it is easy to trivialize this step due to perceived simplicity, we cannot stress enough the importance of proper preparation and implementation of this activity. The goal here is to collect as much relevant information about the asset as possible. In order to do this, there are several factors that you have to consider:

1. Who do you ask for information?
2. How do you ask for the information?
3. What do you ask for?

Who Do You Ask for Information?

This question is possibly the easiest to answer but it is also the most important one to get right. The quality of the information that you are gathering is only as good as the source. When we discussed the asset inventory and asset scoping activities, one of the most important things that we repeatedly stressed is identifying the asset owner. The asset owner is the person who is responsible for the system. By responsibility, it may not be a technical position and is likely someone with more of a process perspective. Often times, the asset owners are the ones that will be your source of information but in other cases, system owners who may be high up in the organizational hierarchy may delegate the responsibility to one of their managers to act as a system steward. Since the best source of information would be the one closest to the day-to-day operations and use of the system, it is important to know whether the person who has been designated as system owner has actually passed responsibility to another person.

How Do You Ask for the Information?

While we previously indicated that interviews were ideal for information gathering this is one instance where the easiest and most efficient way to go about with the collection of information would be through the use of a survey. In terms of surveys, there are various methods depending on the technology available within the company:

1. Intranet portal—This is probably the most efficient and most convenient way to send a survey. For example, Microsoft SharePoint allows you to create robust surveys and integrate the results into spreadsheets and databases.
2. Third party survey mechanisms—There are many third party survey mechanisms such as sites like Survey Monkey which can also be used. As with all third party services it is important to remember that you will be requesting sensitive information and you need to take into consideration security and privacy concerns related to the use of a third party vendor.
3. Electronic Format—PDF and Word files can also be used to collect information. You can create PDF and Word forms to collect data; however, the main problem

with this method is the tracking of the data collected. This problem can be overcome though as there are various automated ways to collect data from PDFs.

4. Paper—There is always good old-fashioned paper for collecting survey responses; however, you can probably see the limitations of this means of collecting this data. Ultimately, to make it more useable you would have to transpose survey results into digital format so you can properly query the information.

Use of a survey at this point definitely has it's advantages, as it is relatively easy to deploy and provides you an efficient way to consolidate all information gathered. The downside, as with all surveys, is that the information that is collected is only as good as the survey itself. Also, no matter how well constructed the survey is, there will always be recipients that will misinterpret items in the survey or will need additional clarification. Because of this, it is always a good idea to have an open communication channel to the system owner or steward that has received the survey in case they have some questions. In our experience we have found that individual emails or follow-up phone conversations allow you to answer questions that the survey respondent has and the effort you put in to discuss the questions with them will pay off in more accurate and useful answers. Depending on the number of systems that you need to review it is often advisable to have a post-survey interview with the system owner or steward to confirm their answers to the surveys. This allows you to better understand their responses and potentially gain more insight and information about the asset.

Remember, it is never just a good idea to send someone a survey without any background information. It is always important to prepare the recipients for the surveys and the interviews. Before sending out the surveys and meeting with them for the post-survey interviews, it would be prudent to send out several communications. The project sponsor should initiate the initial communication to the system owners and this communication should include a description of what the process is and what is expected of the recipient. This communication could be in the form of an introductory email, short kick-off meeting, or a phone call. The executive that is directly responsible for the system or supervises the designated system owner should always be copied in the communication.

A sample Initial Communications to System Owners is provided in the companion website of this book.

What Do You Ask for?

Knowing what to ask for is the most important part of this activity. Our goal in asset profiling is to gain as much relevant information regarding the asset as is necessary to perform a proper data and risk analysis.

The main goal here is to build a profile of the system; however, it is important to note that the items that will be collected should not only cover the system itself but also the environment housing the system. The information gathered here will give the assessor critical information that is necessary in order to accurately analyze the likelihood and impact of a particular threat for the analysis phase of the assessment. For example, at the minimum, the following items should be collected:

1. System Name—Ask for the system and/or module name. As mentioned in the previous activities, some enterprise systems are composed of multiple modules and the component of the system should be clearly stated if they are being assessed separately.
2. System Description—Ask what business process or processes the system supports.
3. Vendor—Ask who the vendor of the system is. For large enterprise systems that are a combination of the application, OS, and database (e.g. PeopleSoft), this will typically be the application vendor. For example, the vendor for a PeopleSoft application would be PeopleSoft and not the database vendor, which is Oracle.
4. Platform—For an application, ask what Operating System and Database the system is running on.
5. System Owner—Ask who has the primary responsibility for the system, the data of the system, and the process or processes it supports.
6. System Steward—Ask who the responsibilities of day-to-day operations of the system are delegated to. In some cases this may be the same person as the system owner.
7. Technical Contact—Ask the respondent to identify a technical contact who is knowledgeable about the technical aspects of the system. Particularly the security mechanisms and controls that are in place.
8. Data Classification—This is intended to identify the data sensitivity of the information stored or accessed through the system. Organizations would typically have some sort of classification scheme and that should be used to identify the classification of the system. In cases where the organization doesn't have one (which is a definite red flag in our risk assessment), you may be able to use a standard one such as:
   a. Confidential: Information that should only be released on a need to know basis.
   b. Internal: Information that is openly shareable within the organization.
   c. Public: Information that is openly shareable with the public.
   d. Special industry or specific classification such as Personally Identifiable Information (PII), Electronic Protected Health Information (ePHI), or Legally Privileged.
9. Accessibility—Ask how the application is accessed. The primary factors you are trying to identify are whether the application is accessible via:
   a. Internet (Public).
   b. Remote (via VPN or some other remote connection but non-public internet).
   c. Internal only.
10. Location—Ask where the system is located. The location could be:

    a. In the organization's data center.
    b. In the department.
    c. At a vendor location.

11. Data Flow—Ask how and where data is transmitted by the system. Some common data transmission mechanisms could be:
    a. Web Transfer (e.g. HTTP, HTTPS).
    b. File Transfers (e.g. FTP, SFTP).
    c. Removable Media (e.g. USB, CD/DVDs).

For each of the transmission methods, you should also ask where the data is transmitted. For example:
    a. Is it transferred within the organization only?
    b. Is it transferred to a business partner?
    c. Is it transferred to a vendor?
    d. Is it transferred to individual users?

An additional question to ask is if any of the transmissions are encrypted. This may be a difficult question for non-technical system owners to answer and is probably suited for the control survey; however, it does not hurt to include it.

12. Users—How many active users does the system have? You may need to create "buckets" for this question to allow for standardization of the answers (e.g. 0–100, 101–1000, 1001 above).

13. User profile—Ask about who accesses the system. The main focus here is whether the individuals accessing the system and its data are employees of the organization or not. This is highly dependent on the type of organization but some examples are:
    a. Employee.
    b. Contractors.
    c. Vendors.
    d. Visitors.
    e. Students.
    f. Volunteers.
    g. Public.

14. Security Incident—Ask the respondent if they know of any instances of a security incident that had an impact to the system they are responsible for.

15. Security Testing—Ask the respondent if there have been any security tests performed against their system and if so when the testing occurred. Ask to see the results of any such testing.

16. Business impact—This is a difficult question to obtain objective information from since most respondents will say that the system they are responding to is important to the organization. Oftentimes it is easier to go through the Business Impact Analysis (BIA) to obtain this data, if one is available. Even with the possibility that the answer will not be entirely accurate, it is still a good idea to ask the system owner and steward about their views regarding the impact of a compromise or loss of a system as a BIA could miss certain things that a system owner or steward would know based on experience. Though we generally recommend against having open ended questions in a survey, this question should be considered for inclusion as it can allow you to at a minimum gain insight into how the system owner feels with respect to the impact on the organization if something was to happen to their system.

A sample Asset Profile Survey is provided in the companion website of this book.

THE CONTROL SURVEY

The control survey should be thought of as an extension of the Asset Profile Survey. While the asset profile survey focuses on identifying the characteristics of the asset and its environment, the control survey, as the name implies, focuses specifically on controls. The control information gathered in this phase will be critical in the data and risk analysis phase as the identification and measurement of controls plays an integral part in the measurement of risk in most information risk assessment frameworks.

Now at this point you may be asking yourself "Aren't controls technically a characteristic of the asset and environment as well?" The short answer is "Yes." The reason that we separate the control assessment into its own survey has more to do with logistics and implementation. As strange as it may seem, after performing these assessments you'll realize that the people who are knowledgeable about the controls in place over a system are usually different than those who know about the business process aspects of the system. Ultimately, this drives the need for a second survey.

The general principles and activities involved in the control survey follow the same approach as the asset profile survey:

1. Who do you ask for information?
2. How do you ask for the information?
3. What do you ask for?

Who Do You Ask for Information?

Surprisingly, it doesn't always follow that the business/system owners will be knowledgeable about the security controls in place for their system. In many cases, this knowledge is held by those who are more familiar with the technical aspects of the system like an IT Application Administrator, System Administrator, or even the Information Security Officer.

The best way to approach this survey is to provide the survey to the system owner and ask them to answer the questions they are able to and then to pass the others to a technical contact that is more suited to answer the technical questions. Ask the system owner to let you know who the technical contact is so that you can resend the survey to the contact and provide an explanation and overview of your objectives. The risk here is that the business owner tries to answer the questions themselves, gets it wrong, and the technical contact doesn't validate the questions that have already been answered. Thus it is important for the assessor to communicate with the business owner to determine if they are comfortable answering the survey.

In most cases, the technical contact may still not have enough information to answer the complete survey particularly in organizations where certain controls are centralized. For this very reason, the next activity, a "survey results review," is conducted by the Information Security Officer to ensure the accuracy of the answers provided by the system owners, stewards, and technical contacts.

Another approach that may speed up the process would be to gather the group of individuals that need to answer the survey into a conference room and have them answer the questions together. The ability for the respondents to query the assessor directly as they fill out the questions could bring clarity to the responses and thus increase the overall accuracy of the results.

How Do You Ask for Information?

The mechanisms used to record information from the system owners or technical contacts will be exactly the same as those used in the asset profile survey. As mentioned in the previous section, surveys are usually the best mechanism to accomplish data collection when you have to query a large group of individuals. Similar to the asset profile survey, there will always be cases where the recipients will need additional clarification. This is why having open communication with the recipients is so important.

In our experience, we recommend conducting the control survey after the asset profile survey. This allows the system owner to become familiar with the process. Also, if the system owner does not have enough knowledge about the security controls in place, it is likely this survey will be passed on to a technical contact after the asset profile survey.

One of the most important exercises related to the control survey is verifying the accuracy of the answers. Some of the recipients, even the technical ones, do not have enough security knowledge to properly assess the security controls that are in place. A more detailed discussion about the requirements around performing this review are covered in the upcoming section "Post-Survey Results Review."

What Do You Ask for?

The idea here is to prepare a checklist that will allow you to identify the security controls that are in place for a particular system. So, what controls should you be looking for? This all depends on the security standards that the organization is using. For example, if there is a published set of security controls and policies that your organization requires for systems, then that set of controls and policies should be the benchmark used for the survey.

With that said, if the organization does not have documented requirements covering security controls for key systems (another red flag in your risk assessment), a published standard of controls is often a good place to start building the checklist.

Using a published control standard not only makes it easier but also makes your assessment more defensible. The following standards are good sources for controls:

1. ISO 27001—A worldwide standard for Information Security Management Systems. Provides 134 different controls. The control catalog can be found in Annex A of the standard.
2. NIST SP800-53—A security standard for federal agencies. Provides a total number of 198 controls. The control catalog can be found in Appendix F of the standard.
3. SANS Top 20—A prioritized baseline of information security controls. Provides 20 high-level controls and multiple implementation guidelines. The control catalog can be found on the SANS website.

The most obvious question you should be asking yourself here is: will you need to send out a survey to your system owners with 198 or 134 items? This depends on the level of detail the assessor is going for but most of the time it all comes down to the amount of time you have available. Obviously, a more thorough review of controls is better but what if this is the first time the organization was conducting a risk assessment and you have to review 20 systems? That's already over 2000 controls to review if you use the controls from ISO 27001!

Though some would say it is ideal to review all controls, this is usually not possible, so we recommend rationalizing and prioritizing the controls to create a minimum baseline to review. The SANS Top 20 controls provide a good list of what various government agencies and large enterprises consider "critical controls." The organization's Information Security Office and the CIo can create a minimum baseline of controls by picking a subset of controls from the organization's security standards or a published standard.

Organizational vs. System Specific

Since this data collection activity pertains to a specific system, you should only include information system specific controls. Many of the published security control standards include organization level controls such as security policies, enterprisewide network controls, data center controls, and asset management controls, as well as many others. Though all of these are important to consider when performing the risk assessment, these controls are better answered by the Information Security Officer and will be part of the strategic risk analysis process, which is covered later. A system owner would probably have minimal knowledge about them as they are enterprise wide controls and not specific to their system. At the very least, the following system-specific control questions should be included in the control checklist:

1. Data Protection Controls:
    a. Is the system encrypting all transmissions (SSL)?
    b. Is the data in the system encrypted (database encryption, FDE)?

2. Malicious Code Protection:
   a. Are AV/HIPS technologies in place on the operating system supporting the application?
3. Patch and Vulnerability Management:
   a. Is the system being patched regularly, at both the application and OS level?
   b. Is the system being reviewed for vulnerabilities regularly?
4. Authentication and Access Control:
   a. Does the system require a password?
   b. Does the system enforce a complex password?
   c. Does the system utilize two-factor authentication?
   d. Are there generic accounts being used in the system?
5. Security Configuration:
   a. Was the system built using a baseline security standard and has the system undergone a security review before deployment and after major upgrades?
6. User Provisioning and Review:
   a. Does the department have a process to provision users?
   b. Does the department have a process to regularly review user accounts allowed to access the system?
   c. Does the department review administrative account creation and activity in the system?
7. Security Awareness:
   a. Have the users of the systems undergone security awareness training and are they aware of incident and breach notification procedures?
8. Network:
   a. Is the system in a "secured" segment of the network or is the system easily accessible via the normal user network?
9. Auditing:
   a. Does the system have logging and monitoring capabilities (e.g. successful and failed logins, administrative account activities)?
10. Backup and Contingency:
    a. Is the system being backed up regularly?
    b. Is the system part of the disaster recovery and contingency plan?
    c. Are there any redundancy mechanisms for the system (e.g. mirrored or failover servers)?
11. Operational Controls:
    a. Does the department follow a change control process when updating the system?
    b. Does the department have defined roles for the system and have proper segregation of duties been considered when defining those roles?
12. Physical Controls:
    a. Are the physical servers that support the system in a secure location (e.g. in the organizations data center with proper physical and environmental controls)?

Scale vs. Yes or No

Once you have determined the minimum set of controls for your checklist, the next step is to determine how you will ask the respondents to measure them. There are two common ways:

1) Using a scale (e.g. 1–5).
2) Simple "Yes or No."

Measuring using scaling is typically the best approach for measuring controls since this allows the assessor to obtain the level of the control maturity as compared to just asking whether it exists or not. The main issue with using a scale is that by their very nature scales are subjective and prone to misinterpretation. In order to make the scale as standardized as possible, you can use a scale that follows the principle of the Capability Maturity Model (CMM):

1. Initial (score: 1)—The control is new and undocumented.
   * Example: There is no documented process to conduct user access reviews nor is it performed.
2. Repeatable (score: 2)—The control is documented but implementation is incomplete.
   * Example: There are documented procedures on how to conduct user access reviews but the review is not regularly conducted.
3. Defined (score: 3)—The control is documented and implemented.
   * Example: The procedures on how to conduct user access reviews are documented and are conducted on a regular basis.
4. Managed (score: 4)—The control is documented, implemented, and results are tracked and monitored.
   * Example: The procedures on how to conduct user access reviews are documented and are conducted on a regular basis. The results of the review are documented and metrics related to the performance of the reviews are kept.
5. Optimizing (score: 5)—the control is documented, implemented, tracked, monitored, and the process is optimized and improved.
   * Example: The procedures on how to conduct user access reviews are documented and are conducted on a regular basis. The results of the review are documented and metrics related to the performance of the reviews are kept. There is a regular discussion regarding improving the control and incorporating process improvements such as automation.

Using a scale is a good way of measuring the maturity of a control and provides better insight into the strengths and weaknesses of a system. Unfortunately, this is easier said than done. System owners and technical contacts sometimes have insufficient knowledge about security to properly assess the level of controls. For example, some system owners would not know if a particular policy or procedure exists especially if it was written by the security office and was not properly communicated. Another example is where a technical contact might not necessarily know if the system they are maintaining is part of a disaster recovery plan, especially if there is a separate group handling disaster recovery planning. As strange as it may seem, this is not an uncommon occurrence in large decentralized organizations where departments maintain their own IT systems.

Using a "Yes or No" checklist on the other hand is appealing since it is very simple and straightforward; however, there are some pitfalls in using this simplified approach. The problem with this approach mostly arises from how the questions are phrased. For example, the following question is very weak and will not necessarily provide you with the information you are looking for:

- Do you perform user access reviews for your system?

In this example, if the system owners or the technical owners are not aware of the standards in place, they might not know how often these reviews are supposed to be done. It is best to assume that the respondent will not know the details and structure your questions accordingly. What if the standard is a quarterly review yet they only perform the review once every year? What if a sign-off from the system owner is required by the standard and the system owner does not know this? In both cases, due to lack of knowledge from the system owner, they might have said "Yes" to the question but in reality, the control is not being properly conducted. A much better question would be:

- Do you perform quarterly user access review for your system and does the system owner sign-off on the review?

This is a much better-phrased question in terms of trying to isolate the answer you are looking for. The downside with this question comes into play when a group is partially performing a control but can't answer the previous question due to its very specific nature. What do you do if they are performing a review once a year? Their answer would end up being "No"; however, shouldn't the fact that they are operating the control, albeit partially, count for something? This is where relying only on "Yes" or "No" answers could lead to inaccuracies in the results since there is no room for capturing a partial implementation of the control.

The use of scales is ultimately a better approach since it provides a better insight into the level of maturity of the controls that are in place. We have found that the use of a scale is better suited to an organization with a relatively mature security implementation. On the flip side we have also found that a "Yes or No" checklist will be easier to understand for the system owners and technical contact and will give you a more standardized way of measurement which tends to be suited to organizations which have a limited or relatively new security program.

Inquiry vs. Testing

Since we have been recommending the use of surveys throughout this section, you might be wondering, why are we relying on inquiry and not actually testing the controls? Obviously, in a perfect world, the assessor would actually test the controls instead of relying on inquiry alone. It is easy to see why this isn't possible if you just look at the following example. You are using a checklist and testing for 30 controls (indicative of a very minimal set of controls) and you have 10 assets to review. This means you already have 300 controls that you and your team would have to manually test!

Ultimately, whether you test controls or not will be up to the assessor and the project sponsor to determine how much assurance they want for the risk assessment. If they feel that substantive testing is required since they cannot rely on the information from the system owners, stewards, and technical contacts, then testing may be the way to go. Remember that information security risk assessments are not intended to be audits. With proper follow-ups and guidance from the assessors, a properly designed inquiry (e.g. survey) can provide sufficient assurance regarding the controls for the purposes of the assessment. Another thing to consider is that as repeat assessments are performed issues with the answers provided by the business units may be identified. These issues may come to light when different people answer the questions or when the same people answer but forget the answers they previously provided. Issues may also be identified during operational audits, penetration tests, or other security or architecture reviews that could call into question the validity of the answers provided to the risk assessment.

A sample Control Survey is provided in the companion website of this book.

SURVEY SUPPORT ACTIVITIES AND WRAP-UP

Though surveys are convenient, they are not simply a sendout and wait affair. Throughout the process the assessor should have an open communication channel with each of the individuals answering the asset profile and the control surveys. As well designed or written as the surveys may be there will always be questions and clarifications needed so it is always a good idea to be available during the course of the process. In fact, the following activities would increase the possibility of gaining more accurate data from the responders and should be done in support of the survey data collection process.

Before and During the Survey

Meet or talk with the responders before or during the process of answering the surveys. This will allow the assessor to clarify any questions that the individual or individuals completing the survey may have.

Review of Survey Responses

For key assets or instances where the responses appear to be inconsistent it may be a good idea to review and discuss the responses with the Information Security Officer, the project sponsor, and the risk assessment team. In some cases other people, particularly the Information Security Officer, might have additional perspectives and insight regarding the design or operating effectiveness of the control environment supporting the asset. It is not uncommon to review the responses and realize that the responders did not answer correctly. Any potential adjustments and unanswered questions in the surveys should be brought up with the original responders. As an example, if the Information Security Officer thinks that a particular control response was inaccurate, note this for verification in the post-survey verification step.

Post-Survey Verifications

Conducting a post-survey verification allows you to meet or talk with the people who responded to the survey after the risk assessment team has had a chance to review their responses. This step is very important and allows you to verify any of their responses. Any possible inaccuracies identified or discussed in the previous step should be brought up during this time. Relay to the responder the observations that you have with respect to any inaccuracies identified and see if the responder agrees with the adjustment. If they disagree with the adjustment, the issue should be escalated to the Information Security Officer and the Project Sponsor who will be able to make the final determination on what answer to record. For example, if the system owner insists that a control is present but the project team believes that there is no evidence that the control is in place or the answer appears to be inconsistent with other related answers, the Information Security Officer or the project sponsor will usually have the final say on the matter.

After the post-survey verification, you will now have completed and verified data that is ready for consolidation.

A sample of a System Profile Survey and Control Survey is provided in the companion website of this book.

CONSOLIDATION

The objective of the consolidation activities is to bring together all the information gathered into a central repository in order to facilitate efficient analysis. Throughout the data collection phase, we have been collecting information from various sources and by this time, the following should have been collected:

1. Results from the Asset Profile Surveys.
2. Results from the Control Surveys.
3. Documents from the Document Requests List.
4. Notes from the Executive Interviews.

The next step is to bring all of these elements together into our container. This simply means that you need to pull all the collected data together into a single aggregated view. Using the asset surveys as an example, this just means putting all the results in your asset container (whether the container is a spreadsheet or database) in such a way that you can see all the assets and the responses in one single view instead of multiple views.

Let's say the assessor used SharePoint surveys to collect the information for the asset profile survey and the control survey. It is fairly straightforward to extract that information from those surveys into a spreadsheet where each asset is one row and each of the survey questions is a column. A sample of an "Asset Container" is provided in the companion website of this book.

Why go through all this trouble? By putting the data in a consolidated and normalized view, you gain more flexibility in the data analysis phase. This has the following benefits:

1. A consolidated view allows the data to be used as a "reference table."
2. A consolidated view makes it easier to obtain overall statistics.
3. A consolidated view makes updates to the data easier if they are all in one view.

The value of these benefits will become more apparent as we go through the data analysis section in Chapter 4.

THE REAL WORLD

Jane, our Information Security Officer, is now in the thick of things. She has been given the go ahead from her CIO to conduct an information security risk assessment project.

When her CIO told her that the budget committee had approved her resource request she was a bit nervous. She hadn't performed an information security risk assessment before and all her knowledge in the area came from reading the frameworks she was able to download. While she feels like she understands the concepts of risk pretty well, she is unsure of how she will manage a full-blown risk assessment project especially since she's only been at the organization for a few months and has very little organization knowledge to fall back on.

One of the first things she recognizes is that she cannot do this by herself. Being new to the organization further compounds this problem. She knows that first and foremost she needs to have someone who will back her up. She needs a "project sponsor." For Jane, that's a pretty easy choice, who else could it be but her trusty CIO! Her CIO is high enough in the organizational food chain to be able to push things through if they get stuck and dialogue with executives at his peer level to make sure there is appropriate organizational support. Her only reservation with her choice of project sponsor is that she has noticed, in her brief time working with him, that he is a bit impulsive with his decision making. This is offset by the fact that he does have some basic understanding of security and she knows that he will back her up. While not necessarily the perfect candidate she thinks he is definitely the best choice within the organization. That day she schedules a meeting with her CIO to discuss the assessment:

Jane: Hi! As you know, I'm kicking off the information security risk assessment project.

CIO: That's good. I had to jump through hoops to get the budget for this approved, and will have to brief the Board on the results, so I'm really expecting something good. Is there anything you need from me to make sure this is successful?

Jane: Yes, in fact that is what I wanted to meet with you about today. I wanted to discuss with you what I'll need from you for the risk assessment.

CIO: Do you mean me directly or in terms of providing you support? I hope the later since I was under the assumption that you will be taking point on this. You know how busy I am right?

Jane: Yes, I totally understand. You really won't have to do much. I just need you to help set me up meetings with some of the VPs, attend some meetings, and mediate if there are some roadblocks along the way. Mostly, I'll just need to make sure I have strong executive support when I start going through the assessment process.

CIO: Fair enough, I can do that. Though I do hope there won't be any roadblocks or problems. My job is stressful enough as it is.

Jane: I'll try my best to minimize your involvement, and I think with effective communication I should be able to keep it to a minimum, but I'm not making any promises. I'm pretty sure it won't be too bad.

CIO: Sounds good. Just tell me what I can do help.

Jane: Well, speaking of help, I was wondering when we could get approval to hire the security analyst I was requesting for? I'm pretty much a one-woman officer here and it would be great to have some help for the risk assessment.

CIO: Hmmm. That may be a problem. We really have a very limited budget right now. I think you'll probably have to wait till the next fiscal year. But I have the utmost confidence that you will be able to handle everything till that time.

Jane: Uh... ok boss...

CIO: You don't sound happy...

Jane: Oh nope, I'm fine. I... uh... need to get started then.

CIO: Yea, you really should... I promised the other execs that we would have and information security risk assessment in a couple of months.

Jane: Hmm. Speaking of execs, I should start setting up interviews with them in order to obtain their views regarding information security here in the hospital.

CIO: Sure, I can set that up for you. Who would you like to meet with?

Jane: Preferably all the C-Level Executives, VPs, and directors of all departments. Do you think that would be possible?

CIO: Probably not, but I can probably get you a quick meeting with our CEO, COO, and CFO and my administrative assistant may be able to help with setting up some of the other meetings. People know he is my right hand person so that should help getting the attention of the person you want to meet with.

Jane: Sure, that would be great!

CIO: Ok, I'll talk to them later in our executive meeting and give them a heads up regarding the interview that you will be conducting. I'll come to the interview so I can introduce you to them. Just make sure you have all your questions ready. They're really busy and blowing these meetings could really impact our success on the project.

Jane: Of course boss! I'll be ready!

After that meeting, as promised her CIO was able to set up brief meetings with the CEO, CFO, and COO. She was a bit nervous at first but she was able to impress the execs with her knowledge of the different systems and business processes of the hospital even though she had only been working there for a relatively short time. Even her boss was impressed! Her homework really paid off and on top of impressing the executives she also obtained some really good information from the interviews. Knowing she had such a short amount of time with the key leaders of the organization her questions revolved around one theme, which was "What keeps you up at night?"

The CEO mentioned that he wants to ensure that the hospital is not in danger of breaking any federal regulations such as HIPAA in order to prevent any bad publicity for the hospital. The COO wanted to make sure that hospital systems are protected from events that would cause downtime and affect the quality of patient care. The CFO on the other hand wants to make sure that their financial statements are accurate. These brief meetings gave Jane some really good insight into the organizational risk that concern the senior executives.

After the executive interviews, Jane has now started to think about data collection. She knew that in order to assess the risk, she needs information to base her conclusions on. If she is going to report to her boss that certain systems are at high risk she needs to make sure she can substantiate her conclusions. One of the first things that she prepares is a document request list of all the documents she thinks would help her in the assessment. Since she was relatively new to the hospital and didn't know who to send the request to, she sent the request to the CIO who then forwarded it to individuals he felt would best be able to help. Surprisingly, most of the documents that she requested, like past audit reports and some IT metrics, were already in the possession of the CIO.

At this point, Jane has mostly collected data that dealt with security from a high-level organizational perspective. The next step for Jane was to start collecting data on specific systems. But before she can collect data, she needs to first know what systems she needs to review. There are several things that will impact the number of systems that are going to be reviewed. First of all, she only has two months to finish the review. She's also the only available resource to conduct the review. With those things in mind, she thinks that she has to prioritize which systems she will review. Obviously, she has to review the most important systems first. But how does she do that and who decides which the most important systems are?

One of the things she included in her document request list was an asset inventory. Fortunately, the hospitals enterprise architect has done pretty well with documenting all the current applications that the hospital is running. This was a life saver for Jane and she was ecstatic until she opened the listing. Much to her chagrin there are about 50 applications in the asset inventory. So Jane went to her CIO and discussed the situation.

Jane: So I wanted to give you an update on the risk assessment. It seems like I may have hit my first snag.

CIO: Already? What seems to be the problem?

Jane: Well I reviewed the key asset listings for the hospital and there are about 50 applications on the list.

CIO: Sounds good. So have you started on them?

Jane: Nope, that is the problem. That is just way too many. I'm only one person and eight weeks is not enough time to complete 50 applications!

CIO: So how many applications do you think we can finish in eight weeks?

Jane: Hmmm. I'm not sure since this is the first time I'm doing this but I think maybe five??

CIO: That doesn't seem like very many but I guess there is no magic number and I have to trust your judgment.

Jane: Thanks. But that brings me to the next issue. If we're going to do five, which five are we going to do? These should be the 5 most critical applications.
        Ideally we should include systems based on their importance to the business. We need to make sure all those systems are covered.

CIO: Well, I can help you with an easy one. I'm pretty sure that one of them will be our enterprise hospital information management system. That pretty much runs everything here.

Jane: I agree. We should also include our financial system since according to our CFO that's one of the most important systems here.

CIO: Yea, I agree. I just have a feeling that we are doing this too informally. Is there a process or something that we need to follow?

Jane: Good question. Based on what I've read we can use techniques such as Affinity Assessments using Critical Success Factors. But I think that may take too long. From what I've read that's a whole monster by itself. I was hoping to use a Business Impact Analysis as a source for this but unfortunately the one we have has not been updated in 10 years. So, I was thinking I could conduct a workshop with all of the directors and managers.

CIO: Yep, keep going...I like it so far.

Jane: In this workshop, we'll list down the hospitals critical business processes and produce a consensus of 5 critical systems that supports those business processes. We can probably have the managers independently write down the system or systems that they feel supports each of the critical business process and then consolidate everything and see what we've got. I already have a gut feel on what the systems will be but doing it this way will probably be much more formal and defensible.

CIO: Hmmm. Sounds like a good idea. Honestly, I'd really like to do that Critical Success Factor thing but if you say that we really don't have much time, let's do the workshop instead.

So Jane conducted the workshop and it went pretty well. She had fairly good representation from the different business units, which helped in providing different views regarding the business processes and the systems they support. In most cases, the group agreed on the critical systems though she found out that, based on the opinions of the managers, there were way more than five systems that were considered critical. In the end, Jane had to go back to the CIO and have him make an executive decision, trimming the list to five with the assurance that the other systems will be assessed after this initial batch.

Based on the result of the workshop, she now has five critical in-scope systems for the risk assessment. She also now knows who the system owners are for each system as they were also identified as part of the workshop.

Considering that this is the first time Jane and the hospital were conducting an information security risk assessment, five systems is still a fairly large task given that she needs to complete this in two months along with her day-to-day duties as an Information Security Officer. Jane decides that one way to make up for her lack of manpower would be to leverage technology as much as possible.

Based on her review of the different frameworks, she knows that before she can analyze the risk to the hospital and the hospitals critical systems, she needs data. And, in order to get that data, she needs a way to collect it. Fortunately, Jane has a lot of experience in collecting data from when she performed an assessment at her previous employer that dealt with collecting information about PII in systems. What she did during that assessment was utilize the survey component of Microsoft SharePoint to collect the information and consolidated it into spreadsheets. Since this worked well in her previous project, Jane believes that this will be a perfect way to collect data for this project as well.

So now that Jane knows how she will be collecting and consolidating the information she starts planning what the content of the survey will be. For several days, she poured through the different risk frameworks and began putting together a list of questions that she needs to ask the different system owners.

For the questions, she knew that in order to fairly gauge the risk of the system, she needs questions that will give her an understanding of the exposure and likelihood of the system to threats and the potential impact if the system were actually affected. Aside from this, she also knew that she needed to know what controls are in place. Unfortunately, there wasn't really an information security program at the hospital before she got there so there wasn't much of a security control standard in place. In the end she decides to use a critical control listing that she referenced from SANS. She felt that instead of doing a very detailed review of controls and running the risk of not completing the assessment, she should focus on the top security controls that are essential for the organization.

After about a week, she was ready with her questionnaires. Using SharePoint, she was able to send out the questionnaires to the various system owners very easily. Knowing that communication was going to be critical in obtaining accurate answers, as well as limiting the involvement of her boss, Jane did a pretty good job of keeping in touch with the asset owners. She was in constant communication with them and explained to them any items that they were unsure of. This ended up being fortuitous since, to her surprise, there were many items that they were unsure of! It wasn't that Jane's questions were vague; however, since this was the first time many of the respondents were involved with this process they were not familiar with the concepts covered in the questions and sometimes even hesitant about answering the questions. Most of the system owners were familiar with audits, having been through many, and right off the bat many of them perceived these questions as being related to some sort of audit. This perception led them to be very guarded. Jane, being the good communicator that she is, was able to smooth that misunderstanding out and, in the end, the system owners were very cooperative and ended up realizing that they could use the process as a means of relaying their security concerns. Jane realized that it was probably a good idea to open up her meetings or initial communications with a comment indicating that "this assessment is not an audit but instead an exercise intended to identify security risks that could impact the operations of your system." After adopting this approach she noticed a change in the demeanor of the business owners who started realizing this was a vehicle for getting their concerns heard, rather than a witch-hunt to find people not doing their jobs.

Aside from this issue, Jane also noticed that some of the system owners had a difficult time with the control survey since they were not familiar with many of the items covered in the survey. Whenever this happened Jane asked them whether there is a technical contact that she could forward the survey to. For those surveys that were forwarded to technical contacts, Jane did the same thing as before, she kept in touch and answered any questions that they may had.

Finally, after another week, Jane received the completed questionnaires. Since she had stayed closely involved with the system owners and technical contacts throughout the survey process, answering questions and providing guidance, she felt that the answers were fairly accurate. She did go to her project sponsor to obtain some input and verify some of the items but all in all, she felt comfortable with the results.

With the results in hand, Jane began consolidating all the information. Since she used SharePoint for the surveys, it was pretty simple to extract all the survey results into a single file. She considered wether to use a database (Microsoft Access) or a spreadsheet (Microsoft Excel) and ultimately, she decided to go with what she was most familiar with, which in this particular case was the spreadsheet. She made this decision because she felt it was the most portable and could easily be understood by more people. As she started compiling her data she realized that unlike the survey, where she received 100% participation, her document request list was mostly unfulfilled. At first this really bothered her but she realized that she should not be too surprised since the information security function is new for the hospital and not only do most people not know of her or her function within the organization there is also very little in terms of current documentation. Regardless of this small setback, she made sure everything she received was tracked in another spreadsheet and created references for each of the documents received.

Now armed with all this information, Jane is ready for the next phase of the risk assessment - data analysis!

Information Security Risk Assessment: Data Analysis

INFORMATION IN THIS CHAPTER:

- Introduction
- Compiling Observations from Organizational Risk Documents
- Preparation of Threat and Vulnerability Catalogs
- Overview of the System Risk Computation
- Designing the Impact Analysis Scheme
- Designing the Control Analysis Scheme
- Designing the Likelihood Analysis Scheme
- Putting it Together and the Final Risk Score

INTRODUCTION

In the scope of the overall information security risk assessment project, data analysis is the phase where we start trying to make sense of the collected data. In this phase our focus is on consolidating all of the information that we have gathered through the previous data collection activities. We will then display and summarize the information collected into a form that will allow us to make conclusions, based on the data.

At this point, the assessor will have likely collected quite a bit of data stored in various containers. Depending on the container selected, these could be spreadsheets, databases or even an application containing all the data from your interviews, the application survey, the control survey, and the various security documents and statistics collected. Various techniques such as formulas, decision matrices, and computations will then be applied to this data in order to give the assessor a view that will facilitate the development of findings and conclusions which are ultimately the product of the actual risk analysis. Thus, this phase can be considered as a mid-point between raw data collection and extrapolation of the actual findings and conclusions derived from the data.

The risk assessment framework that the assessor has adopted will heavily influence the techniques involved in data analysis. The various risk assessment frameworks such as OCTAVE, NIST FAIR, and ISO provide various formulas and decision matrices, some more prescriptive than others, to allow for the computation of risk. The results of these computations are the final product for the data analysis phase and will play an important part in our analysis of overall risk. In this chapter, we will be leveraging guidance from the NIST framework to compute for risk since it is one of the most flexible; however, we will provide some discussion about how other frameworks approach this step. While we will be leveraging guidance from NIST to illustrate the process our primary objective is to guide you through a method that will allow you to apply our approach to any given risk assessment framework and should not be read as a "how to" on executing a full NIST aligned assessment.

COMPILING OBSERVATIONS FROM ORGANIZATIONAL RISK DOCUMENTS

During the data collection phase, the assessor collected various security related documents from throughout the organization. At this point of the risk assessment, it is time to go over the documents and extract information relevant to the risk assessment in a form that can be useable when we start making conclusions.

The activities involved in compiling observations really just involve hard work, and there is no shortcut or trick that can be taught to make this an easier process. You simply have to take the time to read through each of the collected documents one by one and make structured notes. Focus on using common terminology to annotate your observations as you work through the documents. As you notice situations or issues that share a common root cause you could capture that cause as a common observation category and then make note of which reports have observations related to that category. It is very important that you focus on collecting information from the different documents in a standardized format so it will be easier to review your observations during the risk analysis phase. An approach that works fairly well is to use your "container" of choice, typically the same container used in the previous phase, and to collect your observations in this format:

- Observation/Findings—A one-sentence description of the finding or observation.
- Description—A more detailed narrative of the observation including the cause, management response, risk, and mitigation if available.
- Assessment Area—The security area that the finding pertains to. For example, access control, physical security, etc.
- Source of the Finding—What document was reviewed and who was the author of the particular finding or observation (e.g. internal or external audit).

After the container is ready, it is simply a matter of going through all the documents that you have collected and noting observations that may have security implications to the organization. Here is a list of some of the documents that you may encounter and a brief description of the information that you should be looking for:

1. Previous Information Security Risk Assessments:
   a. Observations that were derived from the risk assessment especially any that concern the control environment around in-scope assets.
   b. Any actions plans or recommendations that resulted from the risk assessment.

2. Previous IT Risk Assessments:
   a. Observations derived from the risk assessment particularly in the area of security, computer operations, access control, change control, and disaster recovery.
   b. Any action plans or recommendations that resulted from the risk assessment.

3. Previous Internal or External Audit Reports:
   a. Any audit findings derived from the audit particularly those related to security, computer operations, access control, change control, and disaster recovery.
   b. Include the management response related to any findings that were identified by the auditors.
   c. Pay particular attention to audit findings concerning in-scope assets.

4. Previous Legal, Regulatory, Insurance, or Framework Driven Assessments:
   a. Note any gaps or noted deficiencies as it relates to alignment with regulations or the particular framework that the assessment covered. Make sure you include management responses and as with previous documents you want to focus particularly on those issues that pertain to security, computer operations, access control, change control, and disaster recovery.

5. Previous Vulnerability Assessments:
   a. Any technical vulnerabilities identified particularly those related to in-scope assets.
   b. Since vulnerability lists can be extremely detailed, the assessor should try to aggregate the findings. For example, if there are multiple patches missing in workstations across the enterprise, the assessor can simply record the finding as "Missing patches in multiple workstations" versus noting the hundreds or even thousands of individual workstations that were missing the particular patch.

6. Previous Penetration Tests:
   a. Any attack vectors that were used to compromise systems in the enterprise particularly if the system compromised was an in-scope system or if the vector lead to enterprise wide access (e.g. able to obtain Windows Domain Administrator level privileges).

7. Current Security Policies, Standards, and Procedures:
   a. Any obvious gaps and deviations from established industry standards such as ISO or NIST. You do not have to perform a full gap assessment but you

should take note of any missing policies that you would expect to see in place if the organization was following a specific framework or standard.

8. Disaster Recovery and Business Contingency Plans:
   a. In instances where there is a lack of a Disaster Recovery Plan (DRP) and/ or Business Continuity Plan (BCP) you would document a finding. Also, if the DRP or BCP is significantly out of date (e.g. has not been refreshed in the last 3 years) you should note a potential issue with the organization's ability to recover from a disaster or continue business operations if a disaster was declared. It is important to determine whether there have been any changes to core systems or processes since the plan was last refreshed as this may determine whether you have an issue or not. If there have been no significant changes to the organization's systems or core processes than there is a possibility that their DRP or BCP did not require a refresh.
   b. Take special note if an in-scope system is not included in the DRP or the BCP.

9. Business Impact Analysis (BIA):
   a. Note if the BIA is missing or has not been conducted. Also, identify when the BIA was last performed and, as with the DRP or BCP, determine whether it should have been refreshed due to any organizational changes (e.g. major system or process modifications).
   b. Note if an in-scope system was not included in the BIA.

10. Asset Inventories:
   a. Organizations should have a process for maintaining an inventory of all IT assets. Lack of capabilities to provide a listing should be noted as an observation. The capability to produce the list, or lack of such capability, should have been apparent during the data collection activities.

11. IT and Information Security Metrics:
   a. If not available, definitely note the lack of security metrics.
   b. If available, note all the security areas where metrics are being collected and evaluate whether the metric value indicates that the control is operating effectively.

12. Facilities Security Plan:
   a. Definitely note if a facilities security plan exists or not. If it does not, identify the organizational function that is responsible for facilities management.

13. Organizational Chart and Contact List:
   a. Check if a security function exists in the organization.
   b. Identify at what level within the organization the security function or position reports to.
   c. Review the roles and responsibilities of the position and determine if they have the appropriate level of authority.

14. Any Previous Security Presentations and Debriefs:
   a. Review the presentations and debriefs and note any issues that are stated in them or any treatment plans that could indicate a potential gap in the security of the organization.

15. Security Program, Plans, and Roadmaps:
   a. Review the security program and see if it is consistent with the security framework/standard the organization is adopting. A full gap assessment is not necessary; however, you should try and perform a high level evaluation to make sure no major components are missing. You should note an observation related to any gaps or discrepancies that you identify.
16. SAS70s/SSAE16:
   a. A review of third party attestation reports could be specific to attestation reports covering operations at your organization or, more than likely, you will be reviewing attestation reports for third parties that provide significant services to your organization. Note any exceptions identified by the auditor as well as management's responses.
17. Vendor Security Accreditations:
   a. Note any issues that were identified during the course of the accreditation. Also identify any action plans pertaining to the issues identified.
18. Technology Configuration and Hardening Guidelines or Checklists:
   a. Note if configuration and hardening guidelines or checklists exists or are being used.
   b. Check if the guidelines are based on an accepted security standard.

A sample observations "container" is provided in the companion website of this book.

PREPARATION OF THREAT AND VULNERABILITY CATALOGS

One of the primary steps in performing data analysis for specific systems is to prepare threat and vulnerability catalogs. As we discussed in Chapter 1, threats and vulnerabilities are cornerstone concepts with respect to any discussion about risk.

Threat Catalog

A threat catalog is very simply a generic list of threats that are considered common information security threats. As discussed in Chapter 1, these threats are events, sources, actions, or inactions that could potentially lead to harm of your organization's information security assets. As security professionals, it is tempting to just start writing down threats facing our organization based on our own knowledge. Before jumping right in and doing that, you should consider referencing some of the standard threat catalogs that are available. As much as you may feel that you know, referencing a standard threat catalogs ensures that you are leveraging information from a broadly accepted standard and that you do not miss any relevant threats for the organization.

The following is a list of threat catalogs that can be used as references:

- BITS Calculator—A very comprehensive list of over 600 threats. This is freely available from the BITS website.
- Microsoft Threat Model—A list of 36 threats focusing on application security risks. This is freely available from the Microsoft website.

- NIST SP800-30—A high level list of 5 human threat sources with 32 corresponding threat actions. This is freely available from the NIST website.
- ISO 27005—A high level list of 8 threat types with 43 corresponding threats in Annex C of the document. This document is available for a fee.
- BSI Base IT Security Manual—A list of 370 threats. This is freely available from the BSI website.

Links to the various threat catalogs are provided in the companion website of this book.

The following is an example of a completed threat listing based on a combination of the ISO 27005 and NIST SP-800 threat catalogs. It is important to note here that the threat itself is composed of two elements, the agent, which is the source of the threat and the action, which is the actual activity performed by the agent (see Table 4.1).

One of the common questions encountered during this phase is: How granular will the list of threats be? For example, BITS has a list of 600 threats while NIST only has 32 so there appears to be a large discrepancy between different standards. Which one should you use? This decision will depend on the applicability of the threat to the organization or the system. For example, if a threat catalog includes threats that are related to outsourced application development and your organization does not use any outsourced developers, then it does not make sense to include those threats in the list of threats. In some cases, some assessors include non-applicable or hypothetical threats as a means to plan and prepare for future threat scenarios. This is often a good approach as it helps to ensure that changes in the organization's strategy or direction (e.g. use of new technology or strategic use of third party vendors) that affect the organization's threat landscape are taken into consideration. This brings us to another decision, how long should the threat catalog be? Really, the length of the threat catalog may ultimately depend on certain project limitations that you encounter in the course of the risk assessment project. It is important to take into consideration the length of time that you have to provide the deliverable as well as the resources that you have to assist with the analysis. As an example, let us take a look at the BITS threat catalog. Do you think you can realistically finish an evaluation of 600 different threat in the time allotted to the project? Ultimately, the decision on what threats to include will be heavily reliant on the judgment of the assessor; however, using standard threat catalogs as references improves the completeness of the threat listing that will be used in the assessment.

Vulnerability Catalog

The vulnerability catalog is simply a list of vulnerabilities that affect or could affect an organization. There are two ways to go about building the catalog:

1. Current vulnerabilities—The current vulnerabilities catalog should be a list of vulnerabilities currently affecting the organization. If you followed the steps in this book, you should already have documented a fairly comprehensive list. Remember, one of the first activities discussed in this chapter was consolidating observations and findings from the various documents that were previously collected. This listing can easily serve as your listing of current vulnerabilities.

Table 4.1 Sample Threat Catalog

Threat Agent	Threat Action
Criminal, Pilferer	Retrieval of data from discarded or recycled equipment
Criminal, Pilferer	Theft of sensitive system data on media through unauthorized access
Criminal, Pilferer	Theft of equipment and sensitive media through unauthorized physical access
External Intruders, Malicious Insiders, Malicious Code	Social engineering of system user
External Intruders, Malicious Insiders, Malicious Code	System intrusion and unauthorized system access
Malicious Code	System intrusion and unauthorized system access
Malicious code, Users	Intentional or accidental denial of service event
Malicious Insider, Users	System sabotage or Software failure or malfunction
Malicious Insider, Users	Unauthorized users performing unauthorized operations
Malicious Insider, Users	Unchecked data viewing or alteration
Natural	Equipment damage or destruction due to natural causes (fire, water, etc.)
Non-Specific	Unrecoverable data due to natural or human error
Non-Specific	Unrecoverable system functionality due to natural or human error
Non-Specific, Natural	Failure of network infrastructure
Non-Specific, Natural	Loss of power
Non-Specific, Users	Equipment failure or malfunction
Users	Abuse of user rights and permissions
Users	Denial of user actions or activity
Users	Eavesdropping and Interception of data
Users	Intentional or accidental transmission of regulated data
Users	Intentional or unintentional violations of the system security policy
Users	Unreported security events regarding system use

2. Hypothetical vulnerabilities—The hypothetical vulnerabilities catalog is a list of vulnerabilities that are unverified but could affect the organization. These vulnerabilities can be determined based on the concerns brought up in various meetings and executive interviews and scenarios derived from the threat listings. You may be asking yourself, why put a hypothetical vulnerability in the catalog? Remember, a risk assessment is not an audit and just because you did not find evidence of the existence of a vulnerability, it does not mean that it does not exist. This is consistent with the concept of risk assessments being focused on probabilities.

The following table is an example of a completed vulnerability catalog based on our hypothetical scenario:

Vulnerability Catalog
Critical System Vulnerabilities in Host Systems due to insufficient patch management
Excessive Privileges due to lack of a user access review
Insufficient authentication mechanism and controls
Insufficient backups
Insufficient change control process leading to unauthorized changes
Insufficient contingency planning
Insufficient enforcement of secure deletion and disposal process
Insufficient incident response plan
Insufficient media encryption
Insufficient physical controls protecting equipment
Insufficient security awareness implementation and enforcement
Lack of Anti-virus and Malware Prevention
Lack of environmental controls
Lack of logging and monitoring controls
Lack of Mechanism to Prevent Data Loss
Lack of network security controls
Lack of redundancy and failover mechanisms for the system
Lack of redundant network infrastructure
Lack of redundant or failover equipment
Lack of redundant power supply
Lack of transmission encryption leading to interception of unencrypted data
Lack of user monitoring and periodic access review
Possible Security Misconfigurations in System due to lack of security and hardening reviews
Possible Weak Passwords due to lack of password complexity controls
Unauthorized user accounts and access to the system due to lack of a formal user provisioning process
Undetected Critical Vulnerabilities in Host Systems due to insufficient vulnerability monitoring and management process
Untraceable user actions due to generic accounts

Though vulnerability catalogs can often be created based on the assessors experience or review of various documents or organizational assessments, a sample vulnerability listing may be useful in creating a more comprehensive list. An excellent sample listing that an assessor may want to utilize can be found in Appendix D of ISO27005.

Threat Vulnerability Pairs

A threat-vulnerability pair is a matrix that matches all the threats in our listing with the current or hypothetical vulnerabilities that could be exploited by the threats.

Table 4.2 Sample Threat and Vulnerability Pairs

Threat (Agent and Action)		Vulnerability
Users	Eavesdropping and Interception of data	Lack of transmission encryption leading to interception of unencrypted data
External Intruders, Malicious Insiders, Malicious Code	System intrusion and unauthorized system access	Possible Weak Passwords due to lack of password complexity controls
Users	Denial of user actions or activity	Untraceable user actions due to generic accounts
Malicious Insider, Users	Unchecked data alteration	Lack of logging and monitoring controls
Non-Specific, Natural	Loss of power	Lack of redundant power supply
Natural	Equipment damage or destruction due to natural causes (fire, water, etc.)	Lack of environmental controls

This is the final product leveraging both the threat listing and vulnerability listing that we have been preparing. Once the threat and vulnerability listings are complete, it is a fairly straightforward exercise to create the Threat and Vulnerability pairs:

1. Assuming that you are using a spreadsheet or a table format, list all the threats in one column.
2. In the following column, write down all the applicable vulnerabilities for each of the threats listed in the first column.
3. Remember that each threat could potentially have multiple vulnerabilities related to it. In this case, create a duplicate threat entry in the subsequent row.

Table 4.2 is a shortened version of a threat and vulnerability pair matrix showing 6 threat and vulnerability pairs:

A sample Threat Vulnerability Pair Matrix is provided in the companion website of this book.

This threat and vulnerability pair matrix will be the cornerstone for your risk computation. Typically, the threat and vulnerability pair matrix is applicable for all assets and can be used as a generic template when computing the risk scores.

OVERVIEW OF THE SYSTEM RISK COMPUTATION

Now is a good time for us to step back a little and do a quick overview of what we learned back in Chapter 1 with regards to computing risk:

1. Identify the Assets.
2. Identify the Threats.

3. Identify the Vulnerabilities.
4. Determine the Impact.
5. Determine the Controls.
6. Determine the Likelihood.

So far, we have covered 50% of the necessary steps to compute our risk score. In the data collection phase, we have prepared the asset listing, and in this chapter, we have identified the possible threats and vulnerabilities through the threat-vulnerability pair matrix. What's left now is for us to determine the impact, controls, and likelihood.

In the following activities, our main goal is to determine the impact, controls, and likelihood for each threat and vulnerability pair for each of the assets identified. The relationship of all these elements can be summed up in the following statement:

The risk value of an asset is directly proportional to the impact and likelihood of a particular threat exploiting a vulnerability after considering the controls in place that are protecting the asset.

The most important thing to remember before continuing to the next activity in the risk analysis process is that you should have threat-vulnerability pair matrices for each of the in-scope assets. If you are using a spreadsheet as your data collection container, it would look something like the sample risk computation spreadsheet that is provided in the companion website of this book.

DESIGNING THE IMPACT ANALYSIS SCHEME

In this activity, we will begin formulating the mechanism for computation of impact. As previously mentioned, impact is one of the primary components for computing risk. An impact analysis scheme provides a means to provide a repeatable process for the calculation of impact.

Note that there are many different ways to do this and contrary to what you may read in some literature, there is no one correct way to determine impact. In this activity we will be focusing on qualitative means of determining impact but this doesn't mean that the assessor can arbitrarily assign numbers or ratings as he or she sees fits. We will be identifying specific elements from the data collected that we can use to consistently compute impact across all assets as well as corresponding threat and vulnerability pairs.

At this point we have gathered a significant amount of information from the data collection phase and it is time to make use of it. In order to compute for impact, it is important to take into consideration the data elements that would illustrate the confidentiality, integrity and availability aspects of the system being assessed.

Confidentiality

The data element that will provide a reliable, consistent and repeatable value for confidentiality would be the asset's data classification rating. This typically reflects the sensitivity of the data stored, processed, or transmitted by the asset and if it has been

Table 4.3 Sample Confidentiality Determination Matrix

Confidentiality Determination Matrix		
Score	**Description**	**Criteria**
5	VERY HIGH	Data Classification = Confidential with an additional classification of Legally Privileged or Regulated Data
4	HIGH	Data Classification = Confidential
3	MEDIUM	Data Classification = Internal
2	LOW	Data Classification = Public
1	VERY LOW	Unclassified

accurately reported to the assessor, should be a good way to determine the potential impact of a confidentiality threat.

As part of the data analysis process, we have to turn this data element into a score that we can apply consistently to all threat and vulnerability pairs across all assets. At this point we will introduce the use of a determination matrix in order to accomplish this objective. The determination matrix is simply a reference table that assists the assessor in assigning a score based on the value of the data element. In this case, the determination matrix for the confidentiality impact would look like Table 4.3.

The sample table above is just an example and other data elements can be incorporated if they are available. For example, you could collect the number of records through the asset profile survey and then consider the number of records as part of the computation for confidentiality impact. In that case, the determination matrix would probably look like Table 4.4.

Using this approach, the assessor may be able to better stratify the data especially in instances where all the systems being reviewed have the same data classification level. In many of the assessments we perform, the number of exact records is often a difficult data element to collect. In many cases the asset owners or stewards are only able to provide estimated values for the number of records so you may end up working with large buckets of numbers like 10,000+, 50,000+, or 100,000+.

Not all organizations will use the same logic in determining impact and there can be many variations of this determination matrix. Whatever you decide on remember that once you have decided it is important that you stick with that method without exception for the rest of the risk. This is to ensure consistency within your risk assessment. During the assessment, though not advisable, there will be times that you may need to adjust the matrix, just keep in mind that whenever you adjust the decision matrix, you will have to re-adjust the scores for all impact values. The idea here is not to make an absolute determination of impact but instead to formulate a repeatable and consistent way to determine impact.

Table 4.4 Sample Confidentiality Determination Matrix

Confidentiality Determination Matrix		
Score	**Description**	**Criteria**
5	VERY HIGH	• Data Classification = Confidential with an additional classification of Legally Privileged or Regulated Data AND • Number of Records = HIGH
4	HIGH	• Data Classification = Confidential with an additional classification of Legally Privileged or Regulated Data AND • Number of Records = MEDIUM OR LOW
3	MEDIUM	• Data Classification = Confidential AND • Number of Records = HIGH
2	LOW	• Data Classification = Confidential AND • Number of Records = MEDIUM OR LOW
1	VERY LOW	• Data Classification = All Non Confidential

Integrity

There are several elements that will help guide you in in scoring the integrity impact:

1. Business Critical—An example of this would be an unauthorized change or corruption of data in a hospital radiology imaging system which could have a serious impact to ongoing patient care and the integrity of the patients medical record. The business criticality ranking should be able to be obtained from asset classification documentation that you should have requested in the data classification phase. Unfortunately, less mature organizations may not have an asset classification document that provides a data element indicating whether the asset is business critical. Another document that may help to determine whether an asset is business critical is the BIA. If available, this document may provide specific rankings or even categorization as to whether a particular asset or application is critical to the organization or not.
2. Financial Materiality or Regulatory Impact—The financial materiality data element can be derived from reviewing audit reports that were collected in the previous data collection phase, especially in organizations that are covered by Sarbanes-Oxley. In financial audits, auditors will review whether an asset is "material" or whether it has a significant impact to the integrity of financial reporting.

Similar to what was performed with the confidentiality impact, the next step is to create a determination matrix that will allow the assessor to perform consistent and repeatable scoring. A sample integrity determination matrix would look like Table 4.5.

More often than not, an assessor will encounter difficulty stratifying business criticality. Unless the organizations asset classification or BIA already provides

Table 4.5 Sample Integrity Determination Matrix

Integrity Determination Matrix		
Score	**Description**	**Criteria**
5	VERY HIGH	• Business Critical = High • Financially Material = YES
4	HIGH	• Business Critical = Moderate OR Low • Financially Material = YES
3	MEDIUM	• Business Critical = Moderate • Financially Material = NO
2	LOW	• Business Critical = NO • Financially Material = NO
1	VERY LOW	• Not Applicable

specific values, sometimes it may not be possible to adequately provide a rating for integrity. If facing this situation it is up to the assessor to remain flexible and adjust based on the data that he or she currently has available. For example, if the assessor only knows whether the asset is business critical or not and financially material or not, the determination matrix could be formulated to look like Table 4.6.

Note that the determination matrices shown in this section are just samples to provide the assessor some guidance for preparation of their own determination tables; however, based on our experience the tables provided here should be sufficient for use in most organizations.

Availability

Similar to integrity, there are several elements that will assist in the determination of the availability impact and in some cases the criteria actually overlaps with the determination of the integrity impact. These are:

1. Business Critical—A threat affecting a business critical asset would have a significant availability impact and as such should be the primary contributor for the availability impact rating. As previously mentioned, this data element can be extracted from the asset classification document or the BIA when available.
2. Number of Users—Though not always the case, in general, the more users that are using the system, the more significant the effect of the loss of availability to the organization. There are of course examples where a mission critical system may only have a small number of users and an impact to availability could be devastating to the organization so the assessor needs to develop a keen understanding of the use of the system within the organization. In most cases though, a significant system will tend to have a high number of users.

Table 4.6 Sample Integrity Determination Matrix

Integrity Determination Matrix		
Score	**Description**	**Criteria**
5	VERY HIGH	• Business Critical = YES • Financially Material = YES
4	HIGH	• Not Applicable
3	MEDIUM	• Business Critical = YES • Financially Material = NO OR • Business Critical = NO • Financially Material = YES
2	LOW	• Not Applicable
1	VERY LOW	• Business Critical = NO • Financially Material = NO

A good example of this situation would be an email system, which may not be "financially material" yet the effects of an outage can be significant to the operations of most companies. The availability data element can typically be derived from the asset profile survey. Obtaining specific data for the number of users of a given system may not be as easy as it sounds; however, an estimate (e.g. 500-1000, 1000-2500, 2500-5000, 5000+) should be fairly easy to obtain.

3. Number of Transactions—A loss in availability for a system with a high transaction volume, such as online ordering systems or financial trading systems, could have a significant impact to the organization. This is a data element that may have some overlap with other elements since a system like this would most likely be rated as business critical as well. As with many of the other elements, obtaining accurate transaction counts may be difficult and the assessor may just want to obtain rough estimates of transaction volume.

In our experience, the data elements supporting availability that are probably the most difficult to gather are the number of users of the system and whether the system is business critical. Using those two factors the determination matrix for the availability impact would look like Table 4.7.

Preparing the Impact Score

Now that we have gone through the process of determining confidentiality, integrity and availability impact scores, we will now apply the impact score in the context of

Table 4.7 Sample Availability Determination Matrix

Availability Determination Matrix		
Score	**Description**	**Criteria**
5	VERY HIGH	• Business Critical = YES • Number of Users = High
4	HIGH	• Business Critical = YES • Number of Users = Medium OR Low
3	MEDIUM	• Business Critical = NO • Number of Users = High
2	LOW	• Business Critical = NO • Number of Users = Medium
1	VERY LOW	• Business Critical = NO • Number of Users = Low

the asset and the threat and vulnerability pair affecting the asset. The basic steps here are:

1. Go through each threat and vulnerability pair matrix for each asset.
2. For each threat and vulnerability pair assign a confidentiality, integrity and availability score using your determination matrices as represented in Table 4.8. Remember that in most cases, one threat would only be applicable to one impact. For instance, eavesdropping and interception is considered more of a confidentiality threat than an availability threat. In cases where the impact does not apply just place a zero in the score.
3. Obtain the highest impact score from the confidentiality, integrity and availability scores. That score will be the impact score.

In the example below, let us assume that we received the following information from our data collection activities:

• Data Classification—Confidential with Regulated Data—Reason: Our surveys indicate that it contains ePHI.
• Business Critical—Yes—Reason: Based on a review of the asset classification and BIA, it is considered by the organization to be business critical.
• Financially Material and Regulatory Impact—Yes—Reason: Since this is a hospital information system that processes ePHI, it is covered by HIPAA requirements.
• Number of Users—High—Reason: According to the system owner, the hospital information system has a high number of users as 75% of all users use the system to conduct their day to day responsibilities.
• Number of Transactions—Unknown.

Table 4.8 Sample Assignment of CIA Impact Scores

Application: Hospital Information System

Threat (Agent and Action)		Vulnerability	C	I	A	Impact Score
Users	Eavesdropping and Interception of data	Lack of transmission encryption leading to interception of unencrypted data	5	0	0	5
External Intruders, Malicious Insiders, Malicious Code	System intrusion and unauthorized system access	Possible Weak Passwords due to lack of password complexity controls	5	5	0	5
Users	Denial of user actions or activity	Untraceable user actions due to generic accounts	0	5	0	5
Malicious Insider, Users	Unchecked data alteration	Lack of logging and monitoring controls	0	5	0	5
Non-Specific, Natural	Loss of power	Lack of redundant power supply	0	0	5	5
Natural	Equipment damage or destruction due to natural causes (fire, water, etc.)	Lack of environmental controls	0	0	5	5

Stepping back we can quickly see that the system is an enterprise hospital information system that contains patient information (ePHI) which is regulated by HIPAA requirements for privacy and security. Even with us just analyzing the information gathered via data collection activities, it is easy to see that this is a major application and not surprisingly, if we use our determination matrix discussed above, our impact scores for this system will be high.

Now lets run this exercise against an asset that is not quite so extreme in its characteristics. Let's assume that we have an Access database used by one of the hospital departments for research and trending purposes. This database contains ePHI. It is an important tool but based on the data collected, is not important enough to be labeled as "business critical," although the department using the database feels that it is. Here is the hypothetical data for this asset (see Table 4.9):

- Data Classification—Confidential with Regulated Data.
- Business Critical—No.
- Financially Material—No.
- Number of Users—Low.
- Number of Transactions—Unknown.

Table 4.9 Sample Assignment of CIA Scores

| Application: Cardiology Research Database | | | | | |
Threat (Agent and Action)		Vulnerability	C	I	A	Impact Score
Users	Eavesdropping and Interception of data	Lack of transmission encryption leading to interception of unencrypted data	5	0	0	5
External Intruders, Malicious Insiders, Malicious Code	System intrusion and unauthorized system access	Possible Weak Passwords due to lack of password complexity controls	5	5	0	5
Users	Denial of user actions or activity	Untraceable user actions due to generic accounts	0	3	0	3
Malicious Insider, Users	Unchecked data alteration	Lack of logging and monitoring controls	0	3	0	3
Non-Specific, Natural	Loss of power	Lack of redundant power supply	0	0	1	1
Natural	Equipment damage or destruction due to natural causes (fire, water, etc.)	Lack of environmental controls	0	0	1	1

As you see in this example, the threats that impact confidentiality are much higher when compared to those that affect integrity and availability. This should make sense since the biggest risk to the organization as a whole that this asset poses would be the intentional or unintentional loss or exposure of the data within the database. This is a good example of an application which has a high data sensitivity rating but low criticality rating.

Practical Tips

Having determination matrices is very important in ensuring that scoring is performed consistently throughout the analysis of all the threat and vulnerability pairs across all assets. Use of these matrices is even more important if there are multiple people involved in the assessment as it provides a guideline for each practitioner to follow in assigning scores. A secondary benefit of building and utilizing these matrices is that they also give the assessor the ability to explain the scores for each and every value that are assigned in the risk assessment. One thing that the assessor needs to always keep in mind is that aside from being consistent and repeatable, the matrices have to also be accurate and easy to use. Looking up the determination matrices and using them to score each asset's threat and vulnerability pair matrices might be feasible for a few assets with only a limited number of threat and vulnerability pairs to analyze; however, performing this exercise for a large number of assets could be challenging.

The answer to this challenge is to use automation. The good thing about creating these determination matrices is it provides you with a blueprint to automate the decision making process. For example, if you are using a spreadsheet to capture this analysis, it is a simple matter to create macros that can allow you to auto-score confidentiality, integrity, and availability ratings based on the criteria outlined in the determination matrices. We will be providing a short discussion regarding automation techniques at the end of this chapter.

DESIGNING THE CONTROL ANALYSIS SCHEME

Another main element required for the computation of risk is likelihood; however, before we focus on likelihood, one value that we will need to obtain in order to properly compute likelihood is the type and maturity of the controls that are in place. The basic premise here is that having good controls will significantly decrease the likelihood that a threat would be able to leverage a weakness or vulnerability.

In our data collection phase, one of the main activities conducted was the execution of a control survey. As mentioned previously, a control survey will be different from organization to organization and is largely dependent on the organization's standards or the specific control framework that is in place. For the sake of our discussion, let's say the assessor utilized the following control categories:

- Data Protection.
- Transmission Encryption.
- AV/HIPS.
- Patch Management.
- Complex Passwords.
- Vulnerability Management.
- Security Configuration.
- Authentication Controls.
- IDS/IPS Monitoring.
- User Provisioning.
- User Access Review.
- Generic Account Management.
- Security Awareness.
- Segment Isolation.
- Administrative Redundancy.
- Logging and Monitoring.
- Equipment Storage Encryption.
- Enterprise Backup.
- Backup Tape Encryption.
- Redundancy and Failover
- BCP/DR.
- Secure Deletion and Disposal.
- Change Control.

- Security Incident Response.
- Physical and Environmental Controls.
- Network Infrastructure Redundancy.
- Power Supply.
- Data Center Controls.

Based on data collection activities conducted earlier, each of these control areas should have been given a score either through the survey or through discussions with the system stewards, technical contacts, or the security officer. As previously discussed, this score could be a simple "Yes/No" or a scale rating similar to the 1–5 point scale presented in the previous chapter and illustrated in the table below. For now, let's skip any detailed discussion about the column labeled "reverse" in the table below, since it will receive more detailed treatment later in this chapter. The main concept to focus on at this point is that the stronger the control the lower the probability that a threat would be able to leverage a vulnerability (see Table 4.10).

Assuming that we have rated all of the control areas, it is now a simple matter of matching the appropriate controls with the threat and vulnerability pairs. This activity does require the practitioner to have a greater degree of security experience.

Table 4.10 Control Level Table

Control Level			
Score	**Reverse**	**Description**	**Criteria**
5	.2	VERY STRONG	Control provides very strong protection against the threat. Threat being successful in leveraging the vulnerability is highly unlikely. Effectiveness of the control is being reviewed constantly. Process is defined and documented. Controls are consistently enforced. Performance is monitored.
4	.4	STRONG	Control provides strong protection against the threat leveraging the vulnerability. Performance of the control is enforced. Process is defined and documented. Controls are consistently enforced.
3	.6	MODERATE	Control provides protection against the threat leveraging the vulnerability but may have exceptions. Control is enforced but not consistently or incorrectly.
2	.8	WEAK	Controls provide some protection against threat leveraging the vulnerability but mostly ineffective. Formal process may exist but control may not be enforced.
1	1	VERY WEAK	No control or control provides protection against the threat leveraging the vulnerability. Formal process and enforcement of controls are ad hoc or non-existent.

The reason for this becomes clear as we walk through an example in the table below. First, let's take a subset of the threat and vulnerability pairs for our Hospital Information System. For each of the threat and vulnerability pairs, the assessor has to match the control or controls that are relevant to the threat and vulnerability pair. See Table 4.11 for an example.

After matching each of the controls to their corresponding threat and vulnerability pair, the next step is to put in the control score obtained in the control survey for the corresponding controls. There are several important aspects that the assessor should consider when performing this activity. These are:

1. In most cases, there is one primary control that by itself can be used to address the threat and vulnerability pair. This control is considered the primary control because it typically summarizes an entire control category and is quicker to score than scoring each individual control within the category. For example, instead of providing control scores for each area of Environmental Controls (e.g. raised floors, flood sensors, fire suppression, humidity controls) you would just score the Environmental Controls category.

Table 4.11 Sample Control Analysis

Application: Hospital Information System

Threat (Agent and Action)		Vulnerability	Controls	Controls Score
Users	Eavesdropping and Interception of data	Lack of transmission encryption leading to interception of unencrypted data	Transmission Encryption	
External Intruders, Malicious Insiders, Malicious Code	System intrusion and unauthorized system access	Possible Weak Passwords due to lack of password complexity controls	Complex Passwords	
Users	Denial of user actions or activity	Untraceable user actions due to generic accounts	Generic Account Use Policies	
Malicious Insider, Users	Unchecked data alteration	Lack of logging and monitoring controls	Logging and Monitoring Controls	
Non-Specific, Natural	Loss of power	Lack of redundant power supply	Alternate Power Supply and Generators	
Natural	Equipment damage or destruction due to natural causes (fire, water, etc.)	Lack of environmental controls	Physical and Environmental Controls	

2. In certain cases, particularly if a more detailed and concise control survey was performed, several supporting or alternative controls may have also been identified. In the example table above, the supporting control survey was rather high level so a single control could consist of multiple individual controls. For example, "physical and environmental controls" can consist of separate individual controls in a more detailed control survey.

3. If a weak primary control is supported by several secondary controls, there could be instances that a combination of those controls could increase the effectiveness of the overall control landscape. In these cases, the assessor can take into consideration these other controls to increase the control score, based on their judgment.

Let us continue our example and assume that we have used a high-level control survey in our data collection activities to fill in the control score using the values discussed earlier (see Table 4.12).

Table 4.12 Sample Control Analysis

Application: Hospital Information System

Threat (Agent and Action)		Vulnerability	Controls	Controls Score
Users	Eavesdropping and Interception of data	Lack of transmission encryption leading to interception of unencrypted data	Transmission Encryption	4
External Intruders, Malicious Insiders, Malicious Code	System intrusion and unauthorized system access	Possible Weak Passwords due to lack of password complexity controls	Complex Passwords	4
Users	Denial of user actions or activity	Untraceable user actions due to generic accounts	Generic Account Use Policies	3
Malicious Insider, Users	Unchecked data alteration	Lack of logging and monitoring controls	Logging and Monitoring Controls	3
Non-Specific, Natural	Loss of power	Lack of redundant power supply	Alternate Power Supply	4
Natural	Equipment damage or destruction due to natural causes (fire, water, etc.)	Lack of environmental controls	Physical and Environmental Controls	4

Obviously, the completed table above is just an example and only represents a small subset of the threat and vulnerability analysis that needs to occur. The accuracy, and ultimately the value, of this activity is highly dependent on the accuracy of the control survey completed in the data collection phase. A well-planned control survey is essential in order to obtain good results as an outcome of this activity. The main challenges that an assessor will encounter in performing this activity are matching the appropriate controls with the commensurate threat and vulnerability pair. Finally, one thing that we would like to bring up again is the important decision as to whether to list out and rate the strength of a control objective (e.g. Environmental Controls are in place and operating effectively) or each of the individual controls that support the control objective (e.g. fire suppression, humidity controls, raised floors).

Practical Tips

The hardest part in completing this activity is to identify which controls affect which vulnerability pairs. As we said, in most cases, there is a primary control (often referred to as a control category) that will be relevant for a vulnerability pair. Once it is identified, it is a simple matter of referencing the control score and putting it into the risk computation. One way of doing this is by creating lookup tables that match vulnerability pairs with the appropriate controls. These lookup tables can be used to automate the assignment of control scores for each of the applications vulnerability pairs. Though there may be cases where manual tweaking is necessary, automating most of the control assignments goes a long way toward efficiently conducting the risk assessment. At the end of the chapter, we will be discussing some automation techniques and have provided some sample spreadsheets and macros on the companion website to this book that can be used to assist with automation of the process.

DESIGNING THE LIKELIHOOD ANALYSIS SCHEME

After preparing the control scores for each of the threat and vulnerability pairs for each of the applications that are in scope for your review, the assessor can now proceed to designing and computing the likelihood scheme.

In this activity, we will begin forming the mechanism that will allow for the computation of likelihood. Likelihood, along with Impact, is one of the primary components for computing risk. A likelihood analysis scheme provides a means to provide a repeatable process for measuring likelihood.

Likelihood in the context of an information security risk assessment is the probability that a threat may be able to exploit a weakness or vulnerability and in so doing, affect the confidentiality, integrity, or availability of the asset. In computing for likelihood, we consider two important elements that affect this probability: Exposure and Frequency.

Exposure

Exposure is the predisposition of the system to the threat based on environmental factors. Certain environments increase the likelihood of a threat. For example, if an asset is exposed to the Internet, then the probability of system intrusions due to external intruders increases. There are many possible factors that could affect the value for exposure. Some of the factors an assessor might want to consider are:

- Accessibility of the Asset—Whether the asset is accessible via the Internet, remotely via VPN, or only accessible through the internal network. An asset that is Internet accessible obviously has a higher exposure to certain forms of external threats.
- Location—Whether the asset is housed in a data center or not. In terms of most physical and environmental threats, the location of your core systems plays a large part in the likelihood determination.
- Data Flow—Whether information is transferred outside or internally within the organization (e.g. web, FTP, removable media). Related to this category is an evaluation of the amount of sensitive data that is transferred. Data flows and transfers of information plays a large part in threats that deal with confidentiality. For example, a system that transfers a large number of sensitive data over the Internet, obviously has a higher exposure in terms of confidentiality threats than a system that transmits data via internal connections only.
- Number of Users—Typically, the greater the number of users, the higher probability of threats to the application, particularly availability and integrity threats. Another related factor could be the amount of activity since the higher the activity levels on the system, the greater the exposure to potential integrity and availability threats.
- User Profile—In some cases, the type of users of a system could increase the probability of certain types of threats, particularly threats affecting integrity and confidentiality. For example, contractors and vendors are considered less "trusted" when compared to the employees of an organization so a system with a large population of external users has a different exposure profile than a system that is only accessed by internal users.
- Previous Incidents—Though not always the case, the presence of previous security incidents or security events related to a particular threat may be an indication of a systemic problem thus increasing the probability of a similar event happening again.
- Documented Issues or Findings—A documented and confirmed weakness increases the exposure for the area affected by the issue or finding and the likelihood that a threat may be able to successfully leverage weaknesses related to the issue or finding.

The exposure factors are in no way limited to the above list; however, using this list can serve as good starting point or foundation in determining exposure for a particular threat and vulnerability pair. Similar to our Impact analysis, it is important to prepare determination matrices to make the process consistent and repeatable for all assets that are being reviewed. An example exposure determination matrix is captured in Table 4.13 for the threat of "system intrusion."

The rationale for this matrix is a system is more "exposed" to the threat of system intrusion if a system has documented weaknesses or a related security incident for the system has been documented. The possibility of system intrusion also increases if the system is accessible directly via the public Internet and conversely the exposure lessens as the open accessibility of the system lessens. The structure and format of this particular exposure determination matrix can also be applied to other threats.

An example of another determination matrix for the threat of "Equipment Damage" may look something like Table 4.14.

In this example, our rationale is centered on the premise that the threat of equipment damage increases as the system is placed in a more public environment. This rationale applies to many other physical threats and, as an example, would probably be an appropriate exposure determination matrix for the threat of theft as well.

Table 4.13 Sample Exposure Determination Matrix

Exposure Determination Matrix for System Intrusion		
Score	Description	Criteria
5	VERY LIKELY	Previous related security incidents were noted or weaknesses for the system have been noted.
4	LIKELY	System is Internet accessible.
3	MODERATE	System is remotely accessible (e.g. Site-to-Site or Client-to-Site VPN)
2	UNLIKELY	System is accessible only through the internal network
1	VERY UNLIKELY	Anything that does not fall into the LOW criteria.

Table 4.14 Sample Exposure Determination

Exposure Determination Matrix for Equipment Damage		
Score	Description	Criteria
5	VERY LIKELY	Previous Incidents were noted or weaknesses for the system have been noted.
4	LIKELY	System is located in a common user area.
3	MODERATE	System is located in a specific department but is isolated from general public access.
2	UNLIKELY	System is located in a data center.
1	VERY UNLIKELY	Anything that does not fall into the LOW criteria.

For the purposes of providing some more detailed examples, let's say that the Hospital Information System that we are assessing has the following characteristics which were captured via our interviews and surveys:

- Remotely accessible via VPN;
- Located in a secure data center;
- Documented instances of blackouts due to problems with the electrical grid in the area;
- Large number of sensitive data elements are transferred within the organization via the system; and
- There are a high number of users and a high volume of transactional activity. Also, it was noted that one of the departments with very high levels of user activity frequently utilizes a shared account to logon to the system.
- Has a diverse user base (employees, vendors, and contractors).

While reviewing Table 4.15 you will have noticed that we've provided scores in the Exposure column. Let's walk through the exposure determination matrices that

Table 4.15 Computing for Exposure

Application: Hospital Information System					
Threat (Agent and Action)	**Vulnerability**	**Exposure**	**Frequency**	**Control**	**Likelihood**
Users	Eavesdropping and Interception of data	Lack of transmission encryption leading to interception of unencrypted data	3			
External Intruders, Malicious Insiders, Malicious Code	System intrusion and unauthorized system access	Possible Weak Passwords due to lack of password complexity controls	3			
Users	Denial of user actions or activity	Untraceable user actions due to generic accounts	5			
Malicious Insider, Users	Unchecked data alteration	Lack of logging and monitoring controls	5			
Non-Specific, Natural	Loss of power	Lack of redundant power supply	5			
Natural	Equipment damage or destruction due to natural causes (fire, water, etc.)	Lack of environmental controls	2			

were used to identify the exposure scores in the table. The determination matrices in Tables 4.16–4.21 are provided as samples for purposes of discussion, in all likelihood each organization, or even each assessor would utilize different factors when determining the exposure of a system to a threat. The main goal of the practitioner at this point is not to provide an absolute decision tree for each type of threat but to ensure that the determination of the exposure to a threat is consistent throughout all systems so as to make the process repeatable and defensible.

Once determination matrices have been completed for each threat, producing exposure scores should be fairly straightforward. Preparing determination matrices for each individual threat can appear to be a daunting task; however, keep in mind that the work you put forward now will pay off in the long run. These matrices will help facilitate risk assessments in multiple systems as well as future risk assessments. Once built these matrices can be used to build automation via an application or even simple macros within a spreadsheet. Sample macros are provided within the

Table 4.16 Sample Exposure Determination

Exposure Determination Matrix for Eavesdropping and Interception of data		
Score	Description	Criteria
5	VERY LIKELY	Previous incidents or attempted eavesdropping attacks and weaknesses have been documented
4	LIKELY	System transfers sensitive data over the Internet (any number or records)
3	MODERATE	System transfers a large number of sensitive data within the internal network
2	UNLIKELY	System transfers a low number of sensitive data within the internal network
1	VERY UNLIKELY	No data is transferred

Table 4.17 Sample Exposure Determination

Exposure Determination Matrix for System Intrusion and Unauthorized System Access		
Score	Description	Criteria
5	VERY LIKELY	Previous compromises or attempts have been detected
4	LIKELY	System is Internet accessible
3	MODERATE	System is remotely accessible (e.g. via VPN)
2	UNLIKELY	System is accessible only through the internal network
1	VERY UNLIKELY	Anything that does not fall into the UNLIKELY criteria (e.g. a standalone system without network access)

Table 4.18 Sample Exposure Determination

Exposure Determination Matrix for Denial of User Actions or Activity

Score	Description	Criteria
5	VERY LIKELY	System has a high number of users, high activity, and the user population includes users other than employees
4	LIKELY	System has a high number of users, high activity; however, only employees use the system
3	MODERATE	System has a moderate number of users, activity, and only employees use the system
2	UNLIKELY	System has a low number of users, activity, and only employees use the system
1	VERY UNLIKELY	Anything that does not fall into the UNLIKELY criteria (e.g. a non-interactive system)

Table 4.19 Sample Exposure Determination

Exposure Determination Matrix for Unchecked Data Alteration

Score	Description	Criteria
5	VERY LIKELY	System has a high number of users, high activity, and the user population includes users other than employees.
4	LIKELY	System has a high number of users, high activity; however, only employees use the system
3	MODERATE	System has a moderate number of users, activity, and only employees use the system
2	UNLIKELY	System has a low number of users, activity, and only employees use the system
1	VERY UNLIKELY	Anything that does not fall into the UNLIKELY criteria (e.g. a non-interactive system).

Table 4.20 Sample Exposure Determination

Exposure Determination Matrix for Loss of power

Score	Description	Criteria
5	VERY LIKELY	Previous power loss events were noted.
4	LIKELY	Located in a common user area outside a data center
3	MODERATE	Located in a data center
2	UNLIKELY	Located in redundant data centers
1	VERY UNLIKELY	Anything that does not fall into the UNLIKELY criteria (e.g. in an external data center that has a documented service level agreement).

Table 4.21 Sample Exposure Determination

Score	Description	Criteria
Exposure Determination Matrix for Equipment Damage		
5	VERY LIKELY	Previous Incidents were noted or weaknesses for the system have been noted
4	LIKELY	System is located in a common user area
3	MODERATE	System is located in a department specific location; however, is isolated
2	UNLIKELY	System is located in a data center
1	VERY UNLIKELY	Anything that does not fall into the LOW criteria.

templates provided on the companion website to this book. Please refer to the appendices for more details (see Table 4.20).

Frequency

Frequency is the value that we assign to measure how often an event could happen. For each threat to the system, we determine the frequency value. Determination of frequency is never exact though there are sources of information that can help the assessor in determining a value. These sources of information could include but are not limited to:

- Security metrics—Metrics such as the number of detected internal network attacks, anti-virus statistics, patch availability, and number of security incidents help provide estimates on how often a threat is detected or is experienced by the organization. By using these metrics, the assessor can provide a rough estimate of the frequency of a particular threat in the context of the organization.
- Current research and trends—Other valuable sources of information are published research and trends for specific threats. In today's busy security landscape there is no lack of research for various threats. Most security companies and organizations such as the various Computer Emergency Response Teams (CERTs), anti-virus companies, and vulnerability research companies all provide some form of statistics on different areas of security. Although, we believe that the best source to use when doing your analysis are internal statistics since they are specific to your organization. The use of emerging research from external parties does provide the assessor a baseline for what is happening within the industry, or other industries, when determining frequency.

To produce consistent and reproducible frequency scores for each of the threats, it is important to use a frequency matrix like the following (see Table 4.22):

Table 4.22 Frequency Matrix

Frequency Matrix		
Score	**Description**	**Criteria**
5	VERY LIKELY	Could happen on a daily basis
4	LIKELY	Could happen on a weekly basis
3	MODERATE	Could happen on a monthly basis
2	UNLIKELY	Could happen within 1 year
1	VERY UNLIKELY	Could happen within 5 years

Table 4.23 Adding Frequency Scores

Application: Hospital Information System						
Threat (Agent and Action)	**Vulnerability**		**Exposure**	**Frequency**	**Control**	**Likelihood**
Users	Eavesdropping and Interception of data	Lack of transmission encryption leading to interception of unencrypted data	3	3		
External Intruders, Malicious Insiders, Malicious Code	System intrusion and unauthorized system access	Possible Weak Passwords due to lack of password complexity controls	3	5		
Users	Denial of user actions or activity	Untraceable user actions due to generic accounts	5	1		
Malicious Insider, Users	Unchecked data alteration	Lack of logging and monitoring controls	5	2		
Non-Specific, Natural	Loss of power	Lack of redundant power supply	5	2		
Natural	Equipment damage or destruction due to natural causes (fire, water, etc.)	Lack of environmental controls	2	1		

This allows the assessor to produce reproducible scores throughout all threats and systems assessed. Let's use this matrix to provide frequency scores for each of the sample threat and vulnerability pairs in the example we were working on previously (see Table 4.23).

Determining the frequency of a threat is understandably one of the more difficult and subjective aspects of determining likelihood so it is important that the assessor is able to document their rationale to support the assigned score. For example, for system intrusions due to weak passwords, the assessor could reference network attack alerts from the organization's security metrics. If the assessor sees multiple attempts, each day, this could be their rationale for giving a "Very Likely" frequency score. This rationalization approach would apply to all other threat and vulnerability pairs.

Controls

Earlier in the chapter we walked through the process for determining the control score. The reason this calculation is done early in the process is due to the fact that the existence and maturity of controls plays an important part in the computation of likelihood. Basically, there is an inverse relationship between the two. The better the control, the less likely a threat would be able to successfully leverage a given vulnerability. We discussed the control computation in the previous section so now it is just a matter of putting the control score into our table (see Table 4.24):

Table 4.24 Adding Control Scores

Application: Hospital Information System					
Threat (Agent and Action)	**Vulnerability**	**Exposure**	**Frequency**	**Control**	**Likelihood**
Users	Eavesdropping and Interception of data	Lack of transmission encryption leading to interception of unencrypted data	3	3	4	
External Intruders, Malicious Insiders, Malicious Code	System intrusion and unauthorized system access	Possible Weak Passwords due to lack of password complexity controls	3	5	4	
Users	Denial of user actions or activity	Untraceable user actions due to generic accounts	5	1	3	
Malicious Insider, Users	Unchecked data alteration	Lack of logging and monitoring controls	5	2	3	
Non-Specific, Natural	Loss of power	Lack of redundant power supply	5	2	4	
Natural	Equipment damage or destruction due to natural causes (fire, water, etc.)	Lack of environmental controls	2	1	4	

Likelihood

Now, we have scores for all the components needed to compute for likelihood: Exposure, Frequency, and Controls. As with much that we do during this assessment we need to make sure that our decisions and calculations are supported by a process or rationale that can be defended. For computation of likelihood we use the following logic:

- Exposure is proportional to Likelihood. An increase in exposure increases the likelihood that a threat could successfully exploit a given vulnerability. An easily understood example of this rationale comes into play when discussing systems that are accessible via the Internet. If a system is Internet accessible, there is a higher exposure to system intrusion (e.g. hacker attacks) when compared to a standalone system that is not accessible via the Internet.
- Frequency is proportional to Likelihood. An increase in frequency of activities by a threat agent would increase the expected frequency of the risk being realized and thus the likelihood that a threat could exploit a given vulnerability. For example, malicious code (e.g. worms, viruses) are much more common than earthquakes, at least in most areas of the world. Thus threats that could be caused by malicious code are much more likely to occur than threats stemming from earthquakes.
- Strength of Control is inversely proportional to Likelihood. A stronger control decreases the likelihood that a threat would be able to exploit a given vulnerability. For example, if the organization has complex passwords, an intrusion by a hacker using password brute-forcing attacks is less likely to succeed.

Let's spend a little more time discussing exposure and frequency. As seen in previous discussions, the more exposed the system is and the more frequent a threat is, the greater the likelihood that a threat would be able to successfully exploit a vulnerability. Going back to the earlier example of malicious code; if you conducted research on current trends and if you just look at your anti-virus/anti-malware logs, you will see that automated attacks occur almost constantly. We'd be surprised if you don't see an attack every hour on your external perimeter. Therefore, if the system being reviewed is placed within your organizations external perimeter, it is an asset that is frequently under attack and you would assign it a frequency value of VERY LIKELY for threats associated with worms or other automated attacks. As discussed, exposure and frequency are directly proportional to likelihood and could be computationally reflected. This is where the assessment, which has been purely qualitative up to this point, starts to move into using quantitative assessment methods. The following equation allows us to express likelihood as a calculation:

- **Likelihood = (Exposure + Frequency)/2**

Using this equation we are averaging out exposure and frequency. For example, if your organization has been experiencing electrical outages or blackouts which have directly affected the system that is being reviewed, then we can say that the system has a high exposure to the threat. Based on information gathered we know that the frequency of these blackouts is not frequent, maybe at the most once a year, so the frequency value is not likely. So in this formula, increasing either the frequency or the exposure will also increase the likelihood, which is in line with the basic idea so far.

Now let's take into consideration the controls. Assessing for control score is a bit different because the stronger the control, the less likely that the threat will be successful. This is a classic inverse relationship meaning as one value goes up the other must come down and vice versa. This is why in the Control Level matrix created in the previous chapter we actually had a "Reverse" column that reflects the reverse of the control strength (e.g. 1/5 is .2, 2/5 is .4 and so on) (see Table 4.25).

Now, let's incorporate the controls into our likelihood formula based on the rationale that controls would affect likelihood in an inversely proportional way:

- **Likelihood = ((Exposure + Frequency)/2) x (Reverse Control)**

Let's cover some examples to make the logic of this formula clearer:

Table 4.25 Sample Control Levels

Control Level			
Score	**Reverse**	**Description**	**Criteria**
5	.2	VERY STRONG	Control provides very strong protection against the threat. Threat being successful is highly unlikely. Effectiveness of the control is being reviewed constantly. Process is defined and documented. Controls are consistently enforced. Performance is monitored.
4	.4	STRONG	Control provides strong protection against the threat. Performance of the control is enforced. Process is defined and documented. Controls are consistently enforced.
3	.6	MODERATE	Control provides protection against the threat but may have exceptions. Control is enforced but not consistently or incorrectly.
2	.8	WEAK	Controls provide some protection against threat but mostly ineffective. Formal process may exist but control may not be enforced.
1	1	VERY WEAK	No control or control provides very limited protection against the threat. Formal process and enforcement of controls are ad hoc or non-existent.

- System being reviewed has high exposure score, high frequency score and very weak controls score:
  - Computation:
    - Exposure: 5.
    - Frequency: 5.
    - Controls: 1.
    - Control Inverse: 1.
    - Likelihood (without controls) = (5 + 5) /2 = 5.
    - Likelihood (with controls) = 5 * 1 = 5.

  - Rationale: As you see in this case, a system that has ad hoc or no controls in place would have the same likelihood score as if the control score was not even considered. Basically there would be no change in likelihood because the control is insignificant and does not affect the exposure or frequency. For example, a system that is exposed to the Internet (Exposure: 5) and is constantly being attacked (e.g. brute force or password guessing) (Frequency: 5) with weak authentication controls such as default passwords (Controls Inverse 1) will have a very high likelihood (Likelihood: 5) of a threat successful exploiting the system.
- System being reviewed has a high exposure score, high frequency score and very weak controls score.
  - Computation:
    - Exposure: 5.
    - Frequency: 5.
    - Controls: 5.
    - Control Inverse: .2.
    - Likelihood (without controls) = (5 + 5) /2 = 5.
    - Likelihood (with controls) = 5 * .2 = 1.
  - Rationale: In this case, we have a high exposure score (Exposure: 5), high frequency score (Frequency: 5) but very strong controls score (Controls Inverse: .2) so we ended up with a 1, which is considered highly unlikely (Likelihood: 1). Let's dig into this a little deeper. If a system is exposed to the Internet and is constantly undergoing password attacks yet there are strong authentication controls in place such as the use of complex passwords and two factor authentication, then the likelihood of a compromise via a password brute force vector would be low.

Using this formula, you can now complete the likelihood column in our table (see Table 4.26).

After the computation, you'll notice that we have results with decimals in them which is fine but in order to make it more understandable, it is often a good idea to round up the numbers. Rounding up ensures that you do not have zero values in your likelihood score. Table 4.27 reflects the rounded up likelihood scores.

Let's look at the resulting likelihood values. A good way to see whether the results are logical is to go over one of the example threat and vulnerability pairs (see Table 4.28).

Table 4.26 Sample Computation of Likelihood

Application: Hospital Information System

Threat (Agent and Action)	Vulnerability		Exposure	Frequency	Control	Likelihood
Users	Eavesdropping and Interception of data	Lack of transmission encryption leading to interception of unencrypted data	3	3	4 (.4)	1.2
External Intruders, Malicious Insiders, Malicious Code	System intrusion and unauthorized system access	Possible Weak Passwords due to lack of password complexity controls	3	5	4 (.4)	1.6
Users	Denial of user actions or activity	Untraceable user actions due to generic accounts	5	1	3 (.6)	1.8
Malicious Insider, Users	Unchecked data alteration	Lack of logging and monitoring controls	5	2	3 (.6)	2.1
Non-Specific, Natural	Loss of power	Lack of redundant power supply	5	2	4 (.4)	1.4
Natural	Equipment damage or destruction due to natural causes (fire, water, etc.)	Lack of environmental controls	2	1	4 (.4)	.6

As you can see here, the likelihood that a system intrusion event would occur due to weak password controls is unlikely. Let's walk through the different factors involved in this specific score:

- Exposure is moderate: This is because the system is remotely accessible via VPN. But it is not publicly accessible (e.g. Internet) so the exposure is not as high.
- Frequency is high: Password and other authentication based attacks are very common. There is very minimal skill required to execute the attack so it is one of the most common types of attacks and thus would be assigned a high frequency value.
- Controls are strong: This is based off the data collected from the interviews and surveys. For purposes of this example we'll say that based on the data collected, the system actually enforces strong passwords and uses 2 factor authentication.

Based on our computation, it is unlikely that a threat may be able to successfully leverage the vulnerability. And if you step back and look at it from a common sense

Table 4.27 Sample Computation of Final Likelihood Score

Application: Hospital Information System

Threat (Agent and Action)		Vulnerability	Exposure	Frequency	Control	Likelihood
Users	Eavesdropping and Interception of data	Lack of transmission encryption leading to interception of unencrypted data	3	3	4 (.4)	2
External Intruders, Malicious Insiders, Malicious Code	System intrusion and unauthorized system access	Possible Weak Passwords due to lack of password complexity controls	3	5	4 (.4)	2
Users	Denial of user actions or activity	Untraceable user actions due to generic accounts	5	1	3 (.6)	2
Malicious Insider, Users	Unchecked data alteration	Lack of logging and monitoring controls	5	2	3 (.6)	3
Non-Specific, Natural	Loss of power	Lack of redundant power supply	5	2	4 (.4)	2
Natural	Equipment damage or destruction due to natural causes (fire, water, etc.)	Lack of environmental controls	2	1	4 (.4)	1

Table 4.28 Sample Likelihood Scenario

External Intruders, Malicious Insiders, Malicious Code	System intrusion and unauthorized system access	Possible Weak Passwords due to lack of password complexity controls	3	5	4 (.4)	2

Table 4.29 Sample Likelihood Scenario

External Intruders, Malicious Insiders, Malicious Code	System intrusion and unauthorized system access	Possible Weak Passwords due to lack of password complexity controls	3	5	2 (.8)	4

perspective, the results of the computation work out. A system that is only accessible via VPN with strong authentication controls will be better positioned to defend against password and authentication attacks.

For discussions sake, let's change the situation up a bit. Let's say that we are lacking the controls related to two factor authentication and password complexity and have weak password and authentication controls (e.g. no 2 factor, complex passwords are not enforced) (see Table 4.29).

As you see, the change in the strength of the control changes the likelihood of the threat. This makes sense since a system that is remotely accessible and has weak authentication and password controls has a high likelihood of system intrusion via a password guessing related threat.

Now that we've computed a score for likelihood we have all the elements we need to compute the risk score which we will tackle in the next section.

PUTTING IT TOGETHER AND THE FINAL RISK SCORE

We are now at the final part of the data analysis phase. Let's go over the information we have and look at how it was obtained:

- Threat—This was obtained via the threat catalog. Threat catalogs such as those from BITS, ISO27001, and NIST SP800-30 were used to build an initial list.
- Vulnerability—This was obtained by building a given vulnerability catalog based on sources such as interviews, assessments, and audits identifying potential issues and weaknesses in various controls in the organization. The threat plus the vulnerability give us a threat and vulnerability pair which was structured into a table.
- Impact Score—This was obtained by considering the potential impact of the threat to the confidentiality, integrity, and availability of the system by assigning scores for each of them. The category with the highest impact became the impact score for the threat and vulnerability pair.
- Likelihood Score—This was obtained by assigning scores for the exposure , frequency, and control for each of the threat and vulnerability pairs.

With these, we now have the basic "ingredients" for calculating risk. If we look back to our discussion throughout the previous chapters, ultimately at its most basic form, risk is the product of the likelihood and the impact of a threat exploiting a given vulnerability for a given asset:

- RISK = IMPACT × LIKELIHOOD

The formula above reflects the concept we have discussed in the previous chapters:

- The risk to a system is directly proportional to the impact of a threat exploiting a given vulnerability. For example, the risk of equipment damage is higher for a system that is business critical because its availability is essential to the organization.
- The risk to a system is directly proportional to the likelihood of a threat exploiting a given vulnerability. For example, the risk of equipment damage

Table 4.30 Risk Score Computation Template

Application: Hospital Information System

Threat (Agent and Action)	Vulnerability	Impact Score	Likelihood Score	Risk Score
Users	Eavesdropping and Interception of data	Lack of transmission encryption leading to interception of unencrypted data		
External Intruders, Malicious Insiders, Malicious Code	System intrusion and unauthorized system access	Possible Weak Passwords due to lack of password complexity controls		
Users	Denial of user actions or activity	Untraceable user actions due to generic accounts		
Malicious Insider, Users	Unchecked data alteration	Lack of logging and monitoring controls		
Non-Specific, Natural	Loss of power	Lack of redundant power supply		
Natural	Equipment damage or destruction due to natural causes (fire, water, etc.)	Lack of environmental controls		

is higher for a system that is outside a secure and maintained environment since it is more exposed to potential environmental and physical threats to the system.

- As both impact and likelihood are directly proportional to the risk, we can use the product of the two as the basis of our final risk score.

This formula can be reflected in what ultimately will be our final table for computing system risk. Abow is a template of a table that can be used (see Table 4.30).

Since we have gone through all the necessary steps to identify and compute each individual element of risk, it is a simple matter of obtaining scores and placing them

Table 4.31 Sample Impact Score

Application: Hospital Information System

Threat (Agent and Action)	Vulnerability	Impact Score	Likelihood Score	Risk Score
Users	Eavesdropping and Interception of data	Lack of transmission encryption leading to interception of unencrypted data	5		
External Intruders, Malicious Insiders, Malicious Code	System intrusion and unauthorized system access	Possible Weak Passwords due to lack of password complexity controls	5		
Users	Denial of user actions or activity	Untraceable user actions due to generic accounts	5		
Malicious Insider, Users	Unchecked data alteration	Lack of logging and monitoring controls	5		
Non-Specific, Natural	Loss of power	Lack of redundant power supply	5		
Natural	Equipment damage or destruction due to natural causes (fire, water, etc.)	Lack of environmental controls	5		

in the table. First, let's put all the appropriate impact scores for each of the threat and vulnerability pairs (see Table 4.31).

The next step is putting the appropriate likelihood score for each of the threat and vulnerability pairs (see Table 4.32).

And finally, using our formula RISK= IMPACT x LIKELIHOOD we simple multiply the impact and likelihood scores to obtain our final risk score as shown in Table 4.33.

We now have the final risk score, and have all the elements that we need to analyze our risk. As part of this book, and located on the companion website, we have

Table 4.32 Sample Likelihood Score

Application: Hospital Information System					
Threat (Agent and Action)	Vulnerability		Impact Score	Likelihood Score	Risk Score
Users	Eavesdropping and Interception of data	Lack of transmission encryption leading to interception of unencrypted data	5	2	
External Intruders, Malicious Insiders, Malicious Code	System intrusion and unauthorized system access	Possible Weak Passwords due to lack of password complexity controls	5	2	
Users	Denial of user actions or activity	Untraceable user actions due to generic accounts	5	2	
Malicious Insider, Users	Unchecked data alteration	Lack of logging and monitoring controls	5	3	
Non-Specific, Natural	Loss of power	Lack of redundant power supply	5	2	
Natural	Equipment damage or destruction due to natural causes (fire, water, etc.)	Lack of environmental controls	5	1	

provided a sample spreadsheet implementation of the techniques that we cover in this book. This includes the tables, decision matrices, macros, and formulas to help facilitate all the computations and decisions that were presented in this chapter.

By taking data captured during the data collection phase we took what were essentially unrelated data elements and brought them together and to a certain extent related them back to risk. This is in no way the end of the road though and we will need to perform analysis and interpretation of the results in order to obtain meaningful conclusions from the information, computations, and values that were derived in this chapter. The next chapter "Risk Analysis" will focus on the interpretation, analysis, and process for ultimately producing conclusions based on the data analysis that we have performed..

Table 4.33 Sample Risk Score

Application: Hospital Information System

Threat (Agent and Action)		Vulnerability	Impact Score	Likelihood Score	Risk Score
Users	Eavesdropping and Interception of data	Lack of transmission encryption leading to interception of unencrypted data	5	2	10
External Intruders, Malicious Insiders, Malicious Code	System intrusion and unauthorized system access	Possible Weak Passwords due to lack of password complexity controls	5	2	10
Users	Denial of user actions or activity	Untraceable user actions due to generic accounts	5	2	10
Malicious Insider, Users	Unchecked data alteration	Lack of logging and monitoring controls	5	3	15
Non-Specific, Natural	Loss of power	Lack of redundant power supply	5	2	10
Natural	Equipment damage or destruction due to natural causes (fire, water, etc.)	Lack of environmental controls	5	1	5

THE REAL WORLD

Jane has had a busy few weeks. She has received all the responses to her request lists, done her interviews, identified the assets that are in scope and collected her surveys. Fortunately, Jane has a very friendly and infectious personality which helped her gain the trust and support of the various stakeholders involved with the security risk analysis process. Although she was initially concerned that data gathering activities were going to be very difficult, by following a structured approach she was able to gather what she needed in a quick and efficient manner; however, she now finds herself confronted with quite a bit of information to review. She realizes that she is going to have to figure out a method for efficiently reviewing and normalizing the information or she is likely to get lost. Indirectly, she has started to formulate some conclusions just based on her initial exposure to the information during the data gathering process but she knows that she has to put the data together in a way to make it structured enough to interpret and more importantly to substantiate any final conclusions that she has.

Jane starts off the process by going through all the documents that she has collected. Though she did not receive all of the requested items, she was pleasantly surprised with the number of documents she was able to collect. She was actually surprised that some of the documents she received were even available since prior to her hiring the organization had no formal security function. Looking through the documents she received she was pleased to see that she received:

- A vulnerability assessment and penetration testing report from the IT Director.
- A huge spreadsheet of IT metrics from the CIO which included some security metrics.
- A list of security events and incident documentation from the help desk.
- Several audit reports from internal and external audit.
- A NIST SP800-66 HIPAA "assessment" that was performed by a consultant.

As she reviews the document she realizes that she's going to need a way to keep track of all her observations so she starts capturing anything that was worth noting in a spreadsheet. This spreadsheet becomes here running list of "observations." While reviewing the penetration testing report, she noted that the testers were able to gain domain administrator level access by leveraging vulnerabilities in some vendor systems. She also noticed that there were various findings in the audit reports related to issues with vendor managed systems. She realizes that these are both prime candidates for inclusion in the "observations" spreadsheet and creates an entry for each item even though they are related since she wants to make sure that she captures the total number of observations before she tries to normalize anything. Since Jane is diligent in her review approach she is fairly confident that she was able to extract all relevant information and observations from the documents she reviewed.

When reviewing NIST guidance she made a note that she was going to have to create a risk assessment for each of the specific systems and to accomplish that she knows that she is going to have to identify the threats and vulnerabilities for each system. Since she has completed her initial review of all the data provided to her in the information gathering phase she figures now is a good time to tackle this task.

Jane starts off this process by cataloging different types of threats that could potentially affect the organization and the systems that she is reviewing. Based on her readings, Jane knows that she could probably utilize some of the standard threat catalogs that are available. After reviewing NIST, BITS, Microsoft, and the ISO27005 catalogs she realizes that the NIST catalog is a bit too generic for her purposes, the BITS catalog seems just way too long, and the Microsoft catalog is just too application specific. The catalog that really seemed to resonate with her was Annex C in ISO27005. As she started using the threat catalog from ISO27005 she realized that she could augment the catalog with some of her own observations developed through the interviews to make it more specific to her organization.

Upon finishing her threat catalog she knows that she will need to build a catalog of vulnerabilities.While she was looking at ISO27005 for the threat catalog, she noticed that there was another section called Annex D that consisted of example vulnerabilities which seemed to be a perfect reference for a vulnerability catalog. After flipping back to Annex D she realizes that it aligns well with what she is trying to accomplish and decides that she will be able to use this as a baseline list for developing her vulnerability catalog.

Based on notes she took while reviewing NIST, she knows that now that she has completed both the threat and vulnerability catalogs she needs to start creating risk scenarios based on threat-vulnerability pairs. Based on her understanding, in order to properly assess risk, she has to run through various risk "scenarios" that she feels apply to the organization and the organizations important assets. To create her threat-vulnerability pair, she lists down the threats and matches up these threats with the different vulnerabilities in another column. This allows her to form a matrix of threat-vulnerability pairs. She puts these in a spreadsheet and creates one for each system that she is reviewing.

As she reviews the risk scenarios (threat and vulnerability pairs), the main thing she begins to wonder is how she is going to determine whether the organization, specifically each asset, is susceptible to a particular risk scenario. She knows that there must be a way to "quantify" these risks so that she can identify which risk scenarios are most applicable based on her knowledge of the organization and the organizations assets. She knows that ultimately a risk is the product of the impact and likelihood of a threat leveraging the vulnerability. This is where Jane has an "Ah-Hah" moment and realizes that she has her threat and vulnerability information and that through her surveys, interviews, and observations she can probably assign a value to impact and likelihood. She knows that ultimately she wants to be able to have a quantified risk value so she is going to need to use a calculation and settles on a simple calculation of risk where $RISK = IMPACT \times LIKELIHOOD$.

She decides to tackle assigning an impact value first. A little known fact about Jane is she has ninja level Excel skills, something that she is quite proud of and doesn't always get to use. Knowing that she'll have to apply some level of decision making to calculate impact, and wanting to make sure that it was consistent, she decides to write an Excel macro. She converts the survey results into a spreadsheet and writes a macro to support her ranking criteria.

Now that she has calculated impact she knows she has to calculate likelihood in order to derive her risk score. Continuing to utilize her Excel skills she creates macros to assign scores to Likelihood. Now, using the same spreadsheet containing the survey results, she creates an algorithm that considers the frequency, exposure, and controls of the asset to produce the likelihood score.

Although it took her days to create the algorithms for the scoring of Impact and Likelihood, once she was able to complete it for one system, it became a simple matter of reusing the same algorithm to analyze the data for the rest of the systems. So ultimately, the algorithm based data analysis mechanism that she prepared made it easier in the long run. Of equal importance is the fact that she was able to standardize and consistently apply her decision making process since it was done quantitatively.

Since she was finished computing for impact and likelihood she was able to stop using her advanced Excel skills and just do a simple multiplication of impact and likelihood in order to derive her risk scores.

It's the end of the week and Jane realizes that although she is tired and has had a few hiccups while developing her automated approach it was all worth it since she now has risk scores for all risk scenarios for all of her systems. She's proud of what she accomplished but she realizes that at the end of the day all she has now are a bunch of numbers. Knowing her boss she knows that if she was to go to him and tell him that the risk of an attacker compromising the email system by leveraging weak passwords is a 5 he would stare at her lie she just grew a second head. She realizes she has to come up with a way to effectively communicate these results but she is satisfied with her progress so far and she knows that the work she has put in up until this point will help support risk identification activities as well as substantiate her final results.

Information Security Risk Assessment: Risk Assessment

5

- System Risk Analysis
- Organizational/Strategic Risk Analysis

INTRODUCTION

So, we have collected the data in our data collection phase and we have structured the data in the data analysis phase. At this point you may be asking yourself, "What is the difference between the previous phase of the process and this one?" The fundamental difference is that the data analysis phase deals with structuring and organizing the data that was collected. Think of it as putting unstructured data, like a survey, into an organized format, such as a table. This phase is really focused on going through the organized data and interpreting it in order to derive and support our conclusions.

At this point of our process, we should have relatively organized data that can be used for a more practical analysis of risk. In the previous phase, we used the data we collected in quantitative analysis to derive figures and various "scores." These scores will be essential inputs as we move into more of a qualitative analysis.

During this risk analysis phase, we will interpret the data, gather findings, and ultimately form conclusions that will be the end result of all our activities so far. At the end of this chapter, the assessor should be able to answer the question "What are our organizational and system specific risks?"

In this chapter we will introduce two related but distinct levels of risk analysis. One is the system risk analysis, where we focus on the risk to a specific system. Many of the activities conducted in the data analysis phase are focused on system risk. The second type of risk analysis that we will be performing is an organizational or "strategic" analysis that provides an overall view of risks as they pertain to the organization. Organizational risk analysis is the most qualitative of the two and the outcome of this analysis is more subject to interpretation and is more heavily influenced by the experience of the practitioner.

SYSTEM RISK ANALYSIS

As stated in our introduction, the system risk analysis is focused on interpreting the data we have gathered in order to derive findings and conclusions for the in-scope systems. This is the critical juncture in our process where we will translate the data we have collected as well as analyze the various values and scores that we obtained in the data analysis phase.

As a quick review, in the last chapter, we structured the data by creating a matrix that showed these important elements:

- Threats.
- Vulnerabilities.
- Likelihood.
- Impact.
- Controls.

Through these elements, we were able to compute a final "risk score" for each of these threat and vulnerability pairs for each system. These risk scores will be the primary data analysis element that we will use in this section. By pivoting these risk scores into different views, we will be able to derive different observations and findings about the systems that we are assessing. What follows are several options and techniques to analyze the data.

Risk Classification

The first thing that we need to do is make sense of the risk scores. Based on the results of our previous activity all we really have are a bunch of numbers. Our challenge is to take these numbers, and transform them into something that is of a more "human readable" format. Going through this process will also provide us with a better perspective of what type of data we have.

A good starting point is to classify the risk scores into different levels of severity classification. Simply put, we will put these scores into "buckets" of HIGH, MEDIUM, and LOW. Though we can just arbitrarily designate buckets by simply dividing the risk score into three ranges, let's instead use a technique patterned after a ranking matrix provided in ISO 27005 Annex E as reflected in this table:

Likelihood						
		1	2	3	4	5
	1	1	2	3	4	5
	2	2	4	6	8	10
Impact	3	3	6	9	12	15
	4	4	8	12	16	20
	5	5	10	15	20	25

This is a fairly straightforward table. If the risk score falls into a specific shaded areas of the chart then you simply assign the risk classification assigned to that area:

Area	Risk Classification
Black	High Risk
Gray	Moderate Risk
White	Low Risk

Let's use our Hospital Information System as an example. Below is the finished risk matrix that we completed in the data analysis phase. For this specific example we only have the risk score. The goal here is to convert the risk scores into something we will be able to interpret.

Application: Hospital Information System					
Threat (Agent and Action)		**Vulnerability**	**Impact Score**	**Likelihood Score**	**Risk Score**
Users	Eavesdropping and Interception of data	Lack of transmission encryption leading to interception of unencrypted data	5	2	10
External Intruders, Malicious Insiders, Malicious Code	System intrusion and unauthorized system access	Possible Weak Passwords due to lack of password complexity controls	5	2	10
Users	Denial of user actions or activity	Untraceable user actions due to generic accounts	5	2	10
Malicious Insider, Users	Unchecked data alteration	Lack of logging and monitoring controls	5	3	15
Non-Specific, Natural	Loss of power	Lack of redundant power supply	5	2	10
Natural	Equipment damage or destruction due to natural causes (fire, water, etc)	Lack of environmental controls	5	1	5

Using the risk classification table presented above, we match the risk scores with the respective area of the table and assign the appropriate risk classification. What we'll end up with will be similar to the table below:

Application: Hospital Information System				
Threat (Agent and Action)		**Vulnerability**	**Risk Score**	**Risk Classification**
Users	Eavesdropping and Interception of data	Lack of transmission encryption leading to interception of unencrypted data	10	Moderate
External Intruders, Malicious Insiders, Malicious Code	System intrusion and unauthorized system access	Possible Weak Passwords due to lack of password complexity controls	10	Moderate
Users	Denial of user actions or activity	Untraceable user actions due to generic accounts	10	Moderate
Malicious Insider, Users	Unchecked data alteration	Lack of logging and monitoring controls	15	High
Non-Specific, Natural	Loss of power	Lack of redundant power supply	10	Moderate
Natural	Equipment damage or destruction due to natural causes (fire, water, etc)	Lack of environmental controls	5	Low

As you see, the table is actually a lot easier to comprehend than simply looking at numbers. Of course, the table above is just a much shorter example of what you will actually have since typically, you will have more than six vulnerability pairs. Keep in mind that no matter how many pairs you have, the process is the same.

You should now focus on completing this process for all threat and vulnerability pairs for all applications. If you used spreadsheets, similar in format to those provided on the companion website to this book, to track things you will have a worksheet for each application and each application will have a list of threat-vulnerability pairs with risk classifications for each.

A sample spreadsheet providing risk computations, risk scores, and risk classifications is provided in the companion website.

Risk Rankings

At this point, we now have a list of systems with different threats classified by risk. Classifying the threats helps when reviewing the various tables since the threats that fall into the category of HIGH begin to stand out.

Something that you will frequently need to do is to compare the systems against each other as this is a helpful way for an assessor to obtain a "gut check" about the validity of the results. The assessor should be able to begin to determine whether the results are consistent and aligned with expectations based on their system specific or organizational knowledge. For example, an assessor who has done multiple assessments within an organization would probably already have some expectations on what the results will be and could easily identify inconsistencies in the results based on these expectations.

At this point, an experienced assessor, would be able to identify issues with the dataset or calculations as there may be unexpected results. Of course in a perfect world, the results should be 100% correct; however, since it is the real world there will be instances where some of the results may need to be looked into or verified. If something stands out, it doesn't mean that the results are inaccurate it may just mean that you have to do some validation and ensure that a data collection mistake wasn't made or that the assumptions or information that you used were correct. This particular point in the process is a good time to do a quality ("gut") check.

As an example, if a relatively isolated database jumps out on the list as having a higher risk than an enterprise information system, it is probably a good idea to investigate the scoring related to the isolated database. Remember, this does not immediately mean that the results are incorrect. In fact, the results could be totally accurate and there is in fact something causing the system to be ranked at such a high level of risk.

Let's walk through a scenario like this using our aforementioned example. You should be able to follow along using the narrative; however, a full sample dataset has been provided on the companion website for reference if you would like to follow along using actual data.

Let's start with how we aggregate risk scores in order to identify HIGH risk systems and potential outliers. The process is fairly simple: (1) obtain the total risk scores for all of the systems, and (2) rank them. Let's go through each of the 5 sample systems and obtain their "Aggregate Risk Ranking":

Hospital Information System

Description: The enterprise information system that handles patient records and has interfaces to other financial and clinical systems.

Threat Agent	Threat Action	Vulnerability	Impact	Likeli-hood	Risk Score	Risk Classification
Users	Eavesdrop-ping and Interception of data	Lack of transmission encryption leading to interception of unencrypted data	5	2	10	Moderate

Threat Agent	Threat Action	Vulnerability	Impact	Likeli-hood	Risk Score	Risk Classification
External Intruders, Malicious Insiders, Malicious Code	System intrusion and unauthorized system access	Possible Weak Passwords due to lack of password complexity controls	5	2	10	Moderate
Users	Denial of user actions or activity	Untraceable user actions due to generic accounts	5	2	10	Moderate
Malicious Insider, Users	Unchecked data alteration	Lack of logging and monitoring controls	5	3	15	High
Non-Specific, Natural	Loss of power	Lack of redundant power supply	5	2	10	Moderate
Natural	Equipment damage or destruction due to natural causes (fire, water, etc.)	Lack of environmental controls	5	1	5	Low
Total					60	

HR Payroll System

Description: A PeopleSoft implementation that handles HR functions and payroll for more than a thousand employees.

Threat Agent	Threat Action	Vulnerability	Impact	Likelihood	Risk Score	Risk Classification
Users	Eavesdropping and Interception of data	Lack of transmission encryption leading to interception of unencrypted data	5	2	10	Moderate
External Intruders, Malicious Insiders, Malicious Code	System intrusion and unauthorized system access	Possible Weak Passwords due to lack of password complexity controls	5	3	15	High

Threat Agent	Threat Action	Vulnerability	Impact	Likelihood	Risk Score	Risk Classification
Users	Denial of user actions or activity	Untraceable user actions due to generic accounts	5	2	10	Moderate
Malicious Insider, Users	Unchecked data alteration	Lack of logging and monitoring controls	5	1	5	Moderate
Non-Specific, Natural	Loss of power	Lack of redundant power supply	5	1	5	Moderate
Natural	Equipment damage or destruction due to natural causes (fire, water, etc.)	Lack of environmental controls	5	1	5	Moderate
Total					50	

Cardiology Database

Description: An MS Access Database containing research material for a pilot project at the hospital.

Threat Agent	Threat Action	Vulnerability	Impact	Likelihood	Risk Score	Risk Classification
Users	Eavesdropping and Interception of data	Lack of transmission encryption leading to interception of unencrypted data	3	3	9	Moderate
External Intruders, Malicious Insiders, Malicious Code	System intrusion and unauthorized system access	Possible Weak Passwords due to lack of password complexity controls	3	4	12	Moderate
Users	Denial of user actions or activity	Untraceable user actions due to generic accounts	5	2	10	Moderate
Malicious Insider, Users	Unchecked data alteration	Lack of logging and monitoring controls	5	2	10	Moderate

Threat Agent	Threat Action	Vulnerability	Impact	Likelihood	Risk Score	Risk Classification
Non-Specific, Natural	Loss of power	Lack of redundant power supply	1	3	3	Low
Natural	Equipment damage or destruction due to natural causes (fire, water, etc.)	Lack of environmental controls	1	3	3	Low
Total					47	

Email System

Description: Microsoft Exchange used by the hospital for internal and external email.

Threat Agent	Threat Action	Vulnerability	Impact	Likelihood	Risk Score	Risk Classification
Users	Eavesdropping and Interception of data	Lack of transmission encryption leading to interception of unencrypted data	5	3	15	High
External Intruders, Malicious Insiders, Malicious Code	System intrusion and unauthorized system access	Possible Weak Passwords due to lack of password complexity controls	5	2	10	Moderate
Users	Denial of user actions or activity	Untraceable user actions due to generic accounts	3	2	6	Moderate
Malicious Insider, Users	Unchecked data alteration	Lack of logging and monitoring controls	3	3	9	Moderate
Non-Specific, Natural	Loss of power	Lack of redundant power supply	3	1	3	Low
Natural	Equipment damage or destruction due to natural causes (fire, water, etc.)	Lack of environmental controls	3	1	3	Low
Total					46	

Imaging System

Description: The hospitals primary radiology imaging application.

Threat Agent	Threat Action	Vulnerability	Impact	Likelihood	Risk Score	Risk Classification
Users	Eavesdropping and Interception of data	Lack of transmission encryption leading to interception of unencrypted data	5	3	15	High
External Intruders, Malicious Insiders, Malicious Code	System intrusion and unauthorized system access	Possible Weak Passwords due to lack of password complexity controls	5	2	10	Moderate
Users	Denial of user actions or activity	Untraceable user actions due to generic accounts	5	1	5	Moderate
Malicious Insider, Users	Unchecked data alteration	Lack of logging and monitoring controls	5	1	5	Moderate
Non-Specific, Natural	Loss of power	Lack of redundant power supply	5	1	5	Moderate
Natural	Equipment damage or destruction due to natural causes (fire, water, etc.)	Lack of environmental controls	5	1	5	Moderate
Total					45	

Ok, so now let's take all the "Aggregate Risk Scores" for each application and rank them according to their aggregate risk score. You should be able to create a table similar to this:

Application	Risk Rank
HIS	60
HR Payroll	50
Cardio Research DB	47
Email	46
Imaging	45

The table above presents a ranking of applications based on their aggregate risk scores (sum of all risk scores of all threat and vulnerability pairs). In theory, the higher the aggregate risk score, the greater the corresponding risk of the system across all threat and vulnerability pairs. By doing a risk ranking, one can immediately see if there are any outliers or particular systems that stand out. Typically, as an assessor gains experience within the environment there are certain things that they expect to observe. For example, the top two systems in the ranking in terms of risk scores are the Hospital Information System and the HR Payroll System which are enterprise systems. In our scenario this would tend to validate our results since enterprise systems would typically have high impact and likelihood scores since they are critical operationally, contain more sensitive data, and generally though not always the case, have more exposure to threats and vulnerabilities due to their user base, size, and complexity.

As we have mentioned numerous times, this is an important time for the assessor to evaluate the results for items that appear out of place or unexpected. Sometimes inaccuracies are from simple mistakes like typos but they can also be related to more complex issues like misunderstandings regarding survey control questions.

In our experience, this review point is typically your first line of quality assurance for your risk assessment. As we mentioned earlier, sometimes skewed results occur and this is a good way to verify if your data and approach are in order. It is often the case, especially in automated software driven assessments, that the assessor takes the results of the automated assessment at face value and doesn't bother to review how the final results are obtained. As such, it is very important for the assessor to not just take the results "as is" after the data analysis phase and that the assessor begin to interpret and verify that the results are accurate.

Now let's go back to our risk rankings:

Application	Risk Rank
HIS	60
HR Payroll	50
Cardio Research DB	47
Email	46
Imaging	45

One thing that should stand out in this example is that the Cardiology Database, which is an Access Database used by a single department, has a high risk ranking based on our process. This would be an example where the assessor should step back from the calculations and look into the factors that could make a department centric Access Database have a higher risk score than some of the organizations largest enterprise systems. In our next step, we will start looking more thoroughly at individual systems in order to determine the rationale for the risk scores that were calculated.

Individual System Risk Reviews

One of the pitfalls in risk analysis is focusing too much on the numbers (e.g. the risk scores) or blindly trusting the numbers. Other risk assessment frameworks rely heavily on various formulas and quantitative computations, but as a practitioner you need to remember that risk assessments are more than just number crunching. Numbers are meant to support the expertise of the assessor and nothing beats an experienced assessor supported by a structured, logical, and data driven approach.

Now that we have a first taste of the data based on the risk rankings established in our previous activity, the next step is to conduct risk reviews of each of the individual systems and their corresponding threats. You could consider this individual system risk review as a "deep dive" for each of the systems that were assessed in order to determine the rationale for the risk assigned to each of those systems. This is meant to answer the following questions:

- How did we obtain the risk score for this system?
- Why did this system rank the way it did?
- What contributed to the risk rating of this system?
- What stands out in this system that made it particularly "risky" in a certain area?

One of the best ways to approach this analysis is to evaluate the environment under which the system operates. This will allow you to understand what factors contributed to the final risk score of the system. Several important things to look into are:

1. Exposure.
2. Users.
3. Data Confidentiality.
4. Criticality.
5. Controls.

Based on reviewing the systems environment, characteristics, and controls, it is relatively straightforward to analyze the rationale for the risk to each system. Let's go over a few examples using our aforementioned Hospital Information System. Our most obvious questions here are: Why does the Hospital Information System rank the highest among the group? What factors contributed to the relative severity of its risk rating? In order to answer that let's go back and took a look at the corresponding risk matrix. Assume that we have in hand the data collected through the various surveys conducted in the data collection phase. If you would like to follow along you can download the sample survey in our "Downloads" section for reference; however, the narrative below is pretty self-explanatory.

Hospital Information System:

Threat Agent	Threat Action	Vulnerability	Impact	Likelihood	Risk Score	Risk Classification
Users	Eavesdropping and Interception of data	Lack of transmission encryption leading to interception of unencrypted data	5	2	10	Moderate
External Intruders, Malicious Insiders, Malicious Code	System intrusion and unauthorized system access	Possible Weak Passwords due to lack of password complexity controls	5	2	10	Moderate
Users	Denial of user actions or activity	Untraceable user actions due to generic accounts	5	2	10	Moderate
Malicious Insider, Users	Unchecked data alteration	Lack of logging and monitoring controls	5	3	15	High
Non-Specific, Natural	Loss of power	Lack of redundant power supply	5	2	10	Moderate
Natural	Equipment damage or destruction due to natural causes (fire, water, etc.)	Lack of environmental controls	5	1	5	Low
Total					60	

Let's discuss impact first. Looking at the table you can see that one of the primary contributors to the relatively high risk ranking for this system is the Impact scores which are 5 throughout. This shouldn't be surprising since this system is the primary information system for the hospital.

Again, assuming that we have in hand the various surveys that were completed during the data collection phase we know the following about the system:

1. Based on the system profile survey, the HIS system contains a significant amount of ePHI data.
2. Based on the system profile survey, the HIS system is the one of the primary systems for the hospital and is critical to hospital operations.
3. Based on the system profile survey, the system supports a high number of users.
4. The system is covered by regulations, specifically HIPAA.

It's pretty obvious that these characteristics explain the high impact scores. Higher impact scores will translate to higher risk scores. Now we'll examine the likelihood scores:

1. The system can be accessed remotely but only through VPN.
2. There are a significant number of users and the system is used by non-employees (vendors and contractors).
3. Large amounts of data are transferred; however, only internally within the organization.
4. The system is located in a secure data center.

Looking at this, one should already start seeing where the risks for this system will likely be. Before we discuss those risk we'll take a look at the controls for the system as well:

1. Based on the control profile survey, the system appears for have strong controls over the following:
   a. Transmission encryption.
   b. Password complexity.
   c. Alternate Power Supplies.
   d. Physical and Environmental Controls

2. Based on the control profile survey, the system appears to have documented exceptions or lack of controls in certain areas:
   a. Logging and Monitoring.
   b. Generic Accounts.

Analyzing the important points, we can derive the following conclusions that explain why the system has the highest aggregate risk:

1. The system is a very high impact system. This by default will increase the risk score across the board is probably one of the main contributors to the level of risk assigned to this system.
2. The system is exposed to integrity concerns as there is a diverse user base with access to the system particularly vendors and contractors.
3. The weakness in logging/monitoring as well as use of generic accounts magnifies the potential integrity risks such as detecting and preventing unauthorized user actions and data alterations to the system.

Let's try another system, this time the one that was a bit unexpected: the Cardiology Database. One main question that you should be asking yourself is why did an MS Access database rank relatively high in our risk assessment?

Threat Agent	Threat Action	Vulnerability	Impact	Likelihood	Risk Score	Risk Classification
Users	Eavesdropping and Interception of data	Lack of transmission encryption leading to interception of unencrypted data	3	3	9	Moderate

Threat Agent	Threat Action	Vulnerability	Impact	Likelihood	Risk Score	Risk Classification
External Intruders, Malicious Insiders, Malicious Code	System intrusion and unauthorized system access	Possible Weak Passwords due to lack of password complexity controls	3	4	12	Moderate
Users	Denial of user actions or activity	Untraceable user actions due to generic accounts	5	2	10	Moderate
Malicious Insider, Users	Unchecked data alteration	Lack of logging and monitoring controls	5	2	10	Moderate
Non-Specific, Natural	Loss of power	Lack of redundant power supply	1	3	3	Low
Natural	Equipment damage or destruction due to natural causes (fire, water, etc.)	Lack of environmental controls	1	3	3	Low
Total					47	

As with the previous example, let's first review the Impact scores. Based on the surveys that should have been completed in the data collection part of the process we know the following:

1. Based on the system profile survey, the Cardiology Database contains confidential and proprietary information, but not regulated data. For purposes of this example, let's assume that the assessor performed a follow-up interview and found out that the patient identifiable information is scrambled within the database.
2. As the Cardiology Database is used in a proprietary hospital study, it is very important to consider the integrity of the data once it's in the database. Any false or inaccurate data could lead to skewing of the study results.
3. Interestingly enough though, based on interviews, it appears that losing the entire database is not a primary concern for the system holders as it is easily recreated from the original sources.
4. There are a relatively small number of users of the database.

Going through these points we see that although it is a standalone database, and not an enterprise system, it appears to support an important study and the integrity of the data appears to be extremely important. Keeping that in mind let's look into the factors affecting likelihood as it relates to the system:

1. The system can only be accessed within the internal network.
2. Transfer of the data is restricted to the internal network.
3. There are a limited number of users and only hospital employees use the Cardiology Database.
4. The system is not located in a data center but on a workstation in the Cardiology department.

Looking at these likelihood factors two things that stand out are the fact that data is transferred to or from the application (albeit internal only) and the database itself resides on a workstation in a department instead of a server in the data center. Let's continue with the control analysis:

1. The survey indicated that most of the controls that would be associated with an enterprise systems are non-existent, likely because it is a standalone database.

So now analyzing the important points, we can derive the following conclusions which explains why the system has a high aggregate risk:

1. As the Cardiology Database is an Access Database stored on a workstations, it suffers from an overall lack of controls that would be common to an enterprise application, which explains the general high values in terms of risk scores.
2. Even though the risk scores are generally high across the board, there is no single risk that actually hits the "High" level since the risk level is generally moderated by the low exposure and low impact scores. These low scores were primarily because the system can only be accessed internally and other than the accuracy requirements surrounding the data, the confidentiality and availability factors were not deemed to be that important.
3. There are some scenarios that are worth looking into specific to this application and its characteristics:
   a. The Access Database currently does not have any access controls (e.g. password protection). Even though it does not contain regulated data, the data is still considered confidential and proprietary and the lack of proper access controls could lead to unauthorized access to the database.
   b. Since accuracy of the data is the most important aspect of this system, the lack of logging and the general lack of controls on accounting for changes will be of relatively high concern.

We highly recommend that the practitioner should go over each system and conduct this type of review. The review of the Cardiology Database proved to be valuable as we were able to quickly establish that, based on a variety of factors, it did belong on the listing and the high score was valid due to a general lack of controls. This will not only allow you to start to develop the rationale for the various risk scores that are assigned but will also provide you with the background to defend or justify your observations and conclusions to other people such as auditors or other departments within the organization.

Threat and Vulnerability Review

We have conducted individual risk reviews and by this time have a high level understanding of why the risk rankings are what they are. At this point, we will now focus our attention on the threat and vulnerability pairs.

There are two approaches to performing this review:

1. Identify HIGH risk threats across all systems—This is fairly straightforward. This allows the assessor to quickly identify threats that have the highest risk for the systems reviewed.
2. Obtain aggregate threat and vulnerability pair scores across all systems—This is a little more subtle of an approach. This allows the assessor to see beyond just HIGH risk items and identify potential systemic problems across all systems.

Let's focus on the first approach before moving on to the second. In the first approach, we simply identify all the threat and vulnerability pairs that have a HIGH rating then rank them based on the number of systems that are affected.

This approach, unlike simply ranking systems by risk scores, will allow the assessor to immediately identify high risk items for the systems reviewed. These items will ultimately be part of risk treatment activities which we will be dealing with in a later chapter.

Let's work on an example. This process is actually fairly straightforward. First let's go through all the system risk matrices and identify all unique threat and vulnerability pairs that are classified HIGH risk. You'll end up with a table similar to this:

Threat Agent	Threat Action	Vulnerability
Users	Eavesdropping and Interception of data	Lack of transmission encryption leading to interception of unencrypted data
Malicious Insider, Users	Unchecked data alteration	Lack of logging and monitoring controls
External Intruders, Malicious Insiders, Malicious Code	System intrusion and unauthorized system access	Possible Weak Passwords due to lack of password complexity controls

After that, for each threat and vulnerability pair, identify all systems that have HIGH risk ratings for that particular pairing. You will end up with something like this:

Threat Agent	Threat Action	Vulnerability	Affected Systems
Users	Eavesdropping and Interception of data	Lack of transmission encryption leading to interception of unencrypted data	Email, Imaging

Threat Agent	Threat Action	Vulnerability	Affected Systems
Malicious Insider, Users	Unchecked data alteration	Lack of logging and monitoring controls	HIS
External Intruders, Malicious Insiders, Malicious Code	System intrusion and unauthorized system access	Possible Weak Passwords due to lack of password complexity controls	HR Payroll

And there you have it. Through this view, it is fairly easy to see which threats and which systems are the most important to consider in terms of risk. Let's say that we have the system profile and control surveys on hand for each of the systems reviewed. Using the surveys, you could prepare an analysis like the following:

1. There's a high risk of potential disclosure of data from Email and Imaging since both transmit highly confidential and regulated data but the data is not encrypted.
2. HIS has insufficient logging and monitoring controls to detect unauthorized alterations. This is compounded by the fact that the system has a very large and diverse user base (contractors and vendors) and the HIS is absolutely critical to the hospital operations.
3. The HR Payroll System has a high risk of potential unauthorized access because it does not support password complexity. The risk is compounded by the fact that the system contains confidential and regulated data as well as the fact that it is considered highly critical to the organization.

For now, just keep this analysis in mind. This information will be useful when we start preparing risk management treatment plans for specific systems.

Now it's time to discuss the second, more subtle approach. Compared to the previous approach, which focuses on identifying HIGH risk items for specific systems, this approach tries to identify systemic problems across all systems.

The simplest way to do this is to use the aggregate scores for each threat and vulnerability pair across all systems. Let's work through an example. In this table you see all the threat and vulnerability pairs for one system.

Threat Agent	Threat Action	Vulnerability	HIS
Users	Eavesdropping and Interception of data	Lack of transmission encryption leading to interception of unencrypted data	10
External Intruders, Malicious Insiders, Malicious Code	System intrusion and unauthorized system access	Possible Weak Passwords due to lack of password complexity controls	10
Malicious Insider, Users	Unchecked data alteration	Lack of logging and monitoring controls	15

Threat Agent	Threat Action	Vulnerability	HIS
Users	Denial of user actions or activity	Untraceable user actions due to generic accounts	10
Non-Specific, Natural	Loss of power	Lack of redundant power supply	10
Natural	Equipment damage or destruction due to natural causes (fire, water, etc.)	Lack of environmental controls	5

To allow us to review all systems we just create columns and input the scores for each of those systems and then total the score for each threat and vulnerability pair.

Threat Agent	Threat Action	Vulnerability	HIS	Cardio Research	HR Payroll	Email	Imaging	Score
Users	Eavesdropping and Interception of data	Lack of transmission encryption leading to interception of unencrypted data	10	9	10	15	15	59
External Intruders, Malicious Insiders, Malicious Code	System intrusion and unauthorized system access	Possible Weak Passwords due to lack of password complexity controls	10	12	15	10	10	57
Malicious Insider, Users	Unchecked data alteration	Lack of logging and monitoring controls	15	10	5	9	5	44
Users	Denial of user actions or activity	Untraceable user actions due to generic accounts	10	10	10	6	5	41
Non-Specific, Natural	Loss of power	Lack of redundant power supply	10	3	5	3	5	26
Natural	Equipment damage or destruction due to natural causes (fire, water, etc.)	Lack of environmental controls	5	3	5	3	5	21

As a last step, the final aggregate scores are then plotted to each threat and vulnerability pair. We then sort the threat and vulnerability pairs based on the aggregate risk scores and we get:

Threat Agent	Threat Action	Vulnerability	Score
Users	Eavesdropping and Interception of data	Lack of transmission encryption leading to interception of unencrypted data	59
External Intruders, Malicious Insiders, Malicious Code	System intrusion and unauthorized system access	Possible Weak Passwords due to lack of password complexity controls	57
Malicious Insider, Users	Unchecked data alteration	Lack of logging and monitoring controls	44
Users	Denial of user actions or activity	Untraceable user actions due to generic accounts	41
Non-Specific, Natural	Loss of power	Lack of redundant power supply	26
Natural	Equipment damage or destruction due to natural causes (fire, water, etc.)	Lack of environmental controls	21

This view quickly provides us an idea of what appears to be systemic problems that the organization might be encountering across multiple systems. To make this even more helpful, let's add the top two or three systems with the highest scores for each of the threat and vulnerability pair:

Threat Agent	Threat Action	Vulnerability	Score	Affected Systems
Users	Eavesdropping and Interception of data	Lack of transmission encryption leading to interception of unencrypted data	59	Imaging, Email
External Intruders, Malicious Insiders, Malicious Code	System intrusion and unauthorized system access	Possible Weak Passwords due to lack of password complexity controls	57	HR Payroll, Cardiology Research
Malicious Insider, Users	Unchecked data alteration	Lack of logging and monitoring controls	44	HIS, Cardiology Research

Threat Agent	Threat Action	Vulnerability	Score	Affected Systems
Users	Denial of user actions or activity	Untraceable user actions due to generic accounts	41	HIS, HR Payroll, Cardiology Research
Non-Specific, Natural	Loss of power	Lack of redundant power supply	26	HIS
Natural	Equipment damage or destruction due to natural causes (fire, water, etc.)	Lack of environmental controls	21	HIS, Payroll System, Imaging

In this view, we can already derive several important observations about risk across all of the systems reviewed. Here is a sample analysis for the table above:

1. By far, the highest risk to the organization is disclosure of regulated and confidential data. Looking back at our other analysis activities, this is likely due to the fact that two enterprise systems, that transmit large volumes of regulated data, have weak encryption controls.

2. Unauthorized system access due to weak passwords, though only related to one system (Payroll System), actually gets a High rating as several other systems hit a moderate score because of weak controls. For example, the Cardiology Database has weak access controls; however, since it's general exposure is low (as it is not as critical as the payroll database) it does not rank as high as the Payroll System.

3. It is interesting to note that even though the Cardiology Research Database did not have any High risk items, it appears in the top two or three in several of the risk categories. This would be worth making note of as well.

This approach provides the assessor with an overall view of the risks that are pervasive throughout the systems reviewed. When you approach an analysis in this fashion you are able to catch trends in areas of risk that might not be identified if you only focus on items classified as HIGH. The Cardiology Research database is a good example of how this approach pays off. Even though the Cardiology Research database does not have any high risk items, it ranks high in many of the threat and vulnerability pairs. This could be an indication of an overall problem with the application. After quickly diving into the details around the application it becomes obvious that many of these factors are because it is an Access Database that has a general lack of controls.

A common theme throughout the analysis performed here was the use of summing. Using an aggregate approach to analyzing risk is a useful technique to identify outliers and give clues to the assessor on what systems and threats to focus on. Though there are exceptions, most of the time systems with a high score typically indicate that they are both of high value to the organization and suffering from either poor performing or missing controls.

We are often asked whether it is necessary to do this type of assessment over all systems in an enterprise. In our experience such a review is not necessary and may cause the process to become large and unmanageable. There are software packages that will assist with automating these processes to a certain extent; however, there is still significant work that has to go into data collection and entry. It has always been our position that with the right approach and use of a consistent method you can extrapolate the results and, for the most part, assume that if the issue exists in systems that support critical processes at an enterprise level than it is very likely going to exist in a secondary or tertiary system. This may not be true in all cases; however, based on our experience this is typically a very sound approach. It is very important to note all observations and analysis conducted in this part of the process as this will help in creating focus for the risk management plans.

Review Activities for Organizational Risk

The assessment of risk on an organizational level is a review of potential risks as it pertains to the organization as a whole. This assessment is not system specific but reviews risks to an organization on a strategic level based on areas of business or research, company locations, use of technology, and other factors. The review activities for organizational risk are a little bit more unstructured when compared to the system based risk analysis, primarily because this is highly dependent on the sources of information to which an assessor has access.

Typically, for a review that will focus on an organizational perspective of risk, an assessor will be looking for resources such as documents, assessments, and reviews that focus on either organizational controls or a comprehensive assessment that encompasses multiple systems across the enterprise. This is a way to expand beyond the point in time assessment of the systems in scope and extrapolate out the results across the organization.

We have found that the following are fairly common documents that are most likely available within the organization:

- Security Trend Reports.
- Vulnerability Assessment and Penetration Test reports.
- Security Policy Exceptions.
- Security Metrics.
- Third Party IT Audit Reports.
- Other Regulatory Assessments.

These documents, although not always available, are great sources of information for gaining a high level view of what risks the organization faces as a whole. With just these documents, or even a subset of those documents, the following reviews can be conducted:

- Review of current threats and trends to see if the organization is at risk for any of these upcoming threats based on current or future business practices or technology use.

- Review of security incidents to identify any flaws in organizational controls that led to the security incidents.
- Review of third party assessments and audit reports to see what other third party assessors and auditors have identified as control weaknesses or risks to the organization.
- Review of security exceptions to identify gaps in security controls based on these exceptions.
- Review of security metrics to see the possible root causes of some particularly weak metric items.

As we mentioned, this type of review is fairly unstructured and an experienced assessor would likely be able to use additional information resources at their disposal to identify organizational level risks. For now though, we'll focus on these types of documents or sources of information as these are the most common and most likely be available to the assessor.

Review of Security Threats and Trends

Before one can assess organizational risk, one needs to know what threats an organization faces. In the system based risk analysis, we used a threat catalog. The threat catalog is useful but it focuses on system specific threats and focuses on fairly traditional threats rather than emerging threats.

In order to begin the organizational analysis, the assessor must obtain sources of information regarding security trends. This is actually fairly simple since there are quite a few sources for this type of information. This information could be in the form of:

1. Various reports from third party vendors—Some examples are security annual reports that are released from the FBI, SANS, Microsoft, Symantec, McAfee, and Sophos.
2. Reports and statistics from various Computer Emergency Response Teams (CERTs)—The US CERT website has a publications section and the Software Engineering Institute of Carnegie Mellon has a good statistics section.
3. Reports and statistics from various regulatory bodies—This is industry dependent. Various regulatory bodies for specific industries usually provide reports, for example, in health care the US Department of Health and Human Services provides a variety of helpful reports and statistics.
4. Security News and Forums—There are a quite a few of these available. Security Focus and SANS are good places to start when trying to identify relevant forums and emerging security news.

For a more comprehensive list of information resources please refer to the companion website to this book.

Once collected, it is a fairly simple matter of reading and collecting various notes and observations regarding current and emerging threats from the sources reviewed. There will be times when different sources disagree on what constitute the major emerging security risk trends and this is where the experience of the assessor and/or the Information Security Officer will come into play as it may be necessary to make a judgment call as to which source will be used.

As always, this is best illustrated through the use of an example. Let's say that at the time of our analysis, based on reviewing the sources above, we determined that the current and emerging security threats are:

1. Advance Persistent Threats (APTs).
2. Web Application Attacks.
3. Mobile Attack Vectors.
4. Advanced Polymorphic Malware.
5. Loss of Regulated Data.

One of the difficult things that an assessor might encounter is the fact that as security threats become more and more sophisticated, many of the threats become intertwined and chained. For our example above, "APTs" is such a generic term that almost all of the other threats noted above could be included as part of an APT threat. Consolidation of threats should be evaluated on a case-by-case basis using the discretion of the assessor. Another important byproduct of including discussions on current and emerging threats is that it provides a venue for educating and increasing the awareness of the audience of your risk analysis, which typically would include senior executives or board members.

After listing down the threats, the next step is to see how the organizations current or future operations or business plans align with those threats. In order to do this, one has to rely on the information that the assessor has collected in the data collection phase. Often this information comes from the assessor themselves as well as the Information Security Officer and their understanding of the business context of the organization.

For example, we noted above that APTs are an emerging threat. Let's try to analyze how this threat applies to a private mid-sized hospital. Here is an example of what an analysis could be:

> *Based on our research, augmented by findings from various security companies, the recent high profile APTs appear to primarily target government, military, or large high profile organizations with valuable intellectual property. There also appears to be significant focus on attacking control systems. Compared to the organizations that are being attacked our organization (a mid-sized hospital) is not a high profile target so while these threats are still viable they would have a lower likelihood of occurring.*

Obviously, if the assessor is doing a review of a military hospital, this threat will be very relevant and the analysis will be significantly different. Let's try another example. This time here's a sample analysis for Mobile Attack Vectors:

The organization has a moderate exposure to these attacks primarily because there are increasing numbers of mobile devices that connect directly to the production network. There are currently fairly informal control mechanisms to track, monitor, and implement protection mechanisms for these devices within the organization. These types of threats are relatively new and not as prevalent as other threats; however, the area is evolving quickly as the use of these devices explodes within companies.

Obviously "Mobile Attack Vectors" is a fairly generic threat and should probably be expanded a little more but for purposes of our example, the assessor based the review on an analysis of the current environment of the organization and applied that knowledge to discussing the organizations potential exposure to an emerging threat.

It is important for the assessor to have knowledge of current business or technology initiatives so that they can evaluate the organization's exposure against current and emerging threats. This is typically why an individual with significant knowledge of the company's operations and emerging initiatives should be involved in the risk analysis. If someone with limited knowledge of the company's operations or initiatives conducts the review it will likely be less effective unless extensive information gathering is performed.

Review of Audit Findings

One of the things that an assessor has to consider when performing the analysis is whether previous reviews and assessments have been conducted for the organization. Often times, there are other assessments, audits, and reviews that have been conducted that will pertain to information security. Publically traded companies have to undergo Sarbanes-Oxley (SOX) 404 audits and banking companies undergo Gramm-Leach-Bliley Act (GLBA) reviews which would cover some areas of information security. For healthcare, there are various HIPAA audits that may have been conducted and if you are lucky they would have been performed based on NIST SP800-66. If the organization is a service provider, they may have undergone a SSAE16 (Statement on Standards for Attestation Engagements No. 16 - Reporting on Controls at a Service Organization) review or even obtained ISO 27001 certification.

A good way to approach reviewing this information is to create a table where you list down the name of the audit or assessment report for the organization, the third party auditor or regulator who performed the review, and the assessor's findings and observations. The most critical component is to capture the specific deficiencies stated in the report.

As an example, let's say that our assessor was able to obtain several audit reports from internal audit and the information security department. A sample analysis of the reports would look something like this:

1. IT Access Control Audit:
   a. Third party auditor has found deficiencies in several key systems such as the use of generic accounts and exceptions in the proper logging and monitoring of access.

    b. Auditor has given a rating of "moderate" risk rating for the systems reviewed.

2. HIPAA NIST SP800-66 Audit:
    a. Based on a third party assessment, there are deficiencies noted in the proper implementation of access controls such as the use of password complexity.
    b. The third party assessor has provided a "moderate" risk rating for the assessment.

3. Third Party Penetration Testing:
    a. The third party assessor was able to obtain Windows domain administrator level access by leveraging vulnerabilities in internal systems, caused by lack of proper patching, that are maintained by vendors.
    b. The third party assessor has provided a "high" risk rating for the assessment.

By reviewing the various assessment reports the practitioner can already begin to identify some key risks for the organization. Depending on the type of third party report it may also provide you information on the progress (or lack thereof) of risk mitigation activities, assist in validating the results of the system based assessment, and help the assessor discover other organizational issues that were not detected through the system-based assessments.

Following the case presented above, we can already see that the organization may have some issues regarding:

1. Access control, particularly regarding generic accounts and password complexity.
2. Patch and vulnerability management.

One key thing to remember is that since these assessment happened in the past, the practitioner should take the time to determine whether these issues have been resolved or are in the process of being resolved. Typically, these audits or assessments would include documentation related to management's response and would capture a description of the steps that will be taken to address the issue along with any target dates for completion.

Review of Security Incidents

Another important area to review in order to understand organizational security risk is the organization's collection of security incidents. A well-documented security incident provides great insights into possible flaws or deficiencies in the security controls of a system or the organization as a whole.

Most organizations typically have a way to track security incidents through their incident response process which should be based on a documented incident response plan. These documented reports should be leveraged by the assessor as much as possible as a great source of insights for potential risks since they are often a direct result of some level of control breakdown.

The analysis is fairly straightforward. The assessor should go over the incident documentation and group together common incidents. While we will typically just try to group these together based on common incident types there are tool and standard groupings or "taxonomies" that can be used like Verizon's VERIS taxonomy or MITRE's incident taxonomy. If the organization has had a number of incidents in one particular group it is likely the risk to the organization may still remain high for that area. Once these groups have been identified, one of the important things to do is to analyze the root cause of the incident and determine if the root cause aligns with any of the risks your assessment has already identified.

For example, let's say our assessor found multiple incidents of hospital employees reporting that they have clicked on phishing links. Here's a sample analysis:

> Our review shows multiple instances of **social engineering and phishing incidents** that lead to unauthorized access and ultimately spamming incidents off of the hospital's email system.Based on the incident documentation, it appears that the organization's users were "tricked" into providing their account credentials to an external attacker. The incidents allowed external attackers to send spam through email systems via the compromised accounts.

This is a good example of an organizational threat. Social engineering and phishing attacks take advantage of people and so an organization has to rely on security awareness controls. The level of security awareness is something difficult to define in a system based review since security awareness is more of a strategic and organizational initiative.

Review of Security Exceptions

Very similar to the security incidents, another good location for identifying possible information security risks is within documented security exceptions. If the organization has good tracking and documentation for security exceptions, these exceptions can be used to identify control deficiencies. This is because of the fact that an exception to a security policy indicates that operationally there is some deviation from organizational security standards.

Similar to security incidents, the practitioner would review the security exceptions, grouping common exceptions together, and identifying their root causes. Let's say our assessor performed a review of the organization's security exceptions:

> Based on our review of the documented security exceptions, we noted exceptions filed dealing with:
>
> •   Missing patches and updates—We noted multiple vendor systems without up to date security patches. According to the vendors, they cannot apply OS patches and updates as this will break a legacy component that is used to run the system. The business unit has agreed to sign a security exception as the application is business critical.

- *Security event logging—We noted several legacy applications that do not have security event logging since the application does not have the capability. There are plans to replace the application with a newer one with more features; however, this will not be implemented until a year from now. The business unit has determined that this is a necessary exception since the process the application supports is critical to the organization.*

As you can see, there are already very interesting things that we can derive from the analysis. In our analysis using third party assessment documents, the results of the Penetration Testing indicated that the auditor was able to leverage vulnerabilities, related to unpatched services, in vendor maintained systems. What the review of the exceptions shows is that this may be a pervasive issue with vendor managed systems and the successful penetration of the system may be correlated to this particular exception. As you can see, this review can help feed information into other areas of your assessment as the results may magnify a risk or lower the confidence level of a stated control or compensating control.

Review of Security Metrics

Security metrics are a good source of information for identifying deviations in normal security control implementations. As we mentioned in the data collection phases, security metrics can vary widely from organization to organization; however, some common metrics that are helpful in determining potential risk would be:

- Various Network Performance Statistics.
- Access Control and Access Control Review statistics.
- Security Events and Incidents.
- Vulnerability and Patch Management Statistics.
- Security Exceptions.
- Security Device Statistics (AV, IPS, etc).

Aside from metrics being different from organization to organization, the targets for what each company considers appropriate also differ. For example,

We noted that there is consistently a high number of malware related events reported by the organization's users every reporting period even though the organization uses a commercial anti-malware suite.

We also noted that there are a consistent number of unpatched vulnerabilities which do not appear to decrease over time.

This analysis could be an indication that somewhere there is an issue in the current process or mechanism and such areas might be worth an additional review. For example, in this particular review, it might be worth noting if there were any deficiencies or gaps in terms of host based security controls as well as the organizations patch management process.

THE REAL WORLD

Jane is feeling pretty cross eyed after locking herself away and spending the better part of a week going through the documents that she obtained during her data collection activities. She was heavily focused on identifying observations based on review of the documents, creating her threat and vulnerability catalogs as well as corresponding risk scenarios, and computing risk for all the systems within the scope of her review.

As a result of all her hard work Jane is now armed with:

- A spreadsheet of all findings collected from her document reviews.
- Multiple spreadsheets of risk scores for all risk scenarios for all systems.

Jane finally has an opportunity to stand back and reflect on where she is at in the process and thinks "Wow, I have a lot of information!" While grabbing some coffee and reflecting on the process she realizes she still hasn't figured out the best method for communicating the risk to her boss. For now, all she really has is a bunch of sentences taken from various reports and a bunch of numbers in several worksheets. She has the feeling she is close but knows that she still has to do some more work to make it into something useable.

Jane knows that one of the questions her boss will ask her is "Can you tell me what the highest risks are for our HIS?" Jane remembers seeing a matrix in ISO27005 that is intended to help practitioners to sort risks into Low, Medium, and High categories and thinks that will be a perfect tool to use to help her start structuring her data. Jane remembers seeing a matrix in ISO27005 that is intended to help practitioners sort risks into Low, Medium, and High categories and thinks that will be a perfect tool to use to help her start structuring the data. Since the HIS is considered by everyone, including her boss, to be the most important system to the organization she decides to start on that one first. Following this process she is quickly able to identify the high risk scenarios for the HIS. Seeing how easy it is she quickly completes the process for the other in-scope systems as well. She realizes that her structured approach is really starting to pay off and that the hard work she put in up front is definitely making things easier towards the tail end of the process.

Always wanting to be cautious Jane realizes that she should try to validate some of the risks that have been categorized as High. To do this she goes back to the system profile and the control information related to the system that was captured in the survey and starts documenting the rationale for why each of the high risk findings is valid. Though she knows that this step is not necessary, she is pretty sure that some opinionated people within the organization will likely challenge her scoring and doing this level of documentation at this point, while the analysis is fresh in her head, will really help her defend her findings. Knowing that it's a when and not an if that she'll be questioned, she is going to keep her analysis as a quick and easy way to provide explanations and rationales for each of the high risk scenarios that she identified. She knows this is going to be a lot of work so grabs some more coffee and gets started. She starts her analysis for the first High risk issue for the HIS system which is the risk of possible unchecked data alteration. Reviewing the survey results she notes that the HIS system is noted as being a business critical system and that in the controls section of the survey it was noted that the systems is currently without proper auditing and logging controls. This assessment confirms the results of the risk calculation and subsequent categorization of high risk and she is able to jot down her notes to support that conclusion for future use and support. As she works through the process for each risk she realizes that it is going to be very easy for her to defend all of her conclusions and easily answer questions related to how or why she categorized things a certain way.

After validating all her system specific risk rankings she decides it is a good time to go back and look at the observations listing that she put together during her document review. Although she knows that she could have performed this earlier she felt that identifying risks at a system level would be helpful in her organization risk review and after completing her system review she feels that she made the right choice. Now she can use the information that she derived from her system specific risk review to help her support her organizational review. Digging up the spreadsheet of observations that she compiled while reviewing all the assessments, reports, metrics and other documents that she obtained she decides that she'll start by grouping the findings together based on common themes. The first observation she reviews is related to the results of a third party penetration testing report where the testers were able to compromise the hospital network by exploiting vulnerabilities in vendor managed systems. The second observation she reviews was related to her analysis of bi-monthly vulnerability scanning results where she saw that the vendor segments of the network had an unusually high number of vulnerabilities. Looks like she has struck gold right off the bat and she writes a risk scenario reflecting that there is a high likelihood for system intrusion due to lack of patching on vendor systems. She continues reviewing all her observations and creates common risk scenarios for the rest of her identified issues.

Jane now has a list of useable findings but she knows that she will have to put them together in a neat and orderly way that can be presented to stakeholders. Jane feels pretty good about her progress and knows she is getting close to the end of completing her first Information Security Risk Assessment and that she will be able to easily defend her conclusions.

Risk Prioritization and Risk Treatment

At this point the risk analysis is complete. By now, we should have a good understanding of the information security risks to our systems and the organization. In the next chapter, we will be combining this information into a structured format and start compiling risk treatment plans for each risk.

Information Security Risk Assessment: Risk Prioritization and Treatment

6

INFORMATION IN THIS CHAPTER:

- Organizational Risk Prioritization and Treatment
- System Specific Risk Prioritization and Treatment
- Issues Register

INTRODUCTION

In this chapter we will consolidate and summarize the risks based on the organizational and system specific risks that we have identified in the processes outlined in the previous chapter. Although a separate activity, the practitioner should consider this process as a sub-process of the overall risk analysis process. This part of the risk assessment process is focused on compiling all analysis conducted and presenting it in a structured manner. In fact, the deliverables created after following this process could be considered the "true" deliverables of the whole information security risk assessment process.

The main objective of the processes outlined in this chapter is to be able to present the risks identified in an orderly and prioritized manner. So far we have interpreted the various figures and numbers, reviewed documents, documented our analysis and identified "high risk" items. Now, imagine that at this point in time, you were asked by your boss what the main risks to the organization are? How would you structure and present your answer?

This chapter is focused on providing you an approach to structuring these answers. This chapter focuses on methods for conveying the results of a complex process in a simple yet accurate manner in the form of a "risk register." Remember, it is not enough that you have performed all this work and analyzed all the risk data it is imperative that you be able present the results of all your work in a clear and structured manner especially to the stakeholders of the organization. Failing to clearly communicate the results of the work performed and the methods that were used to derive the results could significantly impact the success of the current assessment as well as future assessments. It is not enough that an assessor provides the stakeholders a bunch of spreadsheets and a list of observations and notes from the process. All of the information and ultimately the work that you did must be presented in a manner that would be easily understandable for those who will need to make decisions about how to address these risks.

Technically, a risk assessment, by its very nature is only meant to "assess" risks; however, we have always found it helpful to provide treatment recommendations for the identified risks. This does not necessarily imply that the assessor should lay out a full-fledged treatment plan for each risk; a high-level recommendation on how to potentially treat the risk can go a long way in helping the stakeholders to place the risk and the actionable items regarding that risk into perspective. Another key part of providing recommendations is to be able clearly present and indicate common actions items and recommendations that address multiple risks or areas of risk.

At the end of this chapter, you will know how to prepare a "risk register" or a compilation of risks derived from the previously accomplished activities. A risk register is really just a list of all the risks that were identified throughout the risk assessment process. This register will be one of the most used references for people trying to understand and address the results of the risk assessment. Although other documents and notes have been created throughout the process this particular deliverable will probably be the most important and will likely serve as a cornerstone of support for discussions after the risk assessment has been completed.

ORGANIZATIONAL RISK PRIORITIZATION AND TREATMENT

In the previous chapter we performed an analysis of organizational risk. As mentioned previously, this form of analysis is a little more unstructured when compared to the system based risk analysis. This is primarily because organizational risk is highly dependent on what sources of information an assessor has access to. We provided several examples of information that can be used for organization level assessments such as:

- Review of Security Threats and Trends.
- Review of Audit Findings.
- Review of Security Incidents.
- Review of Security Exceptions.
- Review of Security Metrics.

In order to for us to properly provide a good example of a risk register for this section, let's assume we have conducted the risk analysis as directed in the previous chapter and create some hypothetical scenarios for a hospital for purposes of working on an example:

Review of Security Threats and Trends

- Based on our analysis, we noted that an emerging trend that the organization appears to have potential exposure to is related to a rise in mobile attack vectors. The exposure to this risk was determined due to a noted increase in the number of employees, especially physicians, using mobile devices to access patient data and hospital information. Based on reviews of current security trends from different security research and publications mobile security risks are increasing at an exponential rate. Contributing factors for this increase are the proliferation of mobile based attack vectors such as mobile malware as well as the natural predisposition of mobile devices to be easily lost or stolen. Frequent discussions amongst senior medical and executive staff about expanding the use of mobile devices within the hospital as well as the possibility of rolling out a "Bring Your Own Device" initiative in the near future make this a risk worth considering for the organization. Improper implementation of expanded mobile device use could lead to possible unauthorized access to hospital information systems as well as data loss.

Review of Audit Findings

- A review of several IT audit and compliance reports from the previous year indicate weaknesses in several areas:

    1. System specific deficiencies concerning the lack of password complexity in a key system containing electronic Protected Health Information (ePHI) based on an IT Access Control Review. During our assessment we noted that this is more of a system specific issue and the system in question is covered in our system specific review so will not be included in the organizational review as an organization wide risk.
    2. Vulnerabilities in vendor maintained systems that led to compromise of the internal network through a Penetration Test. As shown and demonstrated by the penetration test, this weakness could lead to compromise of the whole network including systems containing sensitive patient information. From an organizational perspective, this particular observation could indicate extensive use of vendor systems and immature controls around the governance of those systems.

Review of Security Incidents

- A review of security incident data collected over the past year shows that a large number of the incidents documented were related to some form of phishing or social engineering attack. Either a user provided their user name and credentials or clicked on a malicious link or attachment. This behavior could potentially lead to unauthorized access to hospital systems. From an organizational perspective, this particular observation could indicate a lack of security awareness on the part of the organization's users which could indicate a potentially weak security awareness campaign or lack of security training.

- There were also several incidents noted that resulted in data loss. These data loss incidents were accidental or non-malicious. Some of these incidents included misplaced portable media and data emailed to wrong recipients. Though there were not many occurrences, these represent high risk incidents as the data was sensitive patient information. From an organizational perspective, this particular observation could be indicative of a lack of an overarching data loss prevention initiative or program.

Review of Security Exceptions

- A review of current open security policy exceptions reveal that a large number of exceptions come from vendor-managed systems and is associated with the lack of ability to frequently patch the systems. Based on the information in the security exceptions, there are multiple systems that appear to have operating systems that have low patch levels since the vendors claim that patching would have an adverse effect on the application. This could potentially lead to compromise of these vendor-managed systems. From an organizational perspective, this particular observation could indicate that there are immature controls around the governance of vendor systems.

Review of Security Metrics

- A review of help desk reports and security metrics show that there has been a high number of malware related events reported and tracked over the past year. These could potentially lead to unauthorized access to hospital systems or cause disruptions of services. From an organizational perspective, this observation could indicate a gap in the current enterprise anti-virus and anti-malware solution.
- Vulnerability scanning metrics show that there are a high number of unpatched vulnerabilities within organizational systems. Further research shows that these appear to be the same unpatched systems associated with the vendor managed systems documented in the security exceptions. These vulnerabilities could lead to a compromise of the network as was reflected in the penetration testing report. From an organizational perspective, this observation could indicate several things; the extensive use of vendor systems, immature controls around the governance of those systems, and potentially a gap in the organizations vulnerability management process.

As mentioned, the notes and observations above are based on our hypothetical analysis of a mid-sized hospital. Let's try to extract the essence of each of these observations above to single "risk statements":

1. Mobile Attacks—The organization is facing increasing exposure to mobile attack vectors that could potentially lead to unauthorized access to the hospital network and possible data loss due to the increasing frequency of mobile device use in conducting company business.

2. Security Gaps in Vendor Managed Systems—Potential compromise of hospital network and systems due to vulnerabilities in vendor managed systems.
3. Phishing and Social Engineering—Susceptibility of the organizations users to phishing and social engineering attacks leading to unauthorized access to hospital systems.
4. Data Loss—Insecure or unauthorized transmission of sensitive information without adequate protection increases the likelihood of accidental or intentional data loss of ePHI and other regulated data.
5. Malware—Open Internet filtering rules and the inability of current anti-virus technology to detect polymorphic malware increases the susceptibility of the organization to malware based attacks which could lead to unauthorized access, loss of data, or disruption of service.

Now that we have identified key organizational risks, our next step is to propose high-level recommendations or "initiatives" that would help us address these risks. Let's go over them one by one:

1. Mobile Attacks:
   a. Mobile Device Management.
   b. Security Awareness.
   c. Data Loss Prevention Technology.
2. Security Gaps in Vendor Managed Systems:
   a. Vendor System Security Requirements.
   b. Vendor System Network Isolation.
3. Phishing and Social Engineering:
   a. Security Awareness.
   b. Malware Protection Controls.
   c. Data Loss Prevention Technology.
4. Data Loss:
   a. Data Loss Prevention Technology.
   b. Security Awareness.
   c. Encryption.
5. Malware:
   a. Malware Protection Controls.

Let's go over each of the proposed initiatives in more detail: Looks to be an extra space between the Le and t of the Let's as the first word in the sentence.

1. Mobile Device Management—This is a broad initiative intended to tackle a broad risk. This initiative could include the procurement of a mobile device management suite that will help manage, secure, and standardize controls around the increasing number of mobile devices in the enterprise.
2. Security Awareness—Many of the risks presented above could be reduced through a robust security awareness program. Though the organization may already have a program in place, enhancements could be made to include topics such as data loss, phishing/social engineering, and mobile device use since they appear to be some of the top risks to the organization.

3. Data Loss Prevention—As data loss is one organizational risk identified, data loss prevention will obviously be an important initiative for a hospital due to HIPAA concerns. This is a very broad initiative and could include a myriad of sub initiatives. In this case based on the review, it appears that this initiative should initially focus on media handling and email as these vectors were noted in the security incident review.

4. Malware Protection Controls—Often times, one of the most basic controls that an organization would have is host-based protection such as anti-virus. However, if statistics or review of security incidents shows that malware appears to be a problem, it may be time to review the current solution for deficiencies or implementation flaws, or evaluate the need to augment the current solution. There are also new technologies that may be introduced into the organization, such as mobile devices, which could benefit from malware protection controls but may not have such technology installed.

5. Vendor Security Requirements—Since a major risk was identified on vendor managed systems and was successfully exploited in a third party assessment, it is important to ensure the systems that vendors introduce into the network have the proper security controls in place. These controls could include the implementation of a more comprehensive vendor technology onboarding process and a more stringent enforcement of security requirements for vendor systems.

6. Network Isolation—Often times, there are situations that an organization just cannot control. For example, in this specific case, there were vendors that requested an exception to hospital patching requirements. This may be due to the fact that the vendor applications do not support the patch or upgrade. It is not sufficient to just allow the vulnerability to exist and proper mitigation strategies need to be deployed. One such strategy is isolating the systems that are high risk because of these gaps in their security controls. In this case, whenever vendor systems or even non-vendor systems are unable to comply with the organization's security standards they could be separated from other systems that are compliant.

We have always found that a useful way to present the organizational risks and initiatives in one view is to create a matrix. Since many of the remediation initiatives somewhat overlap and cover multiple risks, a matrix view is a better way to visualize the treatment options:

Organizational Risk					
Recommendation/ Treatment Initiative	Mobile Attacks	Security Gaps in Vendor Systems	Phishing and Social Engineering	Data Loss	Malware
Mobile Device Management	X				
Security Awareness	X	X	X	X	X
Data Loss Prevention	X		X	X	
Malware Protection Controls	X				X

Organizational Risk					
Recommendation/ Treatment Initiative	Mobile Attacks	Security Gaps in Vendor Systems	Phishing and Social Engineering	Data Loss	Malware
Vendor Security Requirements		X			
Network Isolation		X			

The columns in this table show the various risks (mobile attacks, security gaps, etc.) while the rows lists down the different remediation initiatives. This table is helpful in prioritizing some of the organizational initiatives based on the risks that the initiative is trying to address. For example, looking at the table horizontally, all of the risks would benefit from some kind of security awareness initiative. Taking on a security awareness initiative is fairly straightforward and addresses, at least in part, multiple risks; however, depending on the size and complexity of the organization the cost and difficulty of putting together an effective training and awareness program could be very difficult. Even recognizing that this could be a difficult initiative, since it addresses multiple risk areas, this should be considered as one of the first initiatives to implement. Another initiative with a broad reaching effect across several risk areas is data loss prevention; however, as any seasoned security professional will tell you it can be markedly more difficult to roll out an end-to-end data loss prevention program than a security awareness program. Adjusting our view and looking at it vertically, you would see that addressing mobile risks would probably take the most effort, as it requires multiple initiatives.

SYSTEM SPECIFIC RISK PRIORITIZATION AND TREATMENT

In the last chapter, we performed a review of system specific risks. As part of the review, we categorized each risk for the systems being reviewed by using a risk threshold chart as illustrated below. This allowed us to categorize each risk into buckets of HIGH, MEDIUM, and LOW:

		Likelihood				
Impact		1	2	3	4	5
	1	1	2	3	4	5
	2	2	4	6	8	10
	3	3	6	9	12	15
	4	4	8	12	16	20
	5	5	10	15	20	25

Area	Risk Classification
Black	High Risk
Grey	Moderate Risk
White	Low Risk

By utilizing this technique, we were able to prioritize the high risk items for remediation. This does not mean that only HIGH risk items should be remediated. We use this risk classification method as more of a prioritization technique and what would subsequently be targeted for remediation based on this analysis is based on the organization's risk acceptance process. Some organizations may only ever address high risk items while others may choose to address all risks to some extent. For purposes of discussion, our example will mimic a company that is only going to address high risk items.

In the previous chapter, we introduced a risk threshold table that allowed us to categorize the risk based on the risk score. As seen in the sample table, a score of 15 falls within the HIGH risk category based on the risk threshold table:

Application: Hospital Information System				
Threat (Agent and Action)		**Vulnerability**	**Risk Score**	**Risk Classification**
Users	Eavesdropping and Interception of data	Lack of transmission encryption leading to interception of unencrypted data	10	Moderate
External Intruders, Malicious Insiders, Malicious Code	System intrusion and unauthorized system access	Possible Weak Passwords due to lack of password complexity controls	10	Moderate
Users	Denial of user actions or activity	Untraceable user actions due to generic accounts	10	Moderate
Malicious Insider, Users	Unchecked data alteration	Lack of logging and monitoring controls	15	High
Non-Specific, Natural	Loss of power	Lack of redundant power supply	10	Moderate
Natural	Equipment damage or destruction due to natural causes (fire, water, etc.)	Lack of environmental controls	5	Low

After categorizing all the risks, what we did next was to identify ALL high risk items for all of the systems reviewed. In the previous chapter, analysis of our hypothetical scenario led to the creation of this table:

Threat Agent	**Threat Action**	**Vulnerability**	**Affected Systems**
Users	Eavesdropping and Interception of data	Lack of transmission encryption leading to interception of unencrypted data	Email, Imaging
Malicious Insider, Users	Unchecked data alteration	Lack of logging and monitoring controls	HIS

Threat Agent	Threat Action	Vulnerability	Affected Systems
External Intruders, Malicious Insiders, Malicious Code	System intrusion and unauthorized system access	Possible Weak Passwords due to lack of password complexity controls	HR Payroll

These are only hypothetical scenarios used for the purposes of the example and do not necessarily represent the results you may see within your organization. Typically, a practitioner would end up with quite a few threat and vulnerability pairs but for the purposes of the discussions in this chapter, we will assume that these are the only high risk items identified. Like we did with the organizational assessment, let's try to extrapolate the essence of the table above into single "risk statements" based on some hypothetical scenarios:

1. Disclosure of Transmitted Sensitive Data—Potential risk of interception of data and disclosure due to the lack of transmission encryption controls in several key systems (Email and Imaging). The current Email system does not support encryption functionality while the Imaging system transfers data via FTP over the internal network including the Wide Area Network.
2. Data Alteration—Potential unchecked data alteration could occur due to the lack of logging and monitoring controls within the HIS system. The HIS system currently does not have any level of logging or monitoring turned on.
3. System Intrusion—Potential system intrusion and unauthorized access due to lack of password complexity controls in a key system (HR Payroll). The current HR Payroll system does not enforce password complexity.

As we did in the organizational review, our next step is to propose high-level recommendations and initiatives that would help us address these system specific risks. In this case we will have:

1. Disclosure of Transmitted Sensitive Data:
   a. Email Encryption.
   b. Secure FTP Infrastructure.
   c. Security Awareness.
2. Data Alteration:
   a. Logging and Monitoring.
3. System Intrusion:
   a. Password Complexity Enforcement.
   b. Security Awareness.

Your ability to address system specific risks may often be highly dependent on the capabilities of the system. Sometimes, the assessor may not have enough expertise to provide a comprehensive recommendation and remediation plan for the system. As an example, for the lack of encryption functionality in the email system, the assessor may not know if it is just a matter of upgrading the existing system or implementing a completely new system to provide the required functionality. So typically, for system specific recommendations, we recommend that the practitioner use the following process for recommending solutions:

1. Current State Survey—Perform a survey and in-depth analysis of the current controls in place to address the specific risk for the system and the capability of the system to accommodate additional controls if they are required. Using the email system as an example, a good approach for following up on the risk would be to get in touch with the system owners and determine what, if any, options the system has for providing email encryption.
2. Solution Determination—After the survey is completed and the practitioner has a better understanding of the current capabilities of the system, the next step is to determine a solution. This is where the detailed planning for remediating the risk is performed.
3. Implementation—Finally, once a solution has been identified, we implement the solution as part standard operational processes or via a special project.

The takeaway here is that at this point the assessor does not need to provide a detailed recommendation for each of the system risks since this is technically a "risk assessment." The assessor can stay at a high level and provide simple recommendations such as:

1. Explore email encryption solutions for current email system.
2. Consider replacing FTP with SFTP infrastructure.
3. Consider expanded database logging and monitoring solution for HIS.
4. Explore possible password complexity enforcement for systems.
5. Consider additional security awareness training regarding protecting transmissions and utilizing complex passwords.

As was done with the organizational assessment, a useful way to present the system risks and remediation initiatives together is to create a matrix such as the following:

	Email Encryption Initiative	SFTP Infra- structure Initiative	Logging and Monitoring Initiative	Password Complexity Enforcement Initiative	Security Awareness Initiative
Disclosure of Transmit- ted Sensitive Information	Email System	Imaging System			Email System
Unchecked Data Alteration			HIS		
System Intrusion				HR Payroll	HR Payroll

Similar to the table we built for organizational risk we see that the rows are the common risks for the systems and the columns are the initiatives. The content of the cells are the specific systems that are affected by the risk. In this example, you can see that the email system and imaging system are both affected by lack of transmission encryption; however, the initiatives to address this specific issue differ. In the context of our hypothetical scenario, the email system could require a functionality upgrade while for the imaging system, it could be a roll out of an SFTP initiative. These are totally different initiatives but ultimately are trying to address the same type of risk.

Note that later on in the process, additional fields can be added to the table including timeframes for remediation so that the document can become a progress/initiative tracking document as well.

ISSUES REGISTER

Now let's put together the final risk register, our main deliverable, using the tables and lists we created above. For creation of this register, you can use the following format:

Risk ID	
Risk Title	
Scope	
Risk Narrative	
Risk Impact	
Rationale	
Treatment	

1. Risk Identifier—A simple identifier such as a number to help with referencing specific issues.
2. Risk Title—Short title for the risk.
3. Scope—If the risk pertains to an organizational or system specific risk.
4. Risk Impact—A short narrative regarding the potential impact of the risk.
5. Rationale—Items or factors which led to identifying the risk.
6. Treatment—The recommendation proposed by the assessor.

Typically, for purposes of prioritizing our efforts on those areas that have the broadest impact, we start with organizational level risks. With that thought in mind we'll put together our risk register for our organizational risks:

Risk ID	1
Risk Title	Mobile Attacks
Scope	Organizational
Risk Narrative	The organization is facing increasing exposure to mobile attack vectors due to the increasing frequency of mobile device use in conducting company business.

Risk ID	1
Risk Impact	Possible disclosure of sensitive information or unauthorized access to hospital information systems through mobile attack vectors like mobile malware or the accidental loss or theft of the mobile device. Loss of patient information or breach in information systems could lead to significant fines and penalties.
Rationale	• Increasing use of mobile devices in the hospital especially by physicians. • Increasing trend towards mobile attack vectors based on current research and industry reports.
Treatment	Propose initiatives for: • Mobile Device Management. • Security Awareness. • Data Loss Prevention.

Risk ID	2
Risk Title	Security Gaps in Vendor Managed Systems
Scope	Organizational
Risk Narrative	Potential compromise of hospital network and systems due to vulnerabilities in vendor managed systems.
Risk Impact	Possible disclosure of sensitive information or unauthorized access to hospital information systems through weaknesses in vendor managed systems. Loss of patient information or breach in information systems could lead to significant fines and penalties.
Rationale	• Noted multiple security exceptions related to vendor managed systems. • Third party penetration test gained domain administrator access to the internal hospital network due to weaknesses in vendor managed systems.
Treatment	Propose initiatives for: • Vendor Security Requirements. • Network Isolation.

Risk ID	3
Risk Title	Phishing and Social Engineering
Scope	Organizational
Risk Narrative	Susceptibility of the organizations users to phishing and social engineering attacks leading to unauthorized access to hospital systems.

Risk ID	3
Risk Impact	Possible unauthorized access and use of hospital resources leading to increased utilization and degradation of hospital services (e.g. spamming). Targeted attacks could lead to disclosure of sensitive information leading to fines and penalties as well as reputational impacts.
Rationale	• Majority of recorded security incidents were related to successful compromise of hospital user accounts due to phishing and social engineering attacks.
Treatment	Propose initiatives for: • Security Awareness. • Malware Protection controls. • Data Loss Prevention.

Risk ID	4
Risk Title	Data Loss
Scope	Organizational
Risk Narrative	Potential accidental loss of ePHI and regulated data through email or removable media.
Risk Impact	Possible loss of patient information that could lead to significant fines or penalties as well as reputational impacts.
Rationale	• Noted security incidents of data loss via accidental email transmission and loss of removable devices.
Treatment	Propose initiatives for: • Data Loss Prevention. • Security Awareness.

Risk ID	5
Risk Title	Malware
Scope	Organizational
Risk Narrative	Susceptibility of the organization to malware based attacks that could lead to unauthorized access or disruption of hospital network and systems
Risk Impact	Possible unauthorized access and use of hospital resources leading to increased utilization and degradation of hospital services (e.g. spamming). Targeted attacks could lead to disclosure of sensitive information leading to fines, penalties as well as reputational impacts.
Rationale	• Security metrics show high numbers of malware related security events reported through help desk.
Treatment	Propose initiatives for: • Enhanced Malware Protection.

Now, we'll do the same thing for the system specific risks and create risk registers for them:

Risk ID	6
Risk Title	Disclosure of Transmitted Sensitive Data
Scope	• Email System. • Imaging System.
Risk Narrative	Potential risk of interception of data and disclosure due to the lack of protection of transmitted sensitive data in several key systems that transmit ePHI data. Regulatory requirements dictate that transmissions of ePHI be encrypted.
Risk Impact	Possible loss of patient information that could lead to significant fines or penalties as well as reputational impacts.
Rationale	• The current Email system does not support encryption functionality. • Imaging system transfers data via FTP within the internal network.
Treatment	Propose initiatives for: • Email Encryption. • Secure FTP Infrastructure. • Security Awareness.

Risk ID	7
Risk Title	Unchecked Data Alteration
Scope	• HIS.
Risk Narrative	Potential for unchecked data alteration due to lack of logging and monitoring controls in a key systems.
Risk Impact	Inaccurate data due to unchecked alterations could potentially lead to integrity issues and pose significant risks to patient care, diagnosis, billing, or other core hospital processes.
Rationale	• The HIS system currently does not have logging and monitoring enabled.
Treatment	Propose initiatives for: • Logging and Monitoring.

Risk ID	8
Risk Title	System Intrusion
Scope	• HR Payroll.
Risk Narrative	Potential system intrusion and unauthorized access due to lack of password complexity controls in a key system.
Risk Impact	Unauthorized access could lead to significant confidentiality and integrity issues such as disclosure of PII and even changes to payroll data.

Risk ID	8
Rationale	• The current HR Payroll system does not enforce password complexity.
Treatment	Propose initiatives for: • Password Complexity Enforcement. • Security Awareness.

As you can see, the registers are written in a narrative format instead of a "structured" checklist. This makes it easier for stakeholders who are not familiar with the process. The registers are structured in a way that allows the practitioner to easily answer the following questions:

1. What are the risks to our organization?
2. Can you tell us more about the risk?
3. Why should we be concerned about this risk?
4. How did you arrive at this conclusion?
5. What key systems have these risks?

Let's use risk number 2 above as an example for explaining organizational risk items. Using the risk register for risk number 2, we can easily provide a quick overview of the risk to the stakeholders:

Based on our review, we noted that security vulnerabilities in systems connected to our network that are managed by vendors pose a risk to our organization. These security vulnerabilities could lead to unauthorized access to these systems and could even go as far as contribute to compromise of the whole hospital network. In fact, third party assessors were actually able to gain domain admin access to our internal network by leveraging vulnerabilities in a specific vendor managed system. We recommend reviewing and enforcing our security requirements for vendor managed systems and isolating vendor systems that do not conform to our security requirements. We suspect that the issue associated with security vulnerabilities being present on vendor managed equipment indicates that the security programs of the various vendors are not adequate which means that the hospital may be exposed to other risks depending on the services provided by the vendors.

Let's use risk number 6 above as an example for explaining system specific risk items:

Based on our review, we noted that the email system and Imaging system have potential confidentiality and information disclosure issues because data is transmitted in clear text making it susceptible to interception. The current email system does not support any encryption functionality and the Imaging system uses FTP, which transmits data in clear text. Both systems transmit ePHI so if the data was intercepted it would lead to a breach of the data and could result in regulatory fines and loss of customer goodwill. Options for supporting email encryption and the secure transfer of files via a SFTP infrastructure to support internal sensitive data transfers should be evaluated. These technical implementations should be augmented through additional focused security awareness training on the proper transmission of sensitive data.

As you can see, by taking the time to build the tables for each risk, it becomes easy for the practitioner to summarize the risk, factors leading to the identification of the risk, and potential remediation steps. This is important when discussing the risk items with executives, who for all intents and purposes, could probably care less how much analysis was performed in order for you to formulate those few sentences.

The bottom line here is that we should be able to answer the following questions for any of our stakeholders: What is their risk? And what should they do about these risks?

Finally, though these registers are at the heart of the risk analysis process and most likely will be the deliverables that will be reviewed by the organizations stakeholders, it is important to document everything that led to the conclusions provided above. Also note that these issues registers will ultimately be a record of the organizations risks over time. As such, it is recommended that they be placed in a central location (e.g. a Sharepoint portal, a database) so that they can be tracked over time. This centralized documentation and tracking will allow for easier reporting around the status of action items from assessment to assessment. In the next chapter, we will present a report format that can be used to document the whole risk analysis process.

THE REAL WORLD

With all the analyses she has performed, Jane now feels pretty confident that she is ready to put her findings down on paper.

At this point, from a security stand-point, she feels like she pretty much knows the top risks for the organization and important systems. She just needs a way to present her findings and recommendations in a structured but easily understandable way.

She knows that this is really important because ultimately, all the work that she did will really come down to how she presents it.

She starts off with documenting an issues register to capture all her observations. She knows quite a bit about issues registers because in her previous job, she was on the receiving end of many of these from the internal and external auditors of the company. Now, it's her turn to make one!

Based on the techniques that she utilized in the previous chapter, she starts documenting and itemizing each and every one of her findings. She starts off with organizational level findings first and then works her way to the system specific findings.

For each risk item, she decided that capturing the following information will help convey the nature of the risk:

- A unique issue ID so that she can easily reference the risk.
- A title or a short description of the risk.
- The scope, whether it's a high level organizational finding or any specific systems affected by the risk.
- A risk narrative or a long description of the risk.
- The impact of the risk.
- The rationale why it was included in the risk register.

- Some high-level recommendations.

Since she already identified the risks in her previous activities, this really just became a process of writing the risks down into a specific format.

Ultimately, she lists down eight risk areas. Five of which affect the entire organization and three of which were specific to certain systems.

One of the key areas that she added to her risk register was a "rationale" section in order to better substantiate her findings. She hopes that a person reading the register could easily refer to this rationale to better understand her decision process as to why she considered the item a risk to the organization.

After completing the listing she feels very confident about each of the items as they are supported by various documents as well as an analysis of the data that she collected.

Another item that she worked on extensively during this time are the recommendations for addressing each risk. This was a tough exercise because she felt that at this time, it was not feasible to give very detailed and specific action plans. One of the items she was reviewing was related to her observation that data loss is a big risk to the organization. She knows that at a high level, a data loss prevention initiative is needed. Determining how long it will take to implement a whole data loss prevention initiative is going to take input from various parties and will require extensive project planning to discuss feasibility, possible schedules, resourcing and budget. Recognizing this she decides to keep her recommendations at a very high level. She knows that once the findings are communicated to the necessary stakeholders, a more thorough risk treatment initiative can be completed.

In preparing her recommendations, aside from matching up the recommendation with specific risks, she decides to also create a matrix that cross references all risks and initiatives in a way that will allow for easy identification of which recommendations could apply to multiple risks. She knows that this view will make it easier to prioritize treatment areas since an initiative that can mitigate multiple areas would definitely be somewhere to focus efforts on.

Armed with a risk register, Jane feels that she's reached a significant milestone. Having gone through data collection and data analysis, she now has specific risks that she could easily substantiate and present to organizational stakeholders. Before she goes off showing this to everyone, she knows that she should properly document everything that she has done. Right now, she knows that if she just goes to her boss and shows him 8 risks that have been identified, it won't properly reflect all that work that she has put into the process. She realizes that she needs to put together a formal report. The good news is she has all the information she needs; however, she knows that putting together a structured report that will accurately communicate all her findings and reflect the work she has done is not necessarily going to be easy.

Information Security Risk Assessment: Reporting

7

INFORMATION IN THIS CHAPTER:

- Outline
- Risk Analysis Executive Summary
- Methodology
- Results
- Risk Register
- Report Template

INTRODUCTION

In an information security risk assessment, the compilation of all your results into the final information security risk assessment report is often as important as all the fieldwork that the assessor has performed. Some would even argue that it is the most important part of the risk assessment process. This is due to the fact that the final report and related derivative information (e.g. slide decks or summary memos) are the only deliverables that the stakeholders will see. It is essential to the credibility of your entire process that the final report accurately captures all the results and reflects all the time and effort that was put into the process.

Having a cohesive final report will allow the assessor to communicate findings clearly to the stakeholders, allowing them to understand how the findings were identified and ultimately, allow them to "buy" into the process enough to support action plans and remediation activities. A poorly written or structured report can bring into question the credibility of the assessor and ultimately invalidate much of the work that was performed.

This chapter is presented differently from the other chapters up to this point. What we will be providing in this chapter is a report template that an assessor can use in putting together a final information security risk assessment report. In presenting the template, we will be providing an outline first then we will go through each section of the outline. For each section, we will be providing sample content taken from the hypothetical scenarios that we discussed throughout the different chapters of this book.

Note that with all reports; you need to be cognizant of who the reader may be. In many cases the readers of the report, or information derived from the report, could be anyone from executives of the company to system administrators within IT. The sample report presented in this section is structured to allow the executives to gain sufficient information from the executive summary while detailed risk and mitigation discussions are covered in the detail of the report to allow those tasked with addressing risk to have a clear understanding of what was found.

OUTLINE

The report will consist of 6 main sections: Introduction, Methodology, Results, Issues Registers, Conclusion, and Appendices. Here is a quick description of each of these sections:

1. The Executive Summary—needs to provide the reader with answers to the following questions: What is this report? Who was this report written for? Why was this report written? Why is this report important to the organization? What are the findings?
2. Methodology—You don't just want to present the results of your assessment (although that is a key part of the report), it is important to accurately represent the effort that was put into the risk assessment process. Describing the methodology followed helps obtain buy-in from the reader. If the reader cannot understand how you derived your results they are more likely to challenge you. This section should identify the framework that was used (if any) and provide a step-by-step description of the methodology followed as well as the activities performed that support the methodology used.
3. Results—The results section presents the results, or references to the results, for each of the activities that were conducted for the risk assessment. This part of the report should include narratives and evidence on how the assessor ultimately derived the risk findings which will be presented in a consolidated format in the risk register.
4. Risk Register—The risk register is a part of the report that can be considered a standalone section of the report. This risk register may be passed around, independent of the report, as it is basically the list of all the findings that were identified through the entire process.
5. Conclusion—This section allows the assessor to provide their final opinion regarding the outcome of the risk assessment.
6. Appendices—The appendices are the supporting evidences and results for the report. This may include spreadsheets and various documents. This may end up being a rather large section since it may also contain evidence documents that are referenced in the Results section of the report. This is usually due to the fact that the computations and the subsequent results of the computations are too long to integrate into the report itself.

Based on these 6 sections, the actual outline of the information security risk assessment report will look similar to the following:

I. Executive Summary
II. Methodology:
    a. Organizational Assessment.
    b. System Specific Assessment.

III. Results:
    a. Organizational Assessment:
        i. Review of Emerging Threats and Trends.
        ii. Review of Third-Party Assessments.
        iii. Review of Security Incidents.
        iv. Review of Security Exceptions.
        v. Review of Security Metrics.
        vi. […].
        vii. Findings and Recommendations.

    b. System Specific Assessment:
        i. System Characterization.
        ii. Threat Identification.
        iii. Vulnerability Identification.
        iv. Impact Analysis.
        v. Control Analysis.
        vi. Likelihood Determination.
        vii. Risk Determination.
        viii. Control Recommendations.
        ix. Results Documentation.

IV. Risk Register
V. Conclusion
VI. Appendices

Of course, this outline can always be changed to better reflect the actual activities conducted during the risk assessment. For example, organizational assessment activities are relatively fluid depending on the sources available to the assessor so new sections can be added or removed depending on the activities performed. Another area that may change is the system specific assessment section which should be structured depending on the methodology that was used. In our example we relied heavily on the NIST information security risk assessment framework so the subsections of that section of our sample report map closely to NIST.

RISK ANALYSIS EXECUTIVE SUMMARY

A good executive summary is essential in any report. As is often the case, the stakeholders reading the information security risk assessment will likely only have a passing familiarity with the process. Sometimes, all they know is that it was conducted and this report reflects the results of the assessment. Thus it is important to provide several paragraphs of introduction and background in order to prime the reader for what will follow in the report.

Below are examples of several questions that an assessor may want to think about when writing an introduction to the information security risk assessment report:

1. What is an information security risk assessment?
2. What is an information security risk assessment used for?
3. Why did we perform an information security risk assessment?
4. What are the results of the risk assessment?

Here is an example of what a risk assessment introduction could look like based on our hypothetical scenario and organization (hospital) we have been using throughout the book:

> One of the most essential steps in protecting information is evaluating the security posture of an organization. One of the key methods to accomplish this goal is to perform periodic risk assessments of an organization's system threats and vulnerabilities. These assessments provide management measurable feedback as to the current state of information security within an organization, as well as provide a set of recommendations to mitigate identified security vulnerabilities.

> Under the provisions of the Health Insurance Portability and Accountability Act of 1996 (HIPAA), a covered entity, in accordance with 164.306 of the Security Rule, is required to conduct a Risk Analysis. As stated in section §164.308 of HIPAA's Administrative Safeguards (§164.308.a.1.ii.A), an organization shall "Conduct an accurate and thorough assessment of the potential risks and vulnerabilities to the confidentiality, integrity, and availability of electronic protected health information held by the covered entity."

> The US Department of Health and Human Services (HHS) has issued draft Guidance on Risk Analysis for covered entities and business associates. This is provided by HHS to guide organizations in assessing risk to the confidentiality, integrity and availability of electronic Patient Health Information (ePHI), and to fulfill its mandate to provide annual guidance on the most effective and appropriate technical safeguards for carrying out the HIPAA Security Rule standards.

> In an effort to comply with HIPAA and as general security best practice, the Information Security Office (ISO) has conducted a Risk Analysis of the organization's critical information systems.

> Throughout the process, we involved various stakeholders within the organization. These stakeholders include but are not limited to the CEO, CIO, COO, CFO, various department heads, IT managers, and system administrators among others.

> The risk assessment identified five organizational and three system-specific information security risks. The organizational risks were determined using a

risk determination process based on a high level organizational risk review that utilized an analysis of current information security trends, third-party assessments, and a review of various organizational documents, assessments, security metrics and statistics. Based on this review the organization appear to have a relatively high exposure to mobile attacks, social engineering, data loss, malware attacks, and vendor security gaps that could potentially lead to compromise, loss or disruption of the hospitals information systems and resources.

The system specific risks were determined by utilizing the NIST SP800-30 framework which quantifies risks based on likelihood, impact, and the current controls that are in place augmented by threat and vulnerability catalogs from ISO 27005. Based on this review, several critical information systems appear to have a relatively high exposure to disclosure of sensitive data, unchecked data alteration and system intrusion that could potentially affect the confidentiality, integrity and availability of the affected information systems and resources.

As you see in the example, we provided quick descriptions of what the report is about, the importance of a risk assessment, and more importantly, why the organization performed the assessment.

METHODOLOGY

As mentioned previously, aside from just presenting the results, it is important to accurately present the effort that was put into the risk assessment process. This section focuses on discussing how the risk assessment was conducted, which frameworks were used (if any), and which specific activities were involved throughout the whole risk assessment process. The methodology section should be broken down into two sections; the organizational section, and the system-specific section since both phases have different approaches. Below you will find an example of templates for each.

Organizational

A good way to describe the methodology for the organizational review is to list down the major initiatives and then match them with the specific activity performed. This should be fairly easy to do as the content for this section can be extracted from the activities that were discussed in the organizational section covered in Chapter 5.

Here's an example of what the content of the organizational review methodology section could look like based on the hypothetical scenario that we have used throughout the book:

The assessment of risk at an organizational level is at its heart a review of potential risks as it pertains to the organization as a whole. Organization level risk is not to be confused with system specific risk since it is focused on reviewing general risks to an organization at a strategic level. The following table provides a listing of all activities that were performed throughout the organizational risk assessment.

Step	Phase	Activities
1	Review of Security Threats	**1.** Interviews with executive management and the Information Security Officer. **2.** Various reports from third party vendors: a. Ponemon Institute Data Breach Studies. b. SANS Top Cyber Security Risks. c. Microsoft Security Intelligence Report. d. Symantec Internet Security Threat Report. e. Bluecoat Web Security Report. f. McAfee Threats Report. g. Sophos Security Threat Report. h. Symantec—A Window Into Mobile Device Security. **3.** Reports and statistics from various independent security groups: a. US-CERT. b. Local InfraGard Chapter. **4.** Reports and statistics from various regulatory bodies: a. United States Department of Health and Human Services (HHS). **5.** Security News and Forums: a. Security Focus. b. ThreatPost. c. DataLossDB.
2	Review of Audit Findings	**1.** Obtained available audit reports from the Internal Audit Department: a. IT Access Control Audit (External Auditor). b. HIPAA NIST SP800-66 Audit (Internal Auditor). c. Third Party Internal and External Penetration Testing (Security Consulting Company). **2.** Conducted review of the audit reports and determined current status of findings and applicability to security.
3	Review of Security Incidents	**1.** Obtained list of security incidents from the Information Security Officer. **2.** Interviewed the Information Security Officer regarding the details of the incidents obtained. **3.** Reviewed one years worth of security incidents and provided analysis of relevant risks based on the incidents.
4	Review of Security Metrics	**1.** Obtained available security metrics from the Information Security Officer. **2.** Interviewed the Information Security Officer to discuss the security metrics. **3.** Reviewed one years worth of metrics and provided analysis of relevant risks based on the metrics collected.

Step	Phase	Activities
5	Review of Security Exceptions	**1.** Obtained a list of security exceptions from the Information Security Officer.
		2. Interviewed the Information Security Officer to obtain additional details regarding specific security exceptions.
		3. Reviewed results and provided analysis of relevant risks based on interview and exceptions identified.
6	Analysis of Orga-nizational Risks	**1.** Review and consolidation of the various organizational risks that were derived from the previous activities.
		2. Had meetings with Information Security Officer to verify and validate the findings.
		3. Prepared and documented a final list of organizational risk.
7	Control Recom-mendations	**1.** Prepared the final list of organizational risk and recommendations.

As you can see, structuring everything in a table format provides an organized way for the reader to see how the organizational risk review was performed and what specific activities and sources supported the review.

System Specific

The narrative supporting the methodology used in the system specific review is dependent on which information security risk assessment framework was used to conduct the system based risk assessment. Therefore the assessor needs to outline here the activities that were conducted based on the specific framework that was followed. In the case of our hypothetical risk assessment, we followed NIST SP800-30 for the majority of the review so the example below will reflect the phases as it relates to that framework. We also used ISO27005 for some references so it is important that key factors from that standard are reflected in the methodology narrative. For purposes of reference, the phases and activities that are outlined in the table are simply the activities that were covered in Chapters 4 and 5.

> *The US Department of Health and Human Services (HHS) has issued draft* **Guidance on Risk Analysis** *for covered entities and business associates. This is provided by HHS to guide organizations in assessing risk to the confidentiality, integrity and availability of electronic Patient Health Information (ePHI), and to fulfill its mandate to provide annual guidance on the most effective and appropriate technical safeguards for carrying out the HIPAA Security Rule standards.*
>
> *According to the guidance provided by HHS: "There are numerous methods of performing risk analysis and there is no single method or "best practice" that guarantees compliance with the Security Rule. Some examples of steps that might be applied in a risk analysis process are outlined in* **NIST SP 800-30.***"*

This assessment utilized NIST SP800-30 as the standard framework for conducting the system specific risk assessment. NIST SP 800-30 is the Risk Management Guide for Information Technology Systems provided by the National Institute of Standards and Technology (NIST). NISP SP 800-30 represents one of the most broadly accepted US standards regarding information security risk assessment practices.

Another widely accepted risk management framework that was used as a supplementary resource during this assessment is ISO27005—Information Technology Security techniques—Information security risk management. The framework is derived heavily from NIST SP800-30 but includes standard information security threat and vulnerability catalogs which augments NIST's own catalog.

The following table provides a mapping of the NIST SP800-30 recommended phases against the actual activities that were performed for this risk assessment.

Step	Phase	Activities

1	System Characterization	1. Interviewed individuals with executive management responsibilities and asked them what, in their opinion, are the most important systems in the enterprise.
		 2. Obtained listings of various systems in the organization.
		 3. Performed scoping exercises with the CIO, system owners, and IT managers.
		 4. Made final system scoping decisions with the CIO. Limited the system risk assessment to three systems. (Note: Since this is a hypothetical scenario we have selected three systems; however, depending on the size of the organization, there may be a higher or lower number of systems.)
		 5. Sent questionnaires to system owners and various technical contacts around the organization. These included questions and inquiries regarding:
		   a. System Characteristics.
		   b. Security Controls.
		 6. Prepared a Data Collection Matrix (Spreadsheet) as a centralized repository for responses from questionnaires, and interviews.

2	Threat Identification	a. Noted that there was no existing vulnerability catalog. b. Reviewed NIST SP800-30 and ISO27005 (Annex A) threat catalogs. c. Discussed the list with the Information Security Officer and CIO. Customized the catalog based on input. d. Prepared a consolidated listing of common Information Security Threats that cover confidentiality, integrity, and availability.

Step	Phase	Activities
3	Vulnerability Identification	a. Noted that there was no existing vulnerability catalog.
		b. Prepared a vulnerability catalog based on current and potential vulnerability scenarios for the organization.
		c. Prepared a collection of Threat-Vulnerability Pairs based on the threat catalog from the previous step and common vulnerabilities associated with the threats.
4	Impact Analysis	a. Impact was determined based on various Confidentiality, Integrity, and Availability factors that were collected through the various surveys.
		b. Determined the Impact from all threats for each of the applications in scope.
5	Likelihood Determination	a. Likelihood was determined based on Exposure and Frequency. Exposure and Frequency values are somewhat subjective in nature and are largely based on the judgment of the practitioner.
		b. Exposure is the predilection of the system to the threat based on environmental factors.
		c. Frequency is the probability of the threat happening. For each system and each threat to the system, we determined the frequency value.
		d. Determined the final Likelihood value by multiplying Exposure and Frequency values.
6	Control Analysis	a. Matched appropriate control to each threat and vulnerability pair.
		b. For each control, we noted control maturity values using a 5 point scale.
7	Risk Determination	a. Determined inherent risk and residual risk.
		b. Residual Risk is the impact and likelihood tempered with a control value.
8	Control Recommendations	a. Provided recommended treatment options for risks identified.
9	Results Documentation	a. Provided documentation for the following: 1. Final Report. 2. Data Collection Matrix.

In the table above the phase column is fairly consistent with the phases outlined within NIST SP800-30. Most of the frameworks out there provide a lot of flexibility to the assessor as to what phases need to be completed as long as the objectives of the assessment are met. We point this out because the activities that correspond to the particular phase may be different from organization to organization; however, once established, they should remain consistent from assessment to assessment within the organization to allow for trending over time. It is important to note that some frameworks such as OCTAVE and FAIR may be more prescriptive. If you use one of the more prescriptive frameworks then the activities that will be documented under each phase should reflect the activities prescribed by the framework. You cannot say that you have aligned with a specific framework and then disregard key requirements of using that framework. If circumstances lead to deviations from the framework you should ensure that you document any such deviations, and the supporting rationale for the deviation, in case you are questioned.

RESULTS

The goal of the results section is to provide the information and evidence that lead to the findings documented in the risk register which is covered in the section after this one. Think of it as the "proof" of an equation. This is the place where the assessor can include all the rationale that lead to and support the findings of the information security risk assessment.

As with the methodology, the results section is broken into two distinct parts, the organizational analysis and the system-specific analysis. What follows below are examples of each.

Organizational Analysis

In this section, the assessor states proofs, evidence, and rationale in the form of observations that lead to the findings that have strategic implications to the organization. All the information presented in this section is derived from the activities performed in Chapter 6. Here's an example of what an organizational analysis could look like based on the hypothetical scenarios that we used throughout the book:

There are five primary activities involved in the organizational risk analysis. These activities include the following:

- *Review of Security Threats and Trends.*

- *Review of Audit Findings.*

- *Review of Security Incidents.*

- *Review of Security Exceptions.*

- *Review of Security Metrics.*

The following section consolidates the strategic findings collected during the various activities in this phase. Based on the key organizational risks identified in the risk assessment, several key security initiatives were proposed that would mitigate or remediate the strategic risks identified during the assessment.

The table below provides a cross reference for these proposed initiatives and the risk items that each initiative is meant to mitigate and remediate:

Risk Statement	Observation	Recommendation
Mobile Attacks. The organization is facing increasing exposure to mobile attack vectors due to the increasing frequency of mobile device use in conducting company business.	Based on our analysis, we noted that the organization appears to have potential exposures to mobile attack threat vectors. The exposure to this risk was determined due to a noted increase in the number of employees, especially physicians, using mobile devices to access patient data and hospital information. Based on reviews of current security trends from different security researchers and publications, mobile security risks are increasing at an exponential rate. Contributing factors for this increase are the proliferation of mobile-based attack vectors such as mobile malware as well as the natural predisposition of mobile devices to be easily lost or stolen. With frequent discussions about expanding the use of mobile devices within the hospital as well as the possibility of implementing a "Bring Your Own Device" initiative this appears to be a risk worth considering for the organization. Improper implementation of expanded mobile device use could lead to possible unauthorized access to hospital information systems as well as data loss.	Mobile Device Management, Security Awareness, Data Loss Prevention Technology
Security Gaps in Vendor Systems. Potential compromise of hospital network and systems due to vulnerabilities in vendor managed systems.	Vulnerability scanning metrics show that there are a high number of unpatched vulnerabilities within organizational systems. Further research shows that these appear to be the same unpatched systems associated with the vendor managed systems documented within filed security exceptions. These vulnerabilities could potentially lead to compromise of the network, as was demonstrated in a penetration test that was conducted. From an organizational perspective, this particular observation could indicate several things including: the extensive use of vendor systems, immature controls around the governance of those systems, and potentially a gap in the organizations vulnerability management process. Reviews of current open security policy exceptions reveal that a large number of exceptions come from vendor-managed systems and are associated with the lack of ability to frequently patch the systems. Based on the information in the security exceptions, there are multiple systems that appear to have operating systems that have low patch levels since the vendors claim that patching would have an adverse effect on the application. This could potentially lead to compromise of these vendor-managed systems. From an organizational perspective, this particular observation could indicate extensive use of vendor systems and immature controls around the governance of those systems. A penetration test done by an external party showed that hospital systems were able to be compromised and the avenue of compromise was via vendor maintained systems that were unpatched against common vulnerabilities. As demonstrated by the penetration test, this weakness could lead to compromise of the whole network including systems containing sensitive patient information. From an organizational perspective, this particular observation could indicate extensive use of vendor systems and immature controls around the governance of those systems.	Vendor System Security Requirements, Vendor System Network Isolation.

Continued

Risk Statement	Observation	Recommendation
Phishing and Social Engineering Susceptibility of the organization's users to phishing and social engineering attacks leading to unauthorized access to hospital systems.	A review of security incident data collected over the past year shows that a large number of the incidents documented were related to some form of phishing or social engineering attack. Either a user provided their user name and credentials or clicked on a malicious link or attachment as a result of being targeted with a phishing email. This behavior could potentially lead to unauthorized access to hospital systems. From an organizational perspective, this particular observation could indicate a lack of security awareness by the organization's users that could be directly related to a weak security awareness campaign or insufficient training initiatives.	Security Awareness, Malware Protection controls, Data Loss Prevention Technology
Data Loss Lack of DLP initiative and technology increases the likelihood of accidental or intentional data loss of ePHI and regulated data.	There were also several incidents noted that resulted in data loss. These data loss incidents were accidental or non-malicious. Some of these incidents included misplaced portable media and data emailed to wrong recipients. Though there were not many occurrences, these represent high-risk incidents, as the data lost or exposed was sensitive patient information. From an organizational perspective, this particular observation could indicate a lack of an overarching data loss prevention initiative or program within the organizations.	Data Loss Prevention Technology, Security Awareness, Encryption
Malware Susceptibility of the organization to malware based attacks.	A review of help desk reports and security metrics shows that there have been a high number of malware related events reported and tracked over the past year. These could potentially lead to unauthorized access to hospital systems or cause disruptions of services. From an organizational perspective, this particular observation could indicate a gap in the current enterprise anti-virus and malware solution.	Malware Protection controls

Organizational Risk

Recommendation / Treatment Initiative	**Risks**				
	Mobile Attacks	Security Gaps in Vendor Systems	Phishing and Social Engineering	Data Loss	Malware
Mobile Device Management	X				
Security Awareness	X	X	X		X
Data Loss Prevention	X		X	X	
Malware Protection Controls	X			X	X
Vendor Security Requirements		X			
Network Isolation		X			

You're probably already familiar with much of the content we've just outlined since it is derived from activities and deliverables cover in the previous chapter. The only difference is that in the earlier chapter the information was not presented in a more structured table format but rather in a narrative. As seen in the table with the findings, observations, and recommendations it is fairly straightforward to understand since it basically follows the previously mentioned formula for providing information: What is the finding? How did we come up with the finding? What can we do about the finding?

System Specific

The system specific analysis is a bit more complicated than the organizational analysis and the structure of the write-up is highly dependent on the framework that was used. The main reason for this is because every framework has a different set of phases, sub-phases, and steps and therefore has different types of activities.

As we mentioned in the methodology section, one of the most important parts of your documentation is to list down all the activities required by your chosen framework and to document the results (if any) for each of those activities. We cannot emphasize how important this is, since this will allow the assessor to substantiate and provide evidence of how they arrived at their findings and conclusions.

As with previous sections, and in order to provide a concrete example, we will work off a scenario that used NIST SP800-30 as a framework. In doing so, we will be following the format of the processes within NIST SP800-30 in documenting our results. Remaining consistent with the example our format is:

- Step 1: System Characterization.
- Step 2: Threat Identification.
- Step 3: Vulnerability Identification.
- Step 4: Impact Analysis.
- Step 5: Likelihood Determination.
- Step 6: Control Analysis.
- Step 7: Risk Determination.
- Step 8: Control Recommendations.
- Step 9: Results Documentation.

Unlike the previous sections where we provided a template that flowed in a continuous fashion from start to finish, we will be breaking this section into each of the "steps" of our framework.

The system specific review section should be initiated with a brief background covering the steps of the framework that were used to structure the assessment:

The following system specific risk assessment is based off NIST SP800-30. The steps used in the assessment, and derived directly from NIST SP800-30, include the following:

- *Step 1: System Characterization.*

- *Step 2: Threat Identification.*

- *Step 3: Vulnerability Identification.*

- *Step 4: Impact Analysis.*

- *Step 5: Likelihood Determination.*

- *Step 6: Control Analysis.*

- *Step 7: Risk Determination.*

- *Step 8: Control Recommendations.*

- *Step 9: Results Documentation.*

What follows is step-by-step documentation of the results that were derived by following NIST SP800-30.

System Characterization

We'll cover the individual walkthrough of each section starting with System Characterization. Guidance on how to prepare and obtain the resources for this section is documented in the data collection activities covered in Chapter 3. This was the part of the process where we collected IT Asset Inventories, performed Asset Scoping Workshops, conducted interviews with stakeholders, and collected information about the assets through the asset profile surveys.

Example content for this subsection could look like:

The first step performed in the risk analysis was System Characterization. As part of this step, Asset Scoping Workshops, Interviews, and Asset Profile Surveys were conducted and IT Asset inventories were compiled. Based on these activities, there are five systems in scope for this information security risk assessment:

Asset	Description	Asset Owner
HIS	The main hospital information system for patient record keeping which ties into multiple systems used by various departments.	CIO
Cardiology Research Database	This system supports one of the main research initiatives for the hospital. This system contains one year's worth of research data from the cardiology department.	Dept. Head of Cardiology
HR Payroll System	This system handles payroll for all employees of the hospital.	Dept. Head of HR
Email—Exchange	The email system for the organization which is used by physicians, employees, and contractors of the hospital.	CIO
Imaging	The imaging system for the radiology department. This system processes and contains all radiology images and has an integration component that feeds data into the HIS.	Dept. Head of Radiology

Detailed information about each system is documented in their respective Asset Profile Survey within the Data Collection Matrix provided in the Appendices section of this report.

As you may notice from the example, it is fairly short and straightforward. Your main objective is to let the reader know the process you followed, which systems are in scope, provide a brief description of the business function of those systems, and identify who is responsible for the systems. If further information is needed, the reader can always refer to the appendices that are provided with the report.

Threat Identification

Using the data analysis that was conducted as part of the activities covered in Chapter 4, specifically the Threat Catalog, this subsection should be easy to complete. THe reason is that you should be using a standard threat catalog, as was discussed in our hypothetical scenario. As previously discussed, our threat catalog was a combination of NIST SP800-30 and ISO27005.

It is important to note that in our scenarios, in order to keep the examples brief, we used only a very limited subset of the threat catalogs so the threat catalog presented below may seem a bit unrealistic since it is so limited in scope. Here's an example of what a subsection could look like based on the hypothetical scenarios and activities we conducted in this book:

In order to identify the threats that our organization is exposed to we conducted research on common information security threats for organizations like ours, which led us to utilize standard information security threat catalogs from NIST SP800-30 and ISO27005. The following table documents the Threat Catalog used for this assessment:

Threat Agent	Threat Action
External Intruders, Malicious Insiders, Malicious Code	System intrusion and unauthorized system access
Malicious Insider, Users	Unchecked data viewing or alteration
Non-Specific, Natural	Loss of power
Non-Specific, Users	Equipment failure or malfunction
Users	Denial of user actions or activity
Users	Eavesdropping and Interception of data

This list is not representative of all possible information security threats, just the most common threats for the organization based on its environment and exposure as determined by relevant subject matter experts. Also, as threats continually evolve, part of the on-going risk assessment process is to continually review and update this risk catalog.

As previously mentioned, the threat catalog in the example above was shortened drastically to facilitate discussions throughout the book. In reality, you will have a threat catalog that's more like the following:

Threat Agent	Threat Action
Criminal, Pilferer	Retrieval of data from discarded or recycled equipment
Criminal, Pilferer	Theft leading to unauthorized access to sensitive system data in media
Criminal, Pilferer	Theft leading to unauthorized physical access of equipment and sensitive media
External Intruders, Malicious Insiders, Malicious Code	Social engineering of system user
External Intruders, Malicious Insiders, Malicious Code	System intrusion and unauthorized system access
Malicious Code	System intrusion and unauthorized system access
Malicious code, Users	Intentional or accidental denial of service event
Malicious Insider, Users	System sabotage or Software failure or malfunction
Malicious Insider, Users	Unauthorized users performing unauthorized operations
Malicious Insider, Users	Unchecked data viewing or alteration
Natural	Equipment damage or destruction due to natural causes (fire, water, etc.)
Non-Specific	Unrecoverable data due to natural or human error
Non-Specific	Unrecoverable system functionality due to natural or human error
Non-Specific, Natural	Failure of network infrastructure
Non-Specific, Natural	Loss of power
Non-Specific, Users	Equipment failure or malfunction
Users	Abuse of user rights and permissions
Users	Denial of user actions or activity
Users	Eavesdropping and Interception of data
Users	Intentional or accidental transmission of regulated data
Users	Intentional or unintentional violations of the system security policy
Users	Unreported security events regarding system use

In fact, this list is still considered short when compared to other published threat catalogs. For example, the BITS catalog consists of several hundred threats and if you choose to use that framework it is likely not feasible to include all of the threat catalog items in the body of the report. If a framework with a lengthy catalog is used then the appropriate container (e.g. a spreadsheet) should be referenced within the body of the report.

Vulnerability Identification

When documenting this subsection you can once again refer to the data analysis activities of Chapter 4 wherein you would have prepared a vulnerability catalog based on a combination of current identified vulnerabilities and potential vulnerabilities. Here's an example of content for this subsection:

In this step, the vulnerabilities were identified through discussions with key personnel as well as the review of various third-party assessments and internal documents which were reviewed to identify the following current and potential vulnerabilities for the organization:

Vulnerability Catalog
Critical system vulnerabilities in host systems due to insufficient patch management
Excessive privileges due to lack of a user access review
Insufficient authentication mechanism and controls
Insufficient backups
Insufficient change control process leading to unauthorized changes
Insufficient contingency planning
Insufficient enforcement of secure deletion and disposal process
Insufficient incident response plan
Insufficient media encryption
Insufficient physical controls protecting equipment
Insufficient security awareness implementation and enforcement
Lack of anti-virus and malware prevention
Lack of environmental controls
Lack of logging and monitoring controls
Lack of mechanism to prevent data loss
Lack of network security controls
Lack of redundancy and failover mechanisms for the system
Lack of redundant network infrastructure
Lack of redundant or failover equipment
Lack of redundant power supply
Lack of transmission encryption leading to interception of unencrypted data
Lack of user monitoring and periodic access review
Possible security misconfigurations in system due to lack of security and hardening reviews
Possible weak passwords due to lack of password complexity controls
Unauthorized user accounts and access to the system due to lack of a formal user provisioning process
Undetected critical vulnerabilities in host systems due to insufficient vulnerability monitoring and management process
Untraceable user actions due to generic accounts

Impact Analysis

The Impact Analysis, Likelihood Analysis, and the Control Analysis are all transitory steps towards the final Risk Determination and Control Recommendations. As such, there are no substantial results that can be shown except for the results of the computations conducted during the data analysis activities in Chapter 5.

For Impact Analysis, the results of the activities that were conducted after determining the impact analysis scheme (discussed in Chapter 5) will be the covered in this subsection. Since the related computations are better done in a container like a spreadsheet, it is not recommended to put the entire likelihood computation for all the threats identified across all in scope systems into the body of this report. One thing you can do is put a reference to the related container or include an example as part of the report to give the reader an idea as to how the computations were performed. Here is an example of what this subsection could look like:

An Impact Analysis was conducted for all in scope systems. The following factors were analyzed in order to determine the impact that these vulnerabilities would have to the confidentiality, integrity, and availability of the organization's systems should they ever be exploited by a given threat:

Confidentiality:

- *Data Classification.*

- *Number of Records.*

Integrity:

- *Business Criticality.*

- *Financial Materiality.*

- *Regulatory Impact.*

Availability:

- *Business Criticality.*

- *Number of Users.*

- *Number of Transactions.*

The following table represents the computations for each system that were derived for all threats and vulnerabilities:

Application: Cardiology Research Database						
Threat (Agent and Action)		**Vulnerability**	**C**	**I**	**A**	**Impact Score**
Users	Eavesdropping and Interception of data	Lack of transmission encryption leading to interception of unencrypted data	5	0	0	5
External Intruders, Malicious Insiders, Malicious Code	System intrusion and unauthorized system access	Possible weak passwords due to lack of password complexity controls	5	5	0	5

Continued

Application: Cardiology Research Database						
Threat (Agent and Action)		**Vulnerability**	**C**	**I**	**A**	**Impact Score**
Users	Denial of user actions or activity	Untraceable user actions due to generic accounts	0	3	0	3
Malicious Insider, Users	Unchecked data alteration	Lack of logging and monitoring controls	0	3	0	3
Non-Specific, Natural	Loss of power	Lack of redundant power supply	0	0	1	1
Natural	Equipment damage or destruction due to natural causes (fire, water, etc.)	Lack of environmental controls	0	0	1	1

All Impact scores and computations are documented in the Data Collection and Computation Matrix Spreadsheet provided within the Appendices.

Control Analysis

All activities pertaining to the design and implementation of the Control Analysis scheme are covered in detail within Chapter 4. The data used for the Control Analysis scheme is the data collected from the Control Survey that was discussed in the data collection activities covered in Chapter 3.

As we stated previously, the Control Analysis is a key element used to derive the final Risk Determination. Since it is an intermediary step in the process it is better suited to be presented in its own container (e.g. a spreadsheet) rather than the report body itself.

Similar to the Impact Analysis, an assessor can place a reference to the relevant container or cover an example as part of the report in order to provide the reader with an idea on how the computations were performed. Here is an example of what this subsection could look like:

> *The Control Analysis was conducted for all systems that were in scope of the risk analysis. The purpose of the Control Analysis was to assess the security posture of each system based on the organization's standard IT control catalog. The maturity of each control was identified through a control survey based on the following control items:*

Controls Reviewed
Data Protection
Transmission Encryption
AV/HIPS
Patch Management
Complex Passwords

Controls Reviewed
Vulnerability Management
Security Configuration
Authentication Controls
IDS/IPS Monitoring
User Provisioning
User Access Review
Generic Account Management
Security Awareness
Segment Isolation
Administrative Redundancy
Logging and Monitoring
Equipment Storage Encryption
Enterprise Backup
Backup Tape Encryption
Redundancy and Failover
BCP/DR
Secure Deletion and Disposal
Change Control
Security Incident Response
Physical and Environmental Controls
Network Infrastructure Redundancy
Power Supply
Data Center Controls

The control items were assessed via a survey that included one or more questions regarding the status of the control item. For the results of the survey, please refer to the Controls section of the Data Collection and Computation Matrix within the Appendices.

A large part of this analysis was to identify the current controls that are in place to mitigate the threats we were assessing. The following table provides the control level rating scale used in the control analysis step of the risk analysis:

Control Level			
Score	Reverse	Description	Criteria
5	.2	VERY STRONG	Control provides very strong protection against the threat. Threat being successful is highly unlikely. Effectiveness of the control is being reviewed constantly. Process is defined and documented. Controls are consistently enforced. Performance is monitored.
4	.4	STRONG	Control provides strong protection against the threat. Performance of the control is enforced. Process is defined and documented. Controls are consistently enforced.

Continued

Control Level			
Score	**Reverse**	**Description**	**Criteria**
3	.6	MODERATE	Control provides protection against the threat but may have exceptions. Control is enforced but not consistently or it may be enforced in an incorrect fashion.
2	.8	WEAK	Controls provide some protection against threat but it is mostly ineffective. Formal process may exist but control may not be routinely enforced.
1	1	VERY WEAK	No control or control provides little or no protection against the threat. Formal process and enforcement of controls are ad hoc or non-existent.

The following table represents the computations performed to derive the overall control score for the systems that were in scope for the assessment:

Application: Hospital Information System			
Threat (Agent and Action)		**Vulnerability**	**Controls**	**Controls Score**
Users	Eavesdropping and Interception of data	Lack of transmission encryption leading to interception of unencrypted data	Transmission Encryption	4
External Intruders, Malicious Insiders, Malicious Code	System intrusion and unauthorized system access	Possible Weak Passwords due to lack of password complexity controls	Complex Passwords	4
Users	Denial of user actions or activity	Untraceable user actions due to generic accounts	Generic Account Use Policies	3
Malicious Insider, Users	Unchecked data alteration	Lack of logging and monitoring controls	Logging and Monitoring Controls	3
Non-Specific, Natural	Loss of power	Lack of redundant power supply	Alternate Power Supply	4
Natural	Equipment damage or destruction due to natural causes (fire, water, etc.)	Lack of environmental controls	Physical and Environmental Controls	4

All Control scores and computations are documented in the Data Collection and Computation Matrix Spreadsheet.

Likelihood Analysis

The last of the three intermediate steps before obtaining the final risk computation is the likelihood analysis. Similar to the previous 2 intermediary steps, the actual computations and results for the likelihood analysis are better shown through the container used for the computation.

In our scenarios, the container is the spreadsheet called Data Collection and Computation Matrix. Since the full results will generally be too large to include in the results section, a reference to the container will typically suffice for this subsection. In addition, a quick summary of the process should also be included. The entire process for conducting the Likelihood Analysis is documented and can be referenced in the data analysis activities covered in Chapter 4.

Likelihood determination was conducted through analysis of the Exposure, Frequency, and Control score of the threat based on factors collected through document review, metrics, questionnaires, interviews, and subject matter expert judgment.

The Exposure score was determined through a review of the following system and environmental factors that could affect the security of the system being reviewed:

- *Accessibility of the Asset.*

- *Location.*

- *Data Flow.*

- *Number of Users.*

- *User Profile (Employee, Contractor, Visitor).*

- *Previous Incidents.*

- *Documented Issues or Findings.*

Based on the factors presented above, each system was reviewed for the exposure for each individual threat documented in the threat catalog. The table below represents the analysis conducted:

Exposure Determination Matrix for System intrusion and Unauthorized System Access for HIS		
Score	Description	Criteria
5	VERY LIKELY	Previous compromises or attempts have been detected
4	LIKELY	System is Internet accessible
3	MODERATE	System is remotely accessible (e.g. via VPN)
2	UNLIKELY	System is accessible only through the internal network
1	VERY UNLIKELY	Anything that does not fall into the UNLIKELY criteria (e.g. a standalone system without network access)

The Frequency was determined via a similar analysis using the following table:

Frequency Matrix		
Score	**Description**	**Criteria**
5	VERY LIKELY	Could happen on a daily basis
4	LIKELY	Could happen on a weekly basis
3	MODERATE	Could happen on a monthly basis
2	UNLIKELY	Could happen within one year
1	VERY UNLIKELY	Could happen within five years

The Control scores were extracted from the Control Analysis performed in previous activities. The Likelihood Score was determined through the following formula:

- Likelihood = ((Exposure + Frequency)/2) x (Reverse Control)

The formula will yield the following table for each of the systems that are in scope. Note that the Likelihood score is rounded up (0.4 becomes 1) to ensure that there are no zero values in likelihood score. The table below covers all in scope systems; however, the actual computations and results for each system can be referenced in the Data Collection and Computation Matrix provided in the Appendices of this report.

Application: Hospital Information System					
Threat (Agent and Action)	**Vulnerability**	**Exposure**	**Frequency**	**Control**	**Likeli-hood**
Users Eavesdropping and Interception of data	Lack of transmission encryption leading to interception of unencrypted data	3	3	4 (.4)	2
External Intruders, Malicious Insiders, Malicious Code	System intrusion and unauthorized system access	Possible Weak Passwords due to lack of password complexity controls	3	5	4 (.4)	2
Users	Denial of user actions or activity	Untraceable user actions due to generic accounts	5	1	3 (.6)	2

Application: Hospital Information System						
Threat (Agent and Action)	Vulnerability		Exposure	Frequency	Control	Likeli-hood
Malicious Insider, Users	Unchecked data alteration	Lack of logging and monitoring controls	5	2	3 (.6)	3
Non-Specific, Natural	Loss of power	Lack of redundant power supply	5	2	4 (.4)	2
Natural	Equipment damage or destruction due to natural causes (fire, water, etc.)	Lack of environmental controls	2	1	4 (.4)	1

As you can see, for the three intermediate steps that support the Risk Determination, the full results cannot be documented in the report as they will be too large and unwieldy. If the assessor is reviewing just 5 systems and assessing 20 threats, documenting all the computations and results in the body of the report could lead to several hundred pages of matrices. It is more practical, for these three steps, to include description of the process performed, highlight the top risks identified, and then provide a reference to the relevant container as an Appendix to supplement the results section.

Risk Determination

The Risk Determination section is the final output based on the results of the Impact Analysis and Likelihood Analysis. The final output that is represented in this section is the Risk Score. Since the risk score is computed for all threat and vulnerability pairs for all systems, it is not feasible to put all of the results in the body of the report. As with Impact and Likelihood analysis, the results for this section are better represented in an Appendix. In our case this is a spreadsheet containing the risk computation. As with the previous section we encourage you to provide an example within the body of the report and will provide an example below. It is also a good idea to present some form of aggregate results since the full risk scores cannot be easily presented. The presentation of the aggregate results could be a summation table of all the risk scores as seen in the example below. All of the content for this section can be derived from the data analysis activities covered in Chapter 4. What follows is a template that can be used for this section:

> *Risk Determination provides a quantitative risk value representing the systems exposure to a threat exploiting a particular vulnerability after current controls have been considered. This quantitative value is in the form of a Risk Score. A risk score basically follows the following formula:*

- RISK= IMPACT x LIKELIHOOD

The computation for the risk value is a fairly straightforward multiplication of the Impact and Likelihood scores. This computation was performed for all threat and vulnerability pairs for all systems that were in scope for this assessment. An example of what this looks like for one of the hypothetical in scope systems is captured below:

Application: Hospital Information System					
Threat (Agent and Action)		**Vulnerability**	**Impact Score**	**Likeli-hood Score**	**Risk Score**
Users	Eavesdropping and Intercep-tion of data	Lack of trans-mission encryp-tion leading to interception of unencrypted data	5	2	10
External Intruders, Malicious Insiders, Mali-cious Code	System intrusion and unauthorized system access	Possible Weak Passwords due to lack of pass-word complexity controls	5	2	10
Users	Denial of user actions or activity	Untraceable user actions due to generic accounts	5	2	10
Malicious Insider, Users	Unchecked data alteration	Lack of logging and monitoring controls	5	3	15
Non-Specific, Natural	Loss of power	Lack of redundant power supply	5	2	10
Natural	Equipment damage or destruction due to natural causes (fire, water, etc.)	Lack of environ-mental controls	5	1	5

The following risk categorization table was then used to categorize the distinct system risk scores into risk classification "buckets" of High, Moderate, or Low Risk:

	Likelihood					
Impact		**1**	**2**	**3**	**4**	**5**
	1	1	2	3	4	5
	2	2	4	6	8	10
	3	3	6	9	12	15
	4	4	8	12	16	20
	5	5	10	15	20	25

Area	Risk Classification
Black	High Risk
Grey	Moderate Risk
White	Low Risk

Based on the categorization efforts using the Impact versus Likelihood table above, the following table is an example of high risk items for a system are identified:

Application: Hospital Information System					
Threat (Agent and Action)	**Vulnerability**	**Impact Score**	**Likelihood Score**	**Risk Score**	**Classifi- cation**
Users	Eavesdrop- ping and Intercep- tion of data	Lack of transmission encryption leading to interception of unencrypted data	5	2	10	Moderate
External Intruders, Malicious Insiders, Malicious Code	System intrusion and unau- thorized system access	Possible Weak Passwords due to lack of password complexity controls	5	2	10	Moderate
Users	Denial of user actions or activity	Untraceable user actions due to generic accounts	5	2	10	Moderate
Malicious Insider, Users	Unchecked data alteration	Lack of logging and monitoring controls	5	3	15	High
Non- Specific, Natural	Loss of power	Lack of redun- dant power supply	5	2	10	Moderate
Natural	Equipment damage or destruction due to nat- ural causes (fire, water, etc.)	Lack of environmental controls	5	1	5	Low

For all system risk scores and risk classifications please refer to the Data Collection and Computation matrix in the Appendices of this report.

Based on the risk scores, what follows are aggregate views resulting from the risk determination phase. This table presents a ranking of applications based on their aggregate risk scores (sum of all risk scores for all threat and vulnerability pairs). In theory, the higher the aggregate risk score, the greater the risk to the system.

Risk Rank	Application	Aggregate Risk Score
1	HIS	60
2	HR Payroll	50
3	Cardio Research DB	47
4	Email	46
5	Imaging	45

The following table provides a breakdown of the risk scores per system based on each threat and vulnerability pair. The higher the score for each listed system the greater the risk of the threat exploiting the vulnerability.

Threat Agent	Threat Action	Vulnerability	HIS	Cardio Research	HR Payroll	Email	Imaging	Aggregate Score
Users	Eavesdropping and Interception of data	Lack of transmission encryption leading to interception of unencrypted data	10	9	10	15	15	59
External Intruders, Malicious Insiders, Malicious Code	System intrusion and unauthorized system access	Possible Weak Passwords due to lack of password complexity controls	10	12	15	10	10	57
Malicious Insider, Users	Unchecked data alteration	Lack of logging and monitoring controls	15	10	5	9	5	44
Users	Denial of user actions or activity	Untraceable user actions due to generic accounts	10	10	10	6	5	41
Non-Specific, Natural	Loss of power	Lack of redundant power supply	10	3	5	3	5	26

Threat Agent	Threat Action	Vulnerability	HIS	Cardio Research	HR Payroll	Email	Imaging	Aggregate Score
Natural	Equipment damage or destruction due to natural causes (fire, water, etc.)	Lack of environmental controls	5	3	5	3	5	21

Finally based on the aggregation and categorization effort in the previous tables, the following table identifies the high risk systems for each of the risks represented by a threat and vulnerability pair:

Threat Agent	Threat Action	Vulnerability	Score	High Risk Systems
Users	Eavesdropping and Interception of data	Lack of transmission encryption leading to interception of unencrypted data	59	Imaging, Email
External Intruders, Malicious Insiders, Malicious Code	System intrusion and unauthorized system access	Possible weak Passwords due to lack of password complexity controls	57	HR Payroll
Malicious Insider, Users	Unchecked data alteration	Lack of logging and monitoring controls	44	HIS
Users	Denial of user actions or activity	Untraceable user actions due to generic accounts	41	None
Non-Specific, Natural	Loss of power	Lack of redundant power supply	26	None
Natural	Equipment damage or destruction due to natural causes (fire, water, etc.)	Lack of environmental controls	21	None

As seen in the template, the structure of the Risk Determination section follows a very similar pattern as the three intermediary sections (Impact, Likelihood, and Control Analysis) whereby the full results are referenced in a container as it is not feasible to put everything in the body of the report. A key differentiator is that by virtue of it being the final stage of the computation, there are certain aggregate tables that can be presented.

Control Recommendations

This section is meant to provide control recommendations for the system specific risks. This section is mainly setup as a summary since we are going to be presenting the treatment options in the risk registers in the next section. The content for this section can be derived from the risk prioritization and treatment activities performed in Chapter 6. Here is an example of what the control recommendation section could look like for our hypothetical scenario:

> Based on the key system specific risks identified in the risk assessment, several key security initiatives were proposed that would mitigate or remediate the strategic risks identified during the assessment.

> The table below provides a cross reference of these proposed initiatives, risk items and the target systems that the initiative is meant to target:

	Email Encryption Initiative	SFTP Infrastructure Initiative	Logging and Monitoring Initiative	Password Complexity Enforcement Initiative	Security Awareness Initiative
Lack of Transmission Encryption	Email System	Imaging System			Email System
Unchecked Data Alteration			HIS		
System Intrusion				HR Payroll	HR Payroll

As previously mentioned, the system specific results are highly dependent on the framework that is being used. In this case, we used NIST SP800-30 as our framework so our write-up is broken up into the sections presented above. If another framework was used, the sections may be different and some of the computations may use different formulas.

RISK REGISTER

The risk register is probably the most important section of this report. In fact, if we had to choose one section of the report as the most important it would be the risk register. The risk register is where we present to the reader the consolidation of all the findings that were identified through the information security risk assessment process. The content for this section is based on the activities that we conducted in the risk prioritization and treatment activities covered in chapter 6. What follows is an example template for this section:

This section provides the consolidated results of the risk assessment in the form of a risk register. The risk register identifies the risk and provides an analysis containing the rationale behind the identification based on organizational and system specific factors. The risk register also provides a discussion of current and ongoing remediation activities regarding the risk identified.

Based on the activities conducted in this risk assessment, the following risks have been identified for the organization:

Risk ID	1
Risk Title	Mobile attacks.
Scope	Organizational.
Risk Narrative	The organization is facing increasing exposure to mobile attack vectors due to the increasing frequency of mobile device use in conducting company business.
Risk Impact	Possible disclosure of sensitive information or unauthorized access to hospital information systems through mobile attack vectors like mobile malware or the accidental loss or theft of the mobile device. Loss of patient information or breach in information systems could lead to significant fines and penalties.
Rationale	• Increasing use of mobile devices in the hospital especially by physicians. • Increasing trend towards mobile attack vectors based on current research and industry reports.
Treatment	Propose initiatives for: • Mobile Device Management. • Security Awareness. • Data Loss Prevention.

Risk ID	2
Risk Title	Security Gaps in Vendor Managed Systems.
Scope	Organizational.
Risk Narrative	Potential compromise of hospital network and systems due to vulnerabilities in vendor managed systems.
Risk Impact	Possible disclosure of sensitive information or unauthorized access to hospital information systems through weaknesses in vendor managed systems. Loss of patient information or breach in information systems could lead to significant fines and penalties.

Continued

Risk ID	2
Rationale	• Noted multiple security exceptions related to vendor managed systems. • Third party penetration test gained domain administrator access to the internal hospital network due to weaknesses in vendor managed systems.
Treatment	Propose initiatives for: • Vendor Security Requirements. • Network Isolation.

Risk ID	3
Risk Title	Phishing and social engineering
Scope	Organizational.
Risk Narrative	Susceptibility of the organizations users to phishing and social engineering attacks leading to unauthorized access to hospital systems.
Risk Impact	Possible unauthorized access and use of hospital resources leading to increased utilization and degradation of hospital services (e.g. spamming). Targeted attacks could lead to disclosure of sensitive information leading to fines and penalties as well as reputational impacts.
Rationale	• Majority of recorded security incidents were related to successful compromise of hospital user accounts due to phishing and social engineering attacks.
Treatment	Propose initiatives for: • Security Awareness. • Malware Protection Controls. • Data Loss Prevention Technology.

Risk ID	4
Risk Title	Data loss.
Scope	Organizational.
Risk Narrative	Potential accidental loss of ePHI and regulated data through email or removable media.
Risk Impact	Possible loss of patient information that could lead to significant fines or penalties as well as reputational impacts.
Rationale	• Noted security incidents of data loss via accidental email transmission and loss of removable devices.
Treatment	Propose initiatives for: • Data Loss Prevention Technology. • Security Awareness.

Risk ID	5
Risk Title	Malware.
Scope	Organizational.
Risk Narrative	Susceptibility of the organization to malware based attacks.
Risk Impact	Possible unauthorized access and use of hospital resources leading to increased utilization and degradation of hospital services (e.g. spamming). Targeted attacks could lead to disclosure of sensitive information leading to fines, penalties as well as reputational impacts.
Rationale	• Security metrics show high numbers of malware related security events reported through help desk.
Treatment	Propose initiatives for: • Enhanced Malware Protection.

Risk ID	6
Risk Title	Disclosure of transmitted sensitive data.
Scope	• Email System. • Imaging System.
Risk Narrative	Potential risk of interception of data and disclosure due to the lack of transmission encryption controls in several key systems that transmit ePHI data. Regulatory requirements dictate that transmissions of ePHI be encrypted.
Risk Impact	Possible loss of patient information that could lead to significant fines or penalties as well as reputational impacts.
Rationale	• The current Email system does not support encryption functionality. • Imaging system transfers data via FTP in the internal network.
Treatment	Propose initiatives for: • Email Encryption. • Secure FTP Infrastructure. • Security Awareness.

Risk ID	7
Risk Title	Unchecked data alteration.
Scope	• HIS.
Risk Narrative	Potential for unchecked data alteration due to lack of logging and monitoring controls in a key system.
Risk Impact	Inaccurate data due to unchecked alterations could potentially lead to integrity issues and pose significant risks to patient care, diagnosis, billing, or other core hospital processes.

Continued

Risk ID	7
Rationale	• The HIS System currently does not have logging and monitoring enabled.
Treatment	Propose initiatives for: • Logging and Monitoring Initiative.

Risk ID	8
Risk Title	System Intrusion.
Scope	• HR Payroll.
Risk Narrative	Potential system intrusion and unauthorized access due to lack of password complexity controls in a key system.
Risk Impact	Unauthorized access could lead to significant confidentiality and integrity issues such as disclosure of PII and even changes to payroll data.
Rationale	• The current HR Payroll System does not enforce password complexity.
Treatment	Propose initiatives for: • Password Complexity Enforcement. • Security Awareness.

The risk register can be considered as a pull out section of the report, meaning that you could just use this section of the report to guide many of the conversations that you would have around the results of the risk analysis. Based on our experience, most of the discussions that you will have after completion of the analysis will be centered on the information contained within the risk register so it is important that it is presented in a clear and structured format.

CONCLUSION

As with most reports, the final section will be the conclusion. This section provides an area where the assessor can provide their final narrative regarding the information security risk assessment. The conclusion should really just be a short summary of the process and the results. The conclusion can also be used as an opportunity for the assessor to provide some opinions as well as disclaimers regarding the process. What follows below is an example of what the conclusion could look like:

The risk analysis identified 5 organizational and 3 system-specific information security risks. The organizational risks were determined using a risk determination process based on a high level organizational risk review that utilized an analysis of current information security trends, third-party assessments, and a review of various organizational documents, assessments, security metrics and statistics. The system specific risks were determined by utilizing the NIST SP800-30 framework which quantifies risks based on likelihood, impact, and the current controls that are in place augmented by threat and vulnerability catalogs from ISO 27005. Throughout the risk assessment process, the risks identified have been communicated to the organization's CIO and the Information Security Officer. It is also important to acknowledge the valuable participation of various individuals such as the CEO, COO, CFO, various department heads, IT managers, and various other system owners, without whom the risk assessment team could not have completed the assessment

The risks identified in this assessment should be the top priority for remediation activities as these risks are not only the highest risk areas but addressing these risks, particularly those that are strategic and organizational in nature, would provide additional mitigating controls to other identified risks.

It is important to note that the risks identified do not represent all risks to the organization and all information systems, but is representative of the most significant risks and the critical information systems exposed to these risks. In preparing this assessment, we relied upon information provided by various operating unit staff and reports prepared by other entities. Due to the fact that we relied on information provided through interviews and questionnaires we expect some level of inaccuracy in the information. We also expect there may have been improvements or degradations in processes since the date of the assessment. It is also possible that new information may have become available since the completion of this assessment that may supersede the information provided in the risk assessment.

APPENDICES

The appendices are the "containers" which hold our supporting evidence and results. The containers are discussed in the data collection activities covered in chapter 2. These containers may include spreadsheets, databases, documents and links to applications. Typically this section contains the documents that are referenced throughout the Results section of the report. Sections that are heavily supported by this section are the Impact Analysis, Likelihood Analysis, Control Analysis and Risk Determination as they tend to be too large to include in the body of the report. In the case of our hypothetical scenario, we utilized a single spreadsheet with multiple tabas as our container and called it the *"Data Collection and Computation Matrix"* a sample of which can be downloaded off the companion website to this book.

The examples presented in this chapter can be used as templates to build a complete report. Also throughout all the sections walking through the sample report, we have referenced the specific chapter where the examples, methods, guidelines and procedures that need to be followed can be found.

THE REAL WORLD

Jane has come to a point where she feels pretty knowledgeable about the risks that the organization and their critical systems face. She has also developed a risk register that she feels captures the individual risks quite well and is something that she could use to more or less defend and substantiate her findings.

As she sits back and looks at the deliverable representing several weeks of hard work she realizes that her eight identified risks, when put down on paper, fill up a measly 2 pages.

"Hmmm. All that work for 2 pages," Jane thinks to herself.

She knows that she has done a thorough job and she believes that her CIO is aware of how hard she has worked to get to this point. She realizes that she needs something that would truly reflect all the hard work that she's put into the risk assessment. More importantly, she realizes that she needs some kind of way to be able to convey her decision making process to the consumers of her work product.

She knows that if she is asked she can clearly explain her process, but what if she's not there?

Jane decides that she needs to write a report that will clearly communicate her approach as well as capture the work that she has put in for the past couple of weeks. Jane knows that to structure the report properly she needs an outline so starts jotting things down. She's no stranger to reports since she has had to read and prepare quite a few of them and she knows that the one thing she needs to really execute on is her preparation of the Executive Summary portion of the report which will be the first section of her report. Knowing that this may be the only section of the report that any of the executive stakeholders will bother reading she makes it short, sweet, and to the point. She provides a quick overview of what the purpose of the report is, who was involved, the process she followed, and her high level conclusions.

She then goes on to describe the methodology and the activities involved in each "phase" of the assessment. She feels that this section will be a good way to capture her process and the amount of work that was involved in arriving at her conclusions.

After covering the methodology, she starts writing up the results. This is where she decides she should dive deeper into her decision making process. Step-by-step, she breakds down the activities that she discussed in the methodology section and for each activity, she writes a narrative covering the results, insights and observations she came up with while performing each of the activities.

As a final step she includes the issues register in case the reader wants to dive down into the details. Looking over the report she goes through her mental checklist to make sure she has:

- Provided an overview using the executive summary.
- Provided a background of her process and methodology.
- Provided a narrative of what she discovered through all of the activities in the results section.
- Provided a summary, or a "master list," of the risks she was able to identify.

She realizes that she has captured quite a bit of information and that some people might think that the report is too long and not useable; however, she is a firm believer that it is better to have too much information available, if needed, than to have too little which may raise questions. She wants there to be a final deliverable that will be able to stand on its own—or at least that is what she hopes.

She doesn't have any doubts about the results themselves since she was meticulous in her process and fully documented all her findings. She just wants to make sure that she is accurately communicating her findings because she knows that if executives can't understand the content of a report they will begin to question the validity of the entire process and the burden of making them understand is on her shoulders.

Going through the report she feels really good about what she has accomplished and even though it is a long report she found it to be fairly straightforward to write. She was very grateful that she had kept good notes and documented things thoroughly during her process since when it came time to write the report she was, for the most part, copying and pasting information directly from her in-flight write-ups.

Knowing that this report is the first reflection of her work at the organization and may have a positive or negative impact on her perception within the organization she braces herself and sends it off to the CIO!

Information Security Risk Assessment: Maintenance and Wrap Up

INTRODUCTION

Information security is one of the most dynamic and fast changing fields. Security threats are constantly evolving, new vulnerabilities are being discovered, and new exploits are being created to target those vulnerabilities. This ever changing threat landscape requires that your organization and the assessment of your organization's risk to these threats evolve as well. Other than just the rapid pace of external factors it is important not to forget that business changes that aren't directly security related, can often affect the security posture of the organization in some way. The takeaway here is that proactive security risk management requires that you not only monitor external risks but also keep an eye on changes that are occurring within your own organization.

In this chapter, we are going to spend some time reviewing activities that have been previously performed as well as the key deliverables for those activities with a focus on driving toward post-mortem review activities, which will close out the information security risk assessment process.

PROCESS SUMMARY

At this point, we have completed a full information security risk assessment; however, the overall process is not finished. The final part of our information security risk assessment process is to conduct a post-mortem in order to see if there are options and alternatives for improving the process. Before diving into the post-mortem review let's look back at each of the phases of the process:

Data Collection

In the data collection phase our primary focus was to gather information in support of our information security risk assessment. Without adequate data, there is very little value to the risk assessment. If you have been performing a risk assessment as you've read through the book than you have already experienced the fact that the data collection phase is the most rigorous activity within the information security risk assessment process.

Some of the important activities conducted in the data collection phase were:

Preparing the risk assessment team
Identifying the sponsor
Performing executive interviews
Sending document requests
Obtaining asset inventories
Asset scoping
Conducting the asset profile survey
Conducting the control survey

At the end of the data collection phase, the assessor would have "containers" for the data elements that were collected. These "containers" could be a spreadsheet, a database or even just a bunch of files. At this point there is very little structure to the data and it is far from being something useable. This is where the next phase, data analysis, comes into play.

Data Analysis

In this phase, the main goal was to transform the data that we've collected in the data collection phase into something useable. At this point in the process the assessor has collected various forms of data from survey results, interviews, documents, issues registers, and other sources bundled together into one container. The data analysis phase, takes that amalgamated data and adds structure. This is the point where the practitioner moves from just having raw collected data into the actual analysis of risk in the organization and the organization's systems.

Some of the important activities in this phase include:

Compiling observations from the interviews
Compiling observations from documents collected
Preparing the threat/vulnerability catalogs
Performing the Impact Analysis
Performing the Likelihood Analysis
Performing the Control Analysis
Computing for the Risk Score

At the end of this phase, the assessor will have a list of observations, which are typically high level organizational issues, and a list of risk scores for each application that provide a system view of risk. These will be the primary components used for identifying the risk to the organization in the risk analysis phase.

Risk Analysis

At this point, we have collected the data, and then through data analysis, have converted the data into a structured format so that an assessor can perform the actual risk analysis over the organization and the in-scope systems. The main goal of this phase is also the goal of the whole risk assessment process: Determine what the risks are to the organization and its information systems. Simply put, this is where you answer the question: What is our risk?

The main activities that were conducted in this phase were:

Performing a System Specific Risk Review
Performing an Organizational or Strategic Risk Review

At the end of this phase, the assessor will have identified the main risk for each of the in-scope systems (if done correctly), and would begin to have an overall view of the organization's information security risk level as well.

Reporting

During reporting, the assessor documents their findings and communicates to various stakeholders and relevant parties the results of the risk assessment. Though this is a relatively simple part of the overall process, proper reporting could make or break your assessment. We can't stress enough the importance of properly communicating the findings of the assessment. Even if the assessment was done flawlessly, inaccurate reporting of a finding could produce significant issues in the acceptance of your work.

The main activities conducted in this phase are:

Preparing a communication plan
Presenting to the executives
Preparing debriefs to other parties
Preparing and packaging the final report

At the end of this phase, the assessor will have communicated the results of the risk assessment to all relevant parties that have a stake in the process as well as provided the necessary documentation to support all the activities performed so far.

KEY DELIVERABLES

Throughout the process, it is important to keep track of the various deliverables associated with each phase. These deliverables not only serve as the assessors' evidence that the work was performed accurately they also serve as valuable references as the assessor moves through the process. The following table provides a list of the possible deliverables and supporting documentation for each of the phases of the process:

Phase	Deliverables and Supporting Documents
Data Collection	Document Request List
	Record of Interviews
	Asset Inventory
	In-Scope Asset Listing
	Records of Scoping Workshops
	Contact Lists
	System Profile Survey Results
	Control Survey Results
Data Analysis	Issues Observation List and Sources
	Threat Catalog
	Vulnerability Catalog
	Impact Analysis
	Likelihood Analysis
	Control Analysis
	Risk Scores
	Supporting Data and Supporting Matrices
Risk Analysis	List of Organizational and Strategic Findings
	Risk Categorization of Risk Scores
	Finalized System Risk Matrices
Reporting	Final Report
	Support Materials

The main deliverable and supporting documentation for the Risk Analysis phase are actually associated with the Reporting phase; however, in most phases, there are specific stand-alone deliverables that can be used as evidence of the work performed. It is important to keep these deliverables properly cataloged since the results of the risk assessment are likely to be scrutinized by stakeholders and auditors. Being able to provide the deliverables that supported all phses of the process is invaluable.

POST MORTEM

At this point, the assessor would have completed all of the main information security risk assessment processes. All necessary debriefs and meetings have been completed and the final report has been packaged. Depending on a variety of factors, the information security risk assessment could either have gone smoothly or it could have gone very poorly. Regardless of how the process went it is important that the practitioner save some energy for the final part of the process.

As with any major project, it is important to perform a "post-mortem" or a lessons learned analysis. Preferably, this meeting should include the whole risk assessment team as well as the project sponsor, system owners, and various other people involved in the process. It is not always possible to have all individuals who participated in the process attend the post-mortem; however, at a minimum the members who were directly involved in conducting the assessment should attend. The review should happen shortly after the report has been finalized and submitted. The post-mortem activity should apply to every assessment since every assessment, even if it "feels" similar to the last, provides an opportunity to identify areas of improvement that would be helpful in future assessments.

In preparing an agenda for the post-mortem meeting the assessor should consider including the following questions and topics.

Scoping

The primary objective of the scoping activities was for the assessor or the assessment team to have properly identified the systems that were part of the risk assessment. Some of the questions that could be discussed to help determine whether this was properly achieved are:

- What were the objectives of the risk assessment?
- Were we able to identify all systems that should have been in-scope?
- Were there systems excluded from the risk assessment scope? If so, why?
- Were there systems that should not have been part of the risk assessment? If so, why?
- Any feedback regarding the scoping process? Did it work? Are there any suggestions to improve the process?
- How do we update the scoping process to take into consideration future changes in the organization or changes to new or existing systems?
- Did the scope of the assessment satisfy the objective of the risk assessment?

Executive Interviews

The primary objectives of the executive interviews were to ensure that the assessor identified all relevant interviewees for the assessment and that all questions were prepared in a clear and concise way. Some questions that help evaluate whether this objective was met are:

- Were we able to identify all executives that we needed to interview?
- Were there any executives that were excluded from the executive interviews that we need to include in the next iteration? If so, who?
- Did we receive valuable information from the interviews?
- Were there any executives included in the interviews that really did not provide much value to the process? Can they be excluded from future interviews? If so, why?
- Were our questions clear and to the point? Is there anything that we need to add to our questions or change so that they are clearer?

System Owners and Stewards

The primary objective for the identification of system owners and stewards was to ensure that the proper system owners and stewards have been identified based on the scope of the risk assessment. It is critical to the process that the correct people have been identified based on their knowledge of the system. Some of the questions that may assist to verify whether this objective was achieved are:

- Were we able to identify all relevant system owners and stewards?
- Were all the identified system owners and stewards the correct individuals?
- Were the system owners and stewards knowledgeable about their systems?
- Which system owners and stewards had the most difficult time providing information about the system?
- Who among the system owners and stewards was uncooperative?
- Were we able to communicate effectively our goals and requirements to the system owners and stewards?
- Are there any recommendations for improvements with respect to communicating with system owners?

Document Requests

In the document request activities, the primary objective was to ensure all the relevant documents needed for the risk assessment were collected. Some questions to verify whether this objective was achieved are:

- Did we obtain all of the documents we requested?
- What documents did we not receive and why?
- Were the documents we requested sufficient? If not, what other documents should we have requested?
- How do we update the document request list to take into consideration new documents and versions in the future?

System Profile and Control Survey

The primary objective of the system profile and control survey was to ensure that the surveys were distributed, answered and collected efficiently. Some questions that the group may want to discuss to verify whether this objective was achieved are:

- Were there any delays in sending out the surveys? If yes, what caused the delays?
- Did we have all the contact information for the survey recipients?
- Which surveys were forwarded from the steward to another person? Should the contact for that system be updated?
- Was there any feedback regarding our survey distribution mechanism? Any recommendations?

- Were the survey recipients able to complete the survey? If not, what were the problems?
- What systems, system owners, and stewards had the most difficulty with the surveys?
- Was the method of collecting and storing the survey results effective? If not, why and do we have any recommendations or alternatives to improve the process?
- Were all the questions in the survey relevant? Do we need to add other questions to the survey?
- Was our scoring system for the surveys effective?

Analysis

The main objective of the analysis phase was to ensure that all data and risk analysis activities were conducted appropriately. This means that all information necessary to complete the activities were on hand and all techniques used for the analysis were effective in producing the necessary analyses needed. Some questions to verify whether this objective was achieved are:

- Were we able to collect enough information to effectively conduct our analysis? If not, what information do we need to obtain next time?
- Did we encounter any problems extracting observations from the documents collected?
- Did the documents that were collected provide enough information to provide a strategic risk view of the organization?
- Was our threat catalog sufficient to provide enough scope to the assessment? If not, what other alternative catalogs could we use next time?
- Was our vulnerability catalog sufficient? If not, how can we create a better catalog next time?
- What is the process for updating the threat and vulnerability catalog to take into account potential organizational or system changes?
- Did we encounter any inconsistencies in the formulas that we used to calculate various values throughout the process?
- Did our formulas reflect the principles of the framework that we were using?
- Did we encounter any problems or inconsistencies in our Impact and Likelihood decision matrices?
- Were we able to effectively integrate the controls into the analysis?
- Did the resulting risk score appear consistent with the data?
- Were any of the observations or risk scores surprising or unexpected? If yes, why?
- Did our strategic and organizational risk findings reflect the observations seen in other documents (e.g. audits, external risk reports)?
- Did the resulting risk classification for the system risks appear consistent with the data that we collected and analyzed?

Reporting

The main objective of the reporting phase was to ensure that a quality report was produced and to obtain feedback from the stakeholders and other relevant parties regarding the report. Some questions that could assist in verifying if the objective was achieved are:

- How did the various executives or other relevant parties feel or react to the report?
- Were there any suggestions or comments about the final report?
- Were there any issues encountered during the writing of the final report?
- Did the final report accurately and effectively convey the results of the risk assessment?
- Did the final report accurately and effectively convey the process taken to show the results?
- Was there any dissatisfaction with the results of the information security risk assessment or the process that was followed for the information security risk assessment? If yes, who expressed dissatisfaction and why?
- Were there enough supplementary or supporting materials included in the report to provide evidence of the work performed?

General Process

The main objective of the reporting phase was to ensure that the assessor reviews the general process. For example, did the processes in this book work out? Remember that the processes here are not set in stone. There's always room for adjustments and improvements. Some questions that could assist in verifying if the objective was achieved are:

- How long did it take to complete each phase of the risk assessment?
- Did we hit important deadlines and milestones?
- Was there any pushback or dissatisfaction towards the overall information security risk assessment process? If so, who was dissatisfied and why?
- What were the primary bottlenecks in the process?
- Were the team members and skills sufficient for the project?
- Were the tools and techniques that we used, particularly in the collection and analysis process, sufficient? If not, do we need more people or training?
- How do we ensure that our threat/vulnerability catalogs, in-scope assets, and other resources are kept updated for the next iteration of the assessment?

The agenda for the post-mortem should not be limited to the questions above; however, they have been provided as a good baseline to build on. Always remember to take good notes about what was discussed in the post-mortem. If possible, invite someone unrelated to the process to serve as a note taker so that all the active participants can focus on the discussion. Just like an issues register was generated as a part of the risk assessment process, an issues register should be generated for the actual risk assessment process itself so that improvements and recommendations can be incorporated into the next iteration of the assessment.

In terms of how long a post-mortem should take, it really depends on the assessor or the assessment team. Often it may just consist of one meeting but what's important is to make sure that the points discussed in this meeting don't slip through the cracks. Each point discussed and accepted by the team should serve as a valuable input for any subsequent risk assessments.

THE REAL WORLD

After a week of anxiously awaiting for a response from her CIO about the Risk Assessment report her "summons" has arrived. Her "summons" has arrived. Her CIO has had a chance to read through the report and wants her to walk him through the risk assessment report.

Though a little nervous, she feels confident. She knows the report inside and out; however, her CIO always makes her nervous and she hopes that she does a good job of representing and defending her work. She grabs a hard copy of the report and her laptop and thinks: "It's now or never!"

She enters the conference room fifteen minutes before the meeting so that she can be setup by the time he comes in. After hooking up her laptop into the projector and projecting the cover page of her report she reflects for a moment on how satisfying it is seeing the results of months of work up on the big screen.

A few minutes after the hour, her CIO enters the room:

CIO: "Hi Jane! I haven't seen you for a while! I think you've been nose down in your office for weeks now!"

Jane: "Yeah, it's been a hectic couple of months. But I'm really pleased with the results."

CIO: "That's what I like to hear. It's always satisfying when you finish a big task like this and I'm looking forward to having you walk me through the report. I should let you know that I've been asked to present the results of your assessment to our Risk Committee in the next week or so and I'd like to get a better feel for your process and results before I do so."

Jane: "Sure, I think that's a great idea. I'm sure you'll have questions about the report as we walk through this so I'm glad you scheduled this meeting for two hours since it will allow me to address your questions or concerns properly."

CIO: "Exactly what I was thinking about! Since this is our first such assessment I want to make sure I really understand the process and findings since I want to be able to handle any curveballs that might get thrown my way at the Risk Committee. We have some new committee members including this former partner from one of the Big Four firms and I hear he likes to trip up presenters since he has a strong risk management background."

Jane: "Well, I hope you don't find this presumptuous, but since we planned to end at noon today I actually asked your secretary to order us lunch just in case we decide to run past the two hours."

CIO: "Perfect! That's what I like about you, always thinking ahead! I guess that's an attribute you have to have when you think about security risks day in and day out, huh??"

Jane: "Haha. Yes, very true. Well I'm all setup here so if you are ready maybe we can start walking through the report? It is quite long and I want to make the most use of your time."

CIO: "Sure, let's get this going."

Jane feels a lot more comfortable now. Based on their conversation, this appears to be more of a working meeting rather than a full fledged presentation and it seems like the CIO might have actually glanced through the report before the meeting, something that is not always typical with executives that she deals with. She hadn't known that he was going to be presenting the results of the report to the risk management committee but now she knows and so she decides to shift her presentation of the report to follow more of a "teaching" workshop style rather than just a formal presentation of the report. She thinks it will be important that he understand all the key points so he can relate it clearly to the committee and be able to hit those curveballs out of the park.

Jane: "First off, it sounds like you've had a chance to read through the report?"

CIO: "I actually have. But, full disclosure here, I just browsed through it quickly. Honestly, it is a long report; however, I was stricken by the depth of information and explanation that you put into it.I think the committee members will be impressed by the work that you put together, but we're going to need a way to really distill it down to fit into the 30 minutes that they have given me on the agenda."

Jane: "Thanks! So how do you want to go about this? I was thinking that since you've read through it at a high level, maybe I should give you a brief overview of each section and perhaps you can ask me questions if there are things that are vague?"

CIO: "Sure, that sounds good to me."

Jane: "Ok, let's start off with the executive summary. Basically what the executive summary tells you is that this report was performed because of two primary drivers: First HIPAA requires us to have a risk assessment and second, performing risk assessments is good practice for any organization."

CIO: "Sounds good. I did see that you've put in the specific HIPAA clause which I really like but I did see reference to things like NIST SP800-30 and ISO27005. What are those about?"

Jane: "Those are the risk management frameworks that we used to base this risk assessment on."

CIO: "Seems vaguely familiar, I know we talked about this a long time ago when you were starting off with the planning for the assessment but can you refresh my memory real quick?"

Jane: "Definitely. I actually provided an explanation in the executive summary if you want to flip to that section real quick. The important thing to remember when discussing this is that NIST SP800-30 was actually recommended by HHS and I've captured the exact wording from HHS here in the executive summary in case anyone asks."

CIO: "Perfect."

Jane: "Finally, I mentioned that we have identified eight risks. Five of them are organization level risks and three of them are system specific."

CIO: "Ah, ok. This is the first part I'd like to focus some attention on. I know you have it written down but let's cut to the chase and talk about what the risks that we face are?"

Jane: "I'll go into more details when we get to the risk registers but for now, is it ok if I just give you a high level overview?"

CIO:	"Sure. Sounds good."
Jane:	"For the risks that affect the hospital as a whole, we have a relatively high exposure to mobile attacks, social engineering, data loss, malware attacks, and vendor security gaps. Any single one of these, or a combination of these, could actually lead to our information systems and resources being compromised, lost, or stolen."
CIO:	"Ok, right off the bat I can see that I agree that data loss is a problem that we have in the organization. I mean just this morning I had someone asking me if they could use Google Docs to share patient information!"
Jane:	"Oh man, don't even get me started on that subject. It's definitely scary stuff!"
CIO:	"The worst thing is the document had like twenty thousand records in it; I couldn't believe they were asking me if they could throw it up on Google. Anyway, I know we aren't here to talk operational specifics right so I'll get us back on track. Some of those other risks you mentioned are intriguing; however, I'm not entirely sure what they all are so maybe you can explain them to me?"
Jane:	"Yep, of course, I'll walk you through the risk register."
CIO:	"Sounds good. I also noticed you had an observation related to vendor managed systems. I had some sort of inkling that our vendors are not doing their part in maintaining proper security so this affirms what I was thinking. I just didn't know how to prove my premise."
Jane:	"Well then I have just the thing for you! Later, when we go through the risk registers, I actually have a detailed rationale as to why I considered that a risk. But let me continue first with the rest of the risks we identified."
CIO:	"Perfect! Let's continue then."
Jane:	"For system specific risks, there are certain critical systems that have a relatively high exposure to disclosure of sensitive data, unchecked data alteration and system intrusion."
CIO:	"Really? What systems were those?"
Jane:	"Well I don't mention them within the executive summary; however, they are covered in the risk register. As a result of the assessment I was able to identify that our Email and Imaging systems are at a risk for disclosure of sensitive data, the HIS is at risk of unchecked data alteration, and our Payroll system is at a risk of system intrusion."
CIO:	"Hmm.. I understand how email ended up on the list since I'm sure people are using it to send ePHI all that time. I am curious about how you identified the risks with the other systems though. I had no idea we had issues for those."
Jane:	"Did you want me to explain those items now?"
CIO:	"No that's ok, I'm sure you'll discuss them in depth later right?"
Jane:	"Yes we'll get into more detail as we walk through the briefing. So, that pretty much covers the executive summary. Was it clear enough?"
CIO:	"Yes, it was actually eye opening. I'm very interested in how you came up with those conclusions though."
Jane:	"Of course, why don't we take a five minute break and go over the methodology section next?"

CIO:	"Sure, sounds good."
	Jane felt that the discussion about the executive summary went really well. Reflecting on how the discussion went she definitely felt there were some points that she might have explained better. She realizes that she could have expounded more on the different organizational level risks. For instance, she could have explained the risk of "mobile attacks" better since the CIO appeared to have been confused by that item. She notes it down and gets ready to discuss the methodology section.
	After a few minutes, her CIO comes back with a fresh mug of coffee.
Jane:	"Am I making you sleepy?"
CIO:	"Ha ha. Not at all, it's actually all very interesting. So, we're going to talk about the methodology part next right?"
Jane:	"Yes, that's the next one."
CIO:	"Ok, so I have to be honest, if there is one section that is going to make me feel sleepy it's this section. I did read through this section pretty thoroughly and it appears that you were very diligent in recording the activities that you performed and how you went about completing them."
Jane:	"Thanks. I wanted everyone who reads the report to understand the approach I took and how much work went into identifying these risks. Also, I wanted to show everyone that this risk assessment is repeatable and can be performed consistently going forward since we have followed a structured methodology."
CIO:	"Excellent. Since I've read through it and I'm relatively familiar with everything you've been doing the past few months, can you just give me the high level talking points for this section?"
Jane:	"Sure. The first thing that is important to point out when discussing the methodology is the fact that the review really consists of two parts. The first part was an organizational review and the second was a system specific review."
CIO:	"So what's the difference between the two?"
Jane:	"The organizational review was a review of potential risks as it pertained to our organization as a whole. It is by necessity a more general review and approaches the identification of risk from a strategic perspective. As an example, the risk of data loss is an organizational finding and was found to likely affect all of our information systems. Social engineering is also an example of an organizational level risk since all of our employees seem to have a low level of information security awareness."
CIO:	"Ok, that makes sense. What about system specific risk?"
Jane:	"Well system specific, as the name implies, is focused on the specific risks for a specific system. For example, let's take our HIS system. One risk specifically for that system is related to unchecked data alteration. We say that this is system specific because there are specific system security controls missing that could lead to unchecked data alteration. I know for a fact that we have organizational policies in place regarding auditing and logging but the HIS system itself does not have any mechanism for logging or auditing. That makes it system specific."
CIO:	"Ok, got it. Please continue."
Jane:	"Ok, let's talk a little about some of the information sources we leveraged. For the organizational review we relied mostly on interviews and review of organizational documents and resources such as audit reports, third party assessments, and various metrics."

CIO: "I remember you asking me for all those documents. Good to know you actually went through them."

Jane: "Yes, believe it or not I went through each one of those documents and identified any security related observations or findings. I then grouped those findings together in order to identify overarching risks for the organization."

CIO: "What do you mean you grouped them together? Could you explain that a bit more?"

Jane: "Sure, let's talk about a specific example. I noted in one of the penetration testing reports that the testers were able to obtain domain admin access to our network by exploiting weaknesses in a vendor managed system. I also noted that based on the vulnerability assessment reports, the segments containing our vendor managed systems also have a high number of vulnerabilities. Thus, based on this, I was able to conclude that there are gaps in managing the security of vendor systems."

CIO: "Ok, perfect. I see what you mean. That's what I wanted to know. As I said earlier I've been telling everyone that I don't feel that our vendors take security seriously. This provides me the ammunition to actually push this issue!"

Jane: "Glad to be of help! So that's basically an overview of how I went about conducting the organizational review."

CIO: "Sounds good. What about the system specific review?"

Jane: "For the system specific review, I first needed to define the assets in-scope. This was not a very easy task and I'm sure you remember the workshops?"

CIO: "Yes, I remember those. I also remember the interviews you conducted with the CEO, COO, department heads, and IT managers. I distinctly remember your question about "What keeps me up at night." I didn't know where to start!"

Jane: "Well that process allowed us to define the critical systems that should be in-scope for our assessment. After that I had to create threat and vulnerability pairs for each of the systems then..."

CIO: "Wait, hold up on that. What's a threat and vulnerability pair?"

Jane: "Oh, sorry. I definitely need to explain that since it is a core component of our assessment process. Threat and vulnerability pairs are basically "risk scenarios." For example, a hacker gaining access to a system by guessing weak user passwords is an example of a risk scenario. It's called a threat and vulnerability pair because it's a combination of both. In this example the threat is the intrusion by the hacker and the vulnerability is the weak passwords."

CIO: "Ah. So did you just make up your own risk scenarios for each of the system?"

Jane: "Yes and no. I mean I had to create the scenarios, which wasn't easy; however, I was able to leverage threat and vulnerability catalogs or listings from several standards like NIST and ISO27005. I also leveraged information that I was able to extrapolate from reviewing our documents."

CIO: "Ok, got it."

Jane: "So, after I completed that part of the process I started assessing each of the risk scenarios for each of the systems. This was probably the most tedious part of the process since it involved quite a bit of number crunching; however, it was necessary for me to be able to define a risk score that was calculated using a likelihood score and an impact score."

CIO: "Wait up... I got lost there."

Jane:	"Ok, this is a key concept but can also be confusing so I think it will be better if I show you."
	Jane opens up her spreadsheet containing the computation she made for each system and for each risk scenario.
Jane:	"As you can see here, one worksheet covers one system. Each row consists of a risk scenario and there are three columns after each risk scenario. These columns are an impact column, a likelihood column, and a risk score. So basically all I did was assign an impact rating, a likelihood rating, and then multiply them to obtain the risk score."
	Jane shows the spreadsheet to her CIO and walks through the risk computation process.
CIO:	"I get it now. But how did you assign the likelihood and the impact? Did you just arbitrarily assign it by yourself?"
Jane:	"Great question! Actually, I took a very systematic approach. I could have just assigned the values based on how I felt but I decided that for this to be repeatable across all the systems, I should come up with a more structured approach."
CIO:	"Ok, I'm still following you."
Jane:	"In order to accomplish this I actually wrote some macros that used the survey results as the basis of computing for the impact and the likelihood."
	Jane opens up her spreadsheet and shows several of the different macros she wrote.
Jane:	"For example, in this macro for impact, it uses the data I obtained from the surveys such as whether the system contains ePHI, is a business critical system, and the number of users, etc. The macro then uses those data elements to produce a score. This is the same approach I used for calculating likelihood."
CIO:	"Got it. That sounds like quite a bit of work though."
Jane:	"Yes, it was a lot of work initially but ultimately, it worked out for the best since once I finished with one system I just reused the macro so that the same approach applied to all the other systems. I think I actually saved time doing it this way and this will also make all future risk assessments are completed faster and consistent with the previous assessments."
CIO:	"I like to hear that you were thinking ahead to improving the process for future assessments. Good stuff!"
Jane:	"After all of that the final step is very simple. All I had to do was multiply the likelihood and the impact score and I end up with the risk score. The risk score then helped me quantify the risk for each of the scenarios."
CIO:	"Ok, so you have the score, but how did you know what was high risk? It's all just a bunch of numbers to me."
Jane:	"Exactly! Initially, it was all just a bunch of numbers but we use those numbers to start to prioritize the risks. We needed to identify the risks which are high risk. The way I accomplished this was to use a table like this..."
	Jane shows her CIO the risk threshold matrix.
Jane:	"I based this risk threshold matrix on a similar matrix found in ISO27005. Basically, the concept is to use three "buckets" to categorize risks into High, Medium and Low categories. Each bucket is assigned specific ranges. So, when a risk score falls into a specific range, it is assigned to the corresponding bucket. For example, if the risk score is 25, then it falls into the High bucket."
	Jane shows the risk threshold matrix again and points to the area where risks rated with a score of 25 would fall under.

CIO:	"That seems pretty straightforward. It's like my blood pressure. If your blood pressure falls within a certain range, they consider me hypertensive."
Jane:	"Yes, great analogy, it is exactly like that."
CIO:	"Sounds good. So that's how you were able to identify specific risk scenarios for each of the systems?"
Jane:	"Yes, for example, the risk scenario of unchecked data alteration showed up as high in the HIS spreadsheet. That's why it made it into the final risk register."
CIO:	"I'm following so far. What's next?"
Jane:	"Lunch! After that, I'll run you through the results and the risk register."

So after a fairly filling lunch and some discussions about how internal audit is giving the CIO headaches, the CIO and Jane decide to tackle the last leg of the report.

CIO:	"Ok, walk me through these risk registers."
Jane:	"Sure, let's go through them one by one. First off, you see that I've identified mobile attacks as a risk to the organization. When I say mobile attacks, these are attacks against or through mobile devices like phones and tablets"
CIO:	"This one definitely has my attention. We are under a lot of pressure to allow physicians to use their iPad's on the hospital network and our nursing units just purchased 30 iPad's to help with in room charting. I've also seen more and more requests for setting up VPNs to connect to our HIS systems using those things."
Jane:	"Yes, exactly. There is definitely an expectation that people be able to use their tablet devices to do their job. The problem is that currently we have no controls over their use and no policies or procedures governing appropriate use. The majority of the ones that are out there are personal devices meaning we have no ability to secure them without purchasing additional technology. While preparing the risk assessment one of the things I reviewed is a white paper from HHS indicating that this is growing problem in healthcare. A big part of the risk is that these devices are even easier to lose or have stolen than a laptop and who knows what type of data has been placed on the device."
CIO:	"This will certainly be a hot topic of discussion at the committee meeting. Strategically I don't think we can avoid allowing these devices much longer but maybe we can leverage your findings to secure funding to properly support the initiative."
Jane:	"The next issue relates to the gaps in vendor managed systems. I already told you that there are a high number of vulnerabilities in vendor managed systems and the penetration test demonstrated that these vulnerabilities could be exploited to gain extensive access to our network."
CIO:	"Yes, I have a big note about this one in my notebook. I'm definitely going to use your analysis to push this issue."
Jane:	"Next we have risks associated with phishing and social engineering. I was reviewing our documented security incidents and there appear to be a significant number of successful attacks where user accounts were actually compromised."
CIO:	"I'm somewhat aware of those incidents, but didn't they just have access to the users email?"

Jane: "Well remember, we have quite a bit of ePHI information being sent around internally via email so it could lead to a significant data breach and think about a situation where the compromised account also has VPN access. That would mean an external user would be able to potentially log into our VPN and access our internal network directly. One of the compromised users was a VP who had quite a bit of access to clinical systems and sensitive company documents. Think of all the potential data that can be stolen."

CIO: "That explanation helps since I hadn't considered all those angles. This seems like something that really needs to be looked into."

Jane: "Ok, the next one we kind of touched upon already. This is the issue related to data loss as something that we have to think about at an organizational level."

CIO: "Yea, this one is pretty obvious to me. With all the data breaches happening out there I'm positive there is someone in the hospital sending ePHI unprotected probably as we speak. This honestly makes the hairs on the back of my neck stand up. We really need to do something to nip this risk in the butt."

Jane: "Definitely, and I've started to lay out some preliminary plans but let's talk about the last risk. The last risk is related to our susceptibility to compromise via malware."

CIO: "Malware? Why are we at a high risk of compromise via malware? We spent quite a bit on anti-virus, web content filters, and email filters. I believe we probably spend several hundred thousand dollars on these technologies every year."

Jane: "Yes, it is not that we are necessarily doing anything wrong, it's just that the risk landscape is evolving quicker than some of these vendors can keep up and the numbers don't lie. Based on my review of help desk tickets malware contributes to the majority of the trouble tickets that the help desk receives. The scary thing is, the number of security events related to malware continues to rise."

CIO: "Is someone not doing their job? That just seems counter intuitive to me that we would spend that much on something that doesn't appear to be effective. What can we do about it?"

Jane: "Well, part of the risk registers actually includes my recommendations for each of the risks identified. For this specific risk, I'm recommending enhanced malware protection."

CIO: "That seems like a very high-level recommendation. Probably too high-level to obtain any value out of it."

Jane: "Well, at this stage we are focused on risk identification and we'll do a deeper dive into mitigation strategies at the completion of the assessment. I made all the recommendations fairly high level primarily because they should be used to facilitate discussions with various stakeholders. My recommendation here is to put together an initiative for enhanced malware protection. I don't think I have enough information and enough expertise to dictate our solution. It should be discussed more in a project team context."

CIO: "Ok that is fair enough but I can predict that when I present to the committee they are going to want to know what we need to do, how much it will cost, and how long it will take. Anyway, like the other issues I think this is definitely something worth discussing. I didn't know that this was such a problem. Thanks for identifying it."

Jane: "Well that is what you hired me for! I was pleased with the results because it showed that my risk assessment approach is working. If you don't have any other questions on that should we go over the system specific risks?"

CIO:	"Yes, go for it."
Jane:	"The good thing is that we've actually discussed many of these when we were going over the executive summary but let me just give a quick overview. First, the email system and the imaging system are at risk for disclosure of transmitted sensitive data."
CIO:	"As I mentioned earlier, I understand the risk as it relates to the email system. There's probably a ton of ePHI being sent out there but I'm still confused about the imaging system?"
Jane:	"Well, based on my surveys and interviews, one thing I found out was that the imaging system actually transmits data using FTP. It is an internal data transfer; however, the data transfer is traveling in clear text and is transmitting to workstations in the user segment and to clinics over our Wide Area Network."
CIO:	"Really? Wow. I had no idea. So we have a bunch of patient radiology images tat are sent via FTP to workstations out there?"
Jane:	"Yes."
CIO:	"I wonder what they use it for. I think it's something we really need to talk about with the system owner."
Jane:	"Yes, and I've already started dialogs with the system owner and she's very receptive about any suggestions that we have."
CIO:	"Ok, let's put that as an action item then. Please continue."
Jane:	"The next one is related to the risk of unchecked data alteration in the HIS. We talked about this a while ago. We have an enterprise policy in place that requires logging and auditing of all system transactional events for all key systems; however, our HIS doesn't have the capability to do so. At this point I really can't recommend anything specific except to start an initiative and have the system owner be the ones to think of a feasible solution since he knows the system better than any of us."
CIO:	"Very valid point. Actually, I seem to remember this being brought up before by a consultant that we hired a couple of years back. I totally forgot about it. Good catch."
Jane:	"Ok, last but not least, the HR Payroll system may be at risk of intrusion because of the use of weak passwords. The system actually can't enforce password complexity since it's totally separate from our Active Directory and I believe it can only support passwords with six characters."
CIO:	"Why am I only hearing about all of this now?"
Jane:	"Well, this is our first risk assessment. And it's better late than never right?"
CIO:	"Yes, but some of these seem like someone is just blatantly disregarding our operating procedures. We'll need to evaluate if we have a competence issue in IT somewhere. Anyway, are there any others?"
Jane:	"No, that is basically it. I also have some tables in the report that ranks systems and risk scenarios but their real function is to provide support for the items in the risk registers."
CIO:	"Yes, I remember seeing those when I browsed through the report. Well Jane, I have to say, this is very thorough work. It is definitely a little bit long but I understand your rationale and I think this report can stand up very well to any scrutiny. Speaking of which, I know internal audit has been chomping at the bit to get their hands on this so it better!"
Jane:	"Argh. I'm pretty sure that no matter what I did they'll end up with some comments. They always do."

CIO: "Yea, but I think it will go really well with them. This is good work. I am
        sufficiently impressed and I'm really glad that you are on our team."

Jane: "Same here! I'm glad you liked the report."

CIO: "Yes, very much, but it shows how much work we need to do and we need to
        get started fixing all these issues!"

Jane: "True. Especially since we've now officially documented these risks. They
        somehow seem more real after going through this process. The fun's just
        starting."

Index